The TAO of BIRTH DAYS

The TAO of BIRTH DAYS

using the i ching to become
who you were born to be

Denny Sargent

TUTTLE PUBLISHING
BOSTON · RUTLAND, VERMONT · TOKYO

First published in 2000 by Tuttle Publishing, an imprint of Periplus Editions (HK) Ltd, with editorial offices at 153 Milk Street, Boston, Massachusetts 02109.

Library of Congress Cataloging-in-Publication Data
Sargent, Denny, 1956–
   The Tao of birth days : using the I ching to become who you were
born to be / Denny Sargent. -- 1st ed.
      p. cm.
   ISBN 0-8048-3200-5 (hardcover)
   1. I ching. I. Title.
   BF1770.C5S37 2000
133.3'3--dc21   99-40999
                                                       CIP

Distributed by

USA   Japan
Tuttle Publishing   Tuttle Publishing
Distribution Center   RK Building, 2nd Floor
Airport Industrial Park   2-13-10 Shimo-Meguro, Meguro-Ku
364 Innovation Drive   Tokyo 153 0064
North Clarendon, VT 05759-9436   Tel: (03) 5437-0171
Tel: (802) 773-8930   Fax: (03) 5437-0755
Tel: (800) 526-2778

Canada   Southeast Asia
Raincoast Books   Berkeley Books Pte Ltd
8680 Cambie Street   5 Little Road #08-01
Vancouver, British Columbia   Singapore 536983
V6P 6M9   Tel: (65) 280-1330
Tel: (604) 323-7100   Fax: (65) 280-6290
Fax: (604) 323-2600

First edition
06 05 04 03 02 01 00   10 9 8 7 6 5 4 3 2 1

Design by Alicia Cech

Printed in The United States of America

Dedication

This book is dedicated to Shri Guruder Dadaji Mahendranath who taught: "The Will to Love is the Law to Live." And to Sophia, my Shakti, who teaches me daily about the TAO.

CONTENTS

Prologue: Please Read!

Sometimes the simplest is the best; in fact, the goal of the Taoist is *wei wu wei*—"Nothing Doing Nothing." This translates as going with the flow, operating on such a calm, centered, instinctual level that things just work out, are easily accomplished, and the world works together in harmony. Unfortunately for me, I'm not naturally this type of person. Therefore I have written a long—and, I hope, interesting—introduction to this book to help explain the fundamentals of Taoism, the history and meaning of the I Ching, the trigrams and hexagrams, and, finally, how this all relates to the idea of natal I Ching readings.

Yet none of this information is really necessary for you to use this book.

If you just want to discover more about yourself or another person, simply turn to "Finding your Natal Hexagram," do the easy math using the person's birthdate, then look up the hexagram, and read what it says.

There you have it, simple and, I hope, somewhat illuminating.

Then, if you want to know more about this whole cosmic system, go back and read the Introduction, but keep in mind that it is but the tip of the Taoist iceberg. The real sources of wisdom are the core texts of Taoism, which I cannot recommend highly enough: the *I Ching* and the *Tao Teh Ching*. After working with them for twenty-five years, I feel I have only barely scratched the surface!

A few notes:
There are two titles for each natal hexagram.

- The first title is from the Richard Wilhelm and C. F. Baynes translation of the *I Ching* (Bollingen Series, Princeton University Press)—still, to my mind, the definitive translation. I used these titles because they are the best known and so an easy reference.

- The second title of each hexagram is more in tune with people and personality traits. Each one is crafted by me, but many are influenced by new translation work, especially the new edition of the *I Ching* by Rudolph Ritsema and Stephen Karcher (Barnes & Noble Books).

The only other *I Ching* edition that I recommend one hundred percent is that by R. L.Wing (Doubleday and Co.). This is probably the best and most practical modern translation available.

There are numerous translations of the *Tao Teh Ching* available. I have several that I like, but feel free to choose your own—just be sure you get one of them!

Change is the only constant. Enjoy!

—Denny Sargent

Introduction

Since I was a child and became fascinated with ancient cultures, I have sought after myths, legends, and oracles that would help explain the world to me. I have been fascinated, amazed, and constantly involved with studying and using the I Ching for over twenty-five years and I still feel that I have barely scratched the surface! I decided to write this book simply because I could not find anything like it. Before we get to the actual text, and before you delve into what your personal hexagram is, let me give a bit of background on both the I Ching and natal hexagrams.

History of the *I Ching*

The *I Ching* is very likely the oldest book ever written. The actual texts were said to have been written by a legendary emperor of China (Fu Hsi) who existed in prehistory some three to four thousand years ago. Fragments of I Ching symbols (trigrams and hexagrams) have been discovered carved on bones that have been carbon-dated even older than this. It is clear, then, that the I Ching is one of the oldest spiritual and divination systems in the world, if not the oldest. The texts that make up the book called *I Ching*, as we now know them, were written down and annotated by King Wen (translated as "King Writing" or "King Pattern"), the founder of the Chou dynasty, about 1000 B.C.E. He had plenty of time to do this, as he was held captive by an enemy, the tyrant Chou Hsin, for many years. It was King Wen who organized the eight trigrams and the resulting sixty-four hexagrams (more on these later). These symbols and the writings he added roughly resulted in the system we have today.

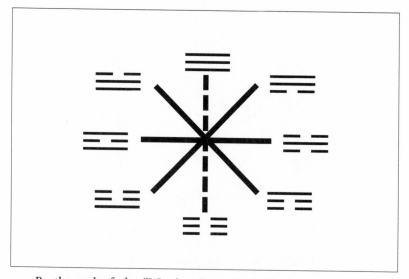

By the end of the "Warring States Period," about 200 B.C.E., the practice of "throwing yarrow sticks" and actually consulting the "official" I Ching was more or less established. The very old primary mode of consulting the spirits had previously centered around touching a hot poker to a tortoiseshell and then reading the cracks that occurred. A legend that ties this together tells of the demigod Fu Hsi contemplating a tortoiseshell one day and seeing in its eight-sectioned back the lines of the eight primal trigrams. What gave form to this mass of visionary information—something we cannot avoid discussing—is the root religion/ philosophy called Taoism.

The Tao and Taoism

Taoism, the root-philosophy of all Asia is extremely easy to embrace once one has delved into it, and yet it is also one of the most difficult things to do! The basis of Taoism is essentially "letting go," a real stretch for most Westerners. Here, then, in a few words, is the paradox of Taoism. Essentially, Taoism is based on the *Tao Teh Ching*, a very slim book of eighty-one short passages written (or dictated) by Lao Tzu, a semimythological Chinese sage who lived, it is said, around 2,500 years ago. Here are some bits and pieces from the *Tao Teh Ching*:

The unnamable is the eternally real . . .

The Tao is like a well; used but never used up
It is like the eternal void: filled with infinite possibilities . . .

The Tao is infinite, eternal.
Why is it eternal? It was never born;
Thus it can never die . . .

Open yourself to the Tao, then trust your natural responses;
and everything will fall into place. *

*   All quotes taken from the *Tao Te Ching: A New English Version*, translated by Stephen Mitchell (New York: HarperCollins, 1992).

This earlier, open-minded, nature-based philosophy imbues and binds the I Ching together, pervading it with cosmic humor and flashes of insight that are far from rational or earthly. It is important to appreciate this spirit of detachment. This is a mysticism that is so basic to Eastern philosophies and spirituality that in order to work with the I Ching in any meaningful way it needs to be understood. Why? Because the I Ching is not a fortune-telling device, nor is it a predictor of the future or a therapeutic device, at least in the Western sense, at least as far as I understand it. To a Taoist, accurately predicting the future is rather beside the point. One should be in the present; that is the goal of living and being. The I Ching was created to help people understand the flow of reality (Tao) about them, to better "go with the flow" to live a real life.

This brings us to the huge subject we have not mentioned, the most important point yet, to wit: What exactly is the I Ching?

The System of the I Ching

To understand a thing, a good place to begin is the name. I Ching literally means "Book [Ching] of Changes [I]." Often this book is simply called by the Chinese ideogram "I." In Chinese, the character "I" is often translated as "Changes," as we have, but "changes" is not exactly correct. It doesn't refer to change as we usually think of it, like the changing of the seasons or the changing of ice into water. In this case the character "I" means "forces of change that are unknowable, mysterious . . ." it indicates a way of dealing with Fate, with the "flow of the Tao," with calamity or things that just happen to you.*

---

*   See I Ching: The Classic Chinese Oracle of Change, edited by Rudolf Ritsema (London: Element Books, 1994).

In short, in common vulgar slang, the I Ching could be considered the "Book of Shit Happens!" This gets the flavor across rather crudely but pretty clearly.

Now that we have more or less presented the philosophical and magical underpinnings of the I Ching, let's briefly back up and look at its structure.

The Tao is beyond, through, existent in/about/as all reality (and not-reality). It is formless, nameless, beyond all conception, thought, or concept. You probably got this by now. So much for that.

In manifesting the unity of Tao comes to be as duality, Yin and Yang. This Yin/Yang is called Tai Chi. It is a symbol that is roundly misunderstood and replicated by New Agers and all sorts of other people. The

Yin/Yang is a symbol that is made of two areas flowing together: Yin (dark) and Yang (light). Originally, this concept was illustrated using the image of the shadow side of a mountain and the lit-up side of a mountain. This goes far to explaining the idea better than negative and positive, unless one thinks of a magnet. In this sense, we can grasp the idea that all things have two poles, two aspects, two sides, two energies, and all things and people are a combination of these two forces, always changing, always flowing, always dancing in the eternal flow of matter and energy.

All things, events, and people are a combination of Yin and Yang, some just have more of one and less of the other. Yet the essence of all things is change, so one can be more Yin while resting or painting and be more Yang while driving or skiing an hour later. Women are not necessarily more Yin then men, though by their nature they have better access to Yin and a deeper understanding of it. Still, if women were essentially Yin all the time, they would be comatose! If men were completely Yang, they would be rabidly insane whirlwinds of aggression!

Think of the left and right halves of the brain; this is probably the physiological origin of the entire concept of Yin and Yang. The right side is more open, artistic, free-form, holistic, embracing, nurturing. The left side is more logical, linear, structured, sequential, spatial . . . and so on.

The Trigrams and Hexagrams

Each of us is a balance of two ever-changing forces manifested in varied and unique ways. The system works like this:

First, beyond/through/within & without all being and nonbeing is the Tao.

This manifests as the two cosmic forms: Yin and Yang, or:

— —   and   ———

Since every basic manifestation is a three-part combination of these forces—for example, Heaven + Earth = Man or Father + Mother = Child—they are each represented as three lines. These three-line figures, or trigrams, are the most basic elemental forces of nature and exist behind all other manifestations or reality. There are eight primal, or archetypal, trigrams because there are that many combinations of Yin/Yang lines in three-line combinations. To wit:

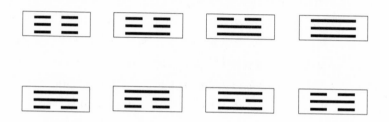

As we descend from pure Tao, we see that the forces of the universe become more and more manifest and more particular. As the eight trigrams form the archetypes, the primal forces that underlie all reality, they can also be combined in pairs (Yin and Yang) to create sixty-four six-line figures known as hexagrams. Here is one:

K'UN

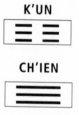

CH'IEN

These sixty-four resulting hexagrams, then, are the images that symbolize all existing things, ideas, concepts, and, most important for this book, people—the "10,000 things" mentioned previously.

These sixty-four hexagrams form the core of the sixty-four chapters of the *I Ching*. When someone does divination or looks for advice from the I Ching, it is one of these sixty-four hexagrams that they end up with, as well as the ancient texts and comments that explain what each hexagram means.

Yet it is important to remember that every hexagram is rooted in the trigrams, the Yin/Yang, and the Tao. To really understand a hexagram, we can retrace these steps from pure Tao to manifest reality. For example, the hexagram above is #11, Prospering. Why? Let me show you.

This hexagram is formed of an equal balance of Yin and Yang lines, this is very good. The trigram in the "Heaven" place (i.e., the top) is Earth, the trigram in the "Earth" place (the bottom half) is Heaven. This is excellent because we have real balance. The Yin power is manifesting in the Yang arena and vice versa.

Interestingly enough, the opposite hexagram (with the two trigrams reversed) is negative. It is called Standstill.

Why Standstill? Because Yin pulls down and this is where the Yin trigram is, Yang pulls upward and this is where the Yang or Heaven trigram is. Thus, like goes to like and there is no union, no blending, no interaction; only a kind of separation and stasis. This is not good! Can you see in this how the I Ching is based on Taoism, with its emphasis on uniting opposites, on flowing, blending, moving, and changing? It is very different from most "fixed" Western ideas and philosophies.

Natal Hexagrams

If we see reality as an ever-shifting, ever-changing flow of forces, then it would follow that as each individual is born, he or she manifests a specific and unique blend of these forces and concepts. This is, in fact, true, and though our lives are what we make of them, it is the natal hexagram that indicates what specific attributes and forces were fixed "in flesh" the moment we came into the world. Thus a person's natal hexagram can be seen much as a natal astrology chart is seen: a pattern set at the moment of birth that indicates the strengths, weaknesses, talents, and, most important, natural tendencies that a person is born with. This doesn't mean anything, however, if that person does nothing with those tendencies or works hard at eliminating the negative ones. For example, if a person has the tendency to be a great artist but never does art, then it has no real meaning. Yet the natal hexagram is very useful in many ways. Let's look first at the trigrams as they relate to natal hexagrams so that you can better understand how one is interpreted and understood.

As we mentioned, trigrams are the basic natural forces of our world, thus their names: Mountain, Wind, Rain, and so on. It is important to realize that these are but symbols for wider-reaching, more intensive forces that include personality traits and deep motivations. Here, then, is a list of the trigrams with some of the traditional attributes as well as some attributes that relate directly to understanding how these trigrams relate to people and how they can be seen in light of natal hexagrams.

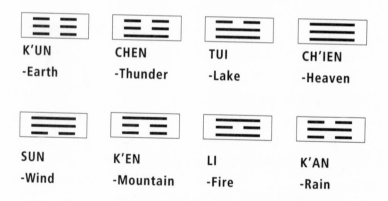

| K'UN | CHEN | TUI | CH'IEN |
| -Earth | -Thunder | -Lake | -Heaven |

| SUN | K'EN | LI | K'AN |
| -Wind | -Mountain | -Fire | -Rain |

When looking at the personal attributes that are connected with natal hexagrams, keep in mind that they are simply forces and indications, some basic feelings and ideas. Thus, a person with K'UN in his or her natal hexagram may not necessarily be weak or yielding; this is only one of many facets that go into an individual's overall character, much as salt is only one ingredient in a complex soup!

With that in mind, here are some of the natal hexagram personality attributes assigned to the trigrams:

K'UN/Earth: Weak, yielding, nourishing, responsive, receptive, adaptive, frugal, supportive, farmer, village-oriented, loving rustic things

CHEN/Thunder: Arousing energy, active, exciting, growing, expanding, stimulating, traveling, quickness, communication, managerial, electric, shocking

TUI/Lake: Satisfied, kind, full, excessive, open, pleasure-loving, hedonistic, singer, erotic, adaptive, entertaining, art-loving, easygoing

CH'IEN/Heaven: Creative, strong, firm, light, ruler, cold, serious, organizing, powerful, intensely focused, centered, aggressive, assertive

SUN/Wind: Simple, gentle, penetrating, gradual, honest, lofty, loquacious, witty, advancing and receding, long-term, soft, ethereal

K'EN/ Mountain: Waiting, calm, immobile, still, stubborn, perverse, family-oriented, meditative, spiritual, questing

LI/Fire: Illuminating, intelligent, conscious, dependent, clarity, teacher, artistic, drawn to beauty, gourmet, dilettante, sharp

K'AN/Rain: Profound, difficult, danger-seeking, anxious, deep, mysterious, dreamer, thief, removes obstacles, intuitive

And what do these trigrams mean in relation to you and me? Well, as we saw, the eight trigrams are considered to be the basic building blocks of the universe, and at the moment of birth two particular trigrams come to the fore and combine to determine our key traits, our physical, mental, and spiritual selves lean toward a specific combination of trigrams. This, then, gives us our natal hexagram.

As mentioned, the Yin and Yang emerge from Tao and the eight trigrams are born from Yin/Yang. From the eight trigrams all the billions of things and people that go to make up reality are created, and these are symbolized by the sixty-four hexagrams.

Of course, we are all a completely unique manifestation of the Tao, of the cosmos. For example, two people, John and Sam, with the same natal hexagram (let's say #11), would still be different people. They may have similar tendencies, they may have similar strengths, weaknesses, talents, and even similar interests. At the very least, if they were to meet, they'd have a lot to talk about, and they would either hit it off because they were so similar or dislike each other because they had similar drawbacks and could see in each other things they disliked about themselves. What each of us does with our natal hexagram tendencies is the key to how we live our lives.

On Reading Natal Hexagrams

In the next section of this book is the method for finding a person's natal hexagram. After you have found your hexagram, and your friend's hexagram, and your enemy's hexagram, you will gain insight into what makes them tick as well as what their potential strengths and weaknesses are. Yet we have to be careful. Having given natal hexagram readings for about fifteen years, I must tell you that the readings in this book are limited. Let me explain why.

A person may be born with a terrible temper, yet the parents may work very hard at helping the child deal with this facet of his or her character to such an extent that it never becomes an issue in adult life. Another problem is that some of the inclinations or tendencies may influence each other, be contradictory, or even cancel each other out! This is why this book is best used with a bit of intuition.

"True will" is the optimal manifestation of the Tao through you in this life. It means strengthening one's positive traits while minimizing or embracing the negative traits in such a way that they are transformed into growth and wisdom. In this sense everyone starts with a certain configuration, symbolized by the natal hexagram, but what each of us makes of our lives is very much up to us. Just because a person has lethargic tendencies does not mean that he or she can't be a pro-baseball player or a ski champion. What I'm trying to say is that the True Will of a person is indicated by a natal hexagram, but it also supersedes the natal hexagram. Thus, the natal hexagram should be seen not as limiting but as a set of indications and a way of understanding.

Keeping these things in mind, the natal hexagram can be very useful for self-discovery as well as for understanding the behavior, viewpoint, and emotional makeup of others. When I know someone's natal hexagram, I intuitively have a grasp on what makes them tick. This helps me deal with them, understand conflicts we may have, and work in a constructive and harmonious way with them.

No quality in and of itself is bad or good, and also no hexagram is completely bad or good as a natal hexagram. Some are easier and some are harder, but easy is not always good. People who have to work more usually have stronger characters, while people with easy hexagrams can be shallow and self-centered. For every light there is a shadow, every peak signals a coming decline, every problem gives way to a necessary and positive change.

Think on these things when reading the natal hexagrams. One more thing: The verses in this book are my ideas, thoughts, and interpretations. They come from my perspective. Some of them may not apply to you, and some, in your opinion, may be completely off the mark. However, I have done my best to intuitively interpret and expound on each natal hexagram. Through great effort and a lot of trial and error (and a whole lot of one-on-one natal hexagram readings), I feel that I have captured the essence of each natal hexagram. As you work with and study this book, other concepts, ideas, and attributes for various hexagrams may come to you: Note them down in the margins! This is always a work-in-progress, just as, in many ways, the I Ching still is. There is no definitive interpretation here; just as the Tao is never seen, never graspable, and never really conceived of, so too is this work elusive and ever-expanding. Use it; do not let it use you. As the *Tao Teh Ching* says: "The world is beyond holding."

FINDING YOUR NATAL HEXAGRAM

Finding A Natal Hexagram

This method of determining a person's natal hexagram was handed down to devotees in the United States of Shri Gurudev Dadaji Mahendranath, a most amazing and erudite tantric holy man. It was first published in *Mandragore* Magazine in 1981. The origins of this system are unclear and how it works is certainly a mystery, yet after working with this system for fifteen years, I am convinced that it yields valid results. Thanks, Dadaji, and may you who use this system have fun and gain a bit of insight as well!

Trigram Chart for Finding Hexagrams

To find the number of your natal hexagram, find the top trigram on the top row and the bottom trigram on the side row. Where they meet in the chart is the number of your natal hexagram.

TOP TRIGRAM / BOTTOM TRIGRAM	CH'IEN	CHEN	K'AN	K'EN	K'UN	SUN	LI	TUI
CH'IEN	1	34	5	26	11	9	14	43
CHEN	25	51	3	27	24	42	21	17
K'AN	6	40	29	4	7	59	64	47
K'EN	33	62	39	52	15	53	56	31
K'UN	12	16	8	23	2	20	35	45
SUN	44	32	48	18	46	57	50	28
LI	13	55	63	22	36	37	30	49
TUI	10	54	60	41	19	61	38	58

To use this table:

• First find what the top trigram of the natal hexagram is by adding the numbers of the birth date across, like so:

> **Example:**
>
> Mr. X was born on April 29, 1911
>
> April 29, 1911= 4/29/1911= 4+2+9+1+9+1+1= 27 and 2+ 7= 9

The final key number must be between 1 and 9.

• Look at the Trigram Key Number Chart on pages 17-18 and find the correct trigram. In the case of our example, the top trigram is # 9:

K'AN

• To get the lower trigram, look up the year of birth on the Date Chart (pages 19-22) and find the key number of the bottom trigram—depending on whether the subject is a man or woman. In the case of our example, the birth date being 1911 and our example being a man, the key number is # 8:

K'EN

• So, the natal hexagram for our example would be a combination of the top and bottom trigrams we found, which you can look up in the Trigram Chart for Finding Hexagrams (page 15) or:

HEXAGRAM 39: OBSTRUCTION (THE PERSEVERING ONE)

Now, look up this hexagram in "The Natal Hexagram Readings" beginning on page 23, and you'll see the reading for Mr. X. Follow the same steps and find your natal hexagram.

You can also look up this hexagram in any other *I Ching* book to get some ideas, thoughts, and feelings about this person's tendencies and influences.

Trigram Key Number Chart

For a better idea of what each trigram means by itself, see the Introduction.

TRIGRAM 1   **LI**

TRIGRAM 2   **K'UN**

TRIGRAM 3   **CHEN**

TRIGRAM 4   **SUN**

TRIGRAM 5* (FOR A MAN)   K'UN

*   Note that Trigram 5 is gender specific.

TRIGRAM 5 (FOR A WOMAN) K'EN

TRIGRAM 6   CH'IEN

TRIGRAM 7   TUI

TRIGRAM 8   K'EN

TRIGRAM 9   K'AN

Date Chart

Year	Man	Woman
1900	1	5
1901	9	6
1902	8	7
1903	7	8
1904	6	9
1905	5	1
1906	4	2
1907	3	3
1908	2	4
1909	1	5
1910	9	6
1911	8	7
1912	7	8
1913	6	9
1914	5	1
1915	4	2
1916	3	3
1917	2	4
1918	1	5
1919	9	6
1920	8	7
1921	7	8
1922	6	9
1923	5	1
1924	4	2
1925	3	3
1926	2	4
1927	1	5
1928	9	6
1929	8	7

Year	Man	Woman
1930	7	8
1931	6	9
1932	5	1
1933	4	2
1934	3	3
1935	2	4
1936	1	5
1937	9	6
1938	8	7
1939	7	8
1940	6	9
1941	5	1
1942	4	2
1943	3	3
1944	2	4
1945	1	5
1946	9	6
1947	8	7
1948	7	8
1949	6	9
1950	5	1
1951	4	2
1952	3	3
1953	2	4
1954	1	5
1955	9	6
1956	8	7
1957	7	8
1958	6	9
1959	5	1
1960	4	2
1961	3	3

Year	Man	Woman
1962	2	4
1963	1	5
1964	9	6
1965	8	7
1966	7	8
1967	6	9
1968	5	1
1969	4	2
1970	3	3
1971	2	4
1972	1	5
1973	9	6
1974	8	7
1975	7	8
1976	6	9
1977	5	1
1978	4	2
1979	3	3
1980	2	4
1981	1	5
1982	9	6
1983	8	7
1984	7	8
1985	6	9
1986	5	1
1987	4	2
1988	3	3
1989	2	4
1990	1	5
1991	9	6
1992	8	7
1993	7	8

Year	Man	Woman
1994	6	9
1995	5	1
1996	4	2
1997	3	3
1998	2	4
1999	1	5
2000	9	6
2001	8	7
2002	7	8
2003	6	9
2004	5	1
2005	4	2
2006	3	3
2007	2	4
2008	1	5
2009	9	6
2010	8	7
2011	7	8
2012	6	9
2013	5	1
2014	4	2
2015	3	3

THE NATAL HEXAGRAM READINGS

An Explanation

This section contains the natal hexagram readings for specific people. If you have followed the previous instructions, you now have the hexagram for a person about whom you are seeking information—or your own. First, a few words on what these readings contain.

1. The first item is the title of the hexagram—for example, Hexagram #1 is The Creative. These are based on the Wilhelm/Baynes translation of the *I Ching*.

2. Following the hexagram title is the title of the personality—for example, #1 is The Original One. This shows the primary personality this hexagram represents and gives us a general "type."

3. The third item is a list of "Traits" that this hexagram embodies, both positive and negative. This is to give a general zen, or quick feel, for the hexagram type.

4. Next is a summarized "Life Lessons." This is a quick synopsis on the key things these people need to work on to grow and become more complete individuals, as indicated by the hexagram.

5. Next are the "Positive Tendencies." As already mentioned, these are only possible tendencies, not literal truth. Keep in mind that a tendency not acted upon or developed never reveals itself. These are natural gifts one is born with; whether one uses them is up to the individual.

6. "Positive Tendencies" are followed by the "Negative Tendencies." The same ideas apply as with the positive tendencies. Some may never surface, others may only be minor problems. These tendencies are not

negative in the sense of being bad; in fact, they are important parts of oneself in that they reveal ways to grow and become a stronger, better, more balanced person.

7.   Last is "Compatibility"—specific natal hexagrams that represent people who may naturally attract or repel initially. Those who are naturally attractive in a positive way may or may not end up becoming important, but they will have better immediate chemistry. People who naturally evoke an immediate negative reaction may, in fact, be great teachers and helpers because they offer the chance for the greatest growth. They may also end up becoming good friends, but it will be more of a challenge getting close to them.

The order that the hexagrams are listed in follows the traditional order as set forth in the Wilhelm/Baynes translation of the *I Ching*.

"Existence and nonexistence produce each other
Difficult and easy complete each other
Long and short contrast each other
High and low attract each other
Pitch and tone harmonize each other
Future and past follow each other. . . ."
      —*Tao Teh Ching, The Tao of Power*, R. L. Wing translation

HEXAGRAM 1
CH'IEN

THE CREATIVE
(THE ORIGINAL ONE)

CH'IEN

Traits

Note, these traits are not given in any particular order and none are considered any more important than any other.

Creative	Genius
"Dragon Power"	Bossy
Great willful energy	Intense
Excellent innovator	Full of *kundalini*
Power of inception	Solid
Great beginning action	Skillful in timing
Powerful	Directed
Momentum	Great initiative
Exceptional	Accelerated growth
Filled with inspiration	Arrogant
Leader or director	Explosive
In charge	

Life Lessons

These people need to learn a little humility, need to share their gifts with others, and need to learn to take more time out for fun.

Positive Tendencies

These are creative and powerful people. Leaders and rulers. People who originate concepts and plans. Movers and shakers. They emanate strong positive Yang energy, and this provides a foundation of greatness for them and others. Grand schemes are very much a part of their character, and all eyes tend to follow them. They are individuals who have that rare combination of charisma, vision, and strength to make things a reality. These are really significant people who truly have indomitable wills. This being the first hexagram, the origin, these people can be looked to as a center of amazing projects, ideas, and leadership. If focused on evolution, on society, and the common good, their dreams and goals will be remarkably fulfilled. Being the center, the one who leads and organizes others, brings these people real happiness. These are very well respected people for whom others would die. They are well loved, even beyond what can be expected, and have tremendous influence over others, which can be used to motivate and propel them forward.

Negative Tendencies

These people can sometimes be overbearing or even violent when crossed. They are capable of being unpredictable. They might have totalitarian tendencies and can be very inflexible. Bossy, they may have a "Godfather" complex and be egocentric. Such people tend to have very little Yin energy, virtually no softness, and this can be hard for others to take day after day. They can be arrogant, impatient with "inferiors," and often have (for good or ill) a sense of their own "manifest destiny."

Compatibility

The following natal hexagrams represent people you naturally tend to have a positive reaction to:

HEXAGRAM **2:**   THE RECEPTIVE
HEXAGRAM **24:**   RETURN
HEXAGRAM **19:**   APPROACH
HEXAGRAM **11:**   PEACE
HEXAGRAM **34:**   THE POWER OF THE GREAT
HEXAGRAM **43:**   BREAKTHROUGH
HEXAGRAM **5:**   WAITING
HEXAGRAM **8:**   HOLDING TOGETHER

The following natal hexagrams represent people you naturally tend to have a negative reaction to:

HEXAGRAM **1:**   THE CREATIVE
HEXAGRAM **44:**   COMING TO MEET
HEXAGRAM **33:**   RETREAT
HEXAGRAM **12:**   STAGNATION

HEXAGRAM 2

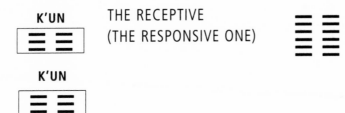

K'UN

THE RECEPTIVE
(THE RESPONSIVE ONE)

K'UN

Traits

The valley spirit	Confused
Open; receptive	Responsive
Actively passive	Pragmatic
Doing without doing	Earthy
Moving inward	Objective
Change within ≠ change without	Great stamina
Sublime	Moral
Connected with unconscious	Self-doubting
Mystical	Calm
Channeling energy	Dependent
Rooted to earth	Quiet
Soft; easy	

Life Lessons

These people need to learn to be more assertive, should try to be more outgoing, and need to learn to make their dreams a reality.

Positive Tendencies

These people are the height of receptivity. They are great at passive accomplishments and artful at "doing without doing." These people develop, plan, and process inwardly, thus changing the outer world. Quiet a lot, alone time is very important for recharging their batteries. They have sublime communication and humor. They are very attuned to the unconscious, dreams, and the psychic realm. They are natural mystics and adept at channeling spiritual information; yet they are almost completely detached from the day-to-day grind. These are great workers who, once directed or motivated by another, can accomplish amazing things. They are very pragmatic, dealing with what is in the real world, not projecting far into the future or spending a lot of time asking "what if." These are also exceptionally moral people who teach by calm example, who do good without a lot of fanfare, and who are empathic, sensitive, and deeply feeling. They are also very earthy people, who love and need nature, gardens, forests, and parks. These are humble, self-effacing people who "work in mysterious ways."

Negative Tendencies

These people are at times passive to the point of absurdity. Sometimes they are perceived as lazy, directionless, self-absorbed, and/or inattentive, though these things may not be true. These are people who are sometimes known for being "spaced out" a lot because they can be so involved with daydreams and inner dialogs that the real world seems unreal. At times, these people have real trouble starting things. Very soft and gentle, they can also be weak in many ways. They can sometimes be manipulated and taken advantage of, and at times may be paralyzed due to poor self-confidence or by overwhelming sympathy for others. Feelings of paranoia, listlessness, and/or depression are possible. Such people must be careful with their psychic abilities; they are very open.

Compatibility

The following natal hexagrams represent people you naturally tend to have a positive reaction to:

HEXAGRAM **1**:   THE CREATIVE

HEXAGRAM **44**:   COMING TO MEET

HEXAGRAM **33**:   RETREAT

HEXAGRAM **12**:   STANDSTILL

HEXAGRAM **20**:   CONTEMPLATION

HEXAGRAM **23**:   SPLITTING APART

HEXAGRAM **35**:   PROGRESS

HEXAGRAM **14**:   POSSESSION IN GREAT MEASURE

The following natal hexagrams represent people you naturally tend to have a negative reaction to:

HEXAGRAM **2**:   THE RECEPTIVE

HEXAGRAM **24**:   RETURN

HEXAGRAM **19**:   APPROACH

HEXAGRAM **11**:   PEACE

HEXAGRAM **34**:   THE POWER OF THE GREAT

HEXAGRAM **43**:   BREAKTHROUGH

HEXAGRAM **5**:   WAITING

HEXAGRAM **8**:   HOLDING TOGETHER

HEXAGRAM 3

K'AN

DIFFICULTY AT THE
BEGINNING

CHEN

(THE SPROUTING ONE)

Traits

Slow to move	Learning to flow
Momentum	Capitalize on luck
Obstacles to overcome	Accepting assistance
Piercing	Of many minds
Breakthrough; success	Scattered
Stop or start	Creatively chaotic
Bursts of growth	Shoulders many tasks
Determined	Overwhelmed
Stubborn	"Type A" personality
Unseeing	Timid
Frustrated, then depressed	Optimistic
Must let it go	

Life Lessons

These people need to learn how to be more of a "self-starter," to reduce the amount of complaining they do, and to work on patience.

Positive Tendencies

Not easily discouraged, these people stay the course and (after much difficulty) emerge the victor. They must be reminded to go farther, to push, and when they do, there's a breakthrough. Personal growth comes in stop-starts, crises, and epiphanies. These are strong people, noble even, heroes and heroines in their own eyes. They have strong follow-throughs when on a roll. When aware, they let things flow in such a way as to create success. This person is constantly surrounded by chaos! They are energizing, exciting, creative, and educational. From this primal brew can emerge almost anything, so they must focus on the project at hand, on one or two things at most at a time. They easily gather interesting and supportive friends and co-workers around to help focus, organize and follow through on all the exciting ideas and energies they bring forth. These people have very important self-realized principles at the core of their character. If held on to tightly, these will carry them through even the stormiest time.

Negative Tendencies

These people can be very chaotic; they may have trouble coping with reality and can have difficulty beginning projects or making important decisions. These are people who may need an outside stimulus, a kick in the pants, as it were. They sometimes moan and groan too much, see problems as insurmountable, get frustrated easily, and may tend to abandon people and projects over problems others don't see as critical. They sometimes hold on to too many things, especially hurts and insults. Sometimes these people feel helpless and out-gunned.

Compatibility

The following natal hexagrams represent people you naturally tend to have a positive reaction to:

HEXAGRAM **30:** THE CLINGING FIRE
HEXAGRAM **56:** THE WANDERER
HEXAGRAM **50:** THE CAULDRON
HEXAGRAM **64:** BEFORE COMPLETION
HEXAGRAM **4:** YOUTHFUL FOLLY
HEXAGRAM **59:** DISPERSION
HEXAGRAM **6:** CONFLICT
HEXAGRAM **13:** FELLOWSHIP WITH MEN

The following natal hexagrams represent people you naturally tend to have a negative reaction to:

HEXAGRAM **29:** THE ABYSMAL
HEXAGRAM **60:** LIMITATION
HEXAGRAM **3:** INITIAL DIFFICULTY
HEXAGRAM **63:** AFTER COMPLETION
HEXAGRAM **49:** REVOLUTION
HEXAGRAM **55:** ABUNDANCE
HEXAGRAM **36:** DARKENING OF THE LIGHT
HEXAGRAM **7:** THE ARMY

HEXAGRAM 4

K'EN

YOUTHFUL FOLLY
(THE ENVELOPING ONE)

K'AN

Traits

Joyful and silly	Fresh
Enthusiastic	New perspectives
Naive	Persistent
Youthful errors	Bubbling
Do it yourselfer...with help	Rude
Needs teachers	Effervescent
Overzealous	Loquacious
Bull in a china shop	Immature
Amazing	Funny
Impetuous	Selfish
Annoying	Innocent
Brave	

Life Lessons

These people need to learn to not get so excited so often. They should work at getting more perspective and on maturing in some areas of their lives.

Positive Tendencies

These are enthusiastic people bubbling over with new ideas, a million interests, and a lot of humor. Young at heart, they never seem to get old-fashioned or stodgy. Always ready to try new things, new ideas, new food, and meet new people, they love to argue, explore, challenge established taboos, and shake things up. They are brave people who seem fearless in dangerous situations, the first person into the burning building, often laughing. They often have a new perspective on things. These are persistent people, almost to the point of insanity, and are usually intensely curious. These people are good talkers, loquacious and witty, and deep only on occasion. They are the life of the party, fun people who bring energy to every undertaking. They are enthusiastic but possibly roaming lovers, people who act sometimes as if they never really grew up. They are people who relate to and love playing with and helping children. Almost too enthusiastic spiritually, these people learn and advance quickly under the wise supervision of a spiritual teacher or guru. In almost all areas of life, they do very well with teachers and supervisors who can direct their almost endless energy and verve.

Negative Tendencies

Enthusiasm can lead these people into trouble, even if it's just to irritate others. This high energy level can lead to overzealousness, even fanaticism, especially if one is shallow, which these people can be. Such people may be impetuous, off-the-top-of-the-head, and generally flippant about some serious things. The key negative is, possibly, immaturity and naïveté. Not meaning any harm, these people can sometimes be a bull in a china shop, destroying projects and relationships, hurting feelings and chances, all without knowing what happened: a true innocent fool. They can also be overly dependent and, if the urge takes them, willing converts to a cult or master of any sort. They may need to question more and to foster independence.

Compatibility

The following natal hexagrams represent people you naturally tend to have a positive reaction to:

HEXAGRAM **30:** THE CLINGING
HEXAGRAM **56:** THE WANDERER

HEXAGRAM **50**: THE CAULDRON

HEXAGRAM **64**: BEFORE COMPLETION

HEXAGRAM **4**:   YOUTHFUL FOLLY

HEXAGRAM **59**: DISPERSION

HEXAGRAM **6**:   CONFLICT

HEXAGRAM **13**: FELLOWSHIP WITH MEN

The following natal hexagrams represent people you naturally tend to have a negative reaction to:

HEXAGRAM **52**: KEEPING STILL

HEXAGRAM **22**: GRACE

HEXAGRAM **26**: TAMING POWER OF THE GREAT

HEXAGRAM **41**: DECREASE

HEXAGRAM **8**:   OPPOSITION

HEXAGRAM **10**: TREADING

HEXAGRAM **61**: INNER TRUTH

HEXAGRAM **53**: DEVELOPMENT

HEXAGRAM 5

K'AN

CH'IEN

WAITING
(THE ATTENTIVE ONE)

Traits

Patient	Muddled
Knows when to wait	Inspired
Draws success to one	Self-centered
Indolent	Stable
Connoisseur	Great worrier
Decadent	Patient
Epicurean	Nurturing
Debauchee	Visionary
Magnet	Coordinator
Manifestor	Counselor
Can't force things	Center of matrix
Natural Taoist	

Life Lessons

These people need to become more motivated; they should work at delaying gratification and on being less fatalistic as well as leading a simpler life.

Positive Tendencies

People of distinction, epicurean in tastes, rarefied in experiences and tastes. These people are patient and accept adversity as learning experiences. They are capable of being very confident and have a very strong connection with the inner self, the deep strength within which can help them wait out adversity and stormy times. Such people can see things factually, clearly, and with great insight. They have a knack for timing, knowing when to pause, when to let go, and when to act. "Good things come to those who wait" applies to these people. They don't believe in forcing things, preferring to take things at their own pace. Natural philosophers, these people see the flow of all things in relation to all other things. They can be visionaries or mystics of sorts. Two things they may often think are "Everything is as it should be" and "Oh well, that's just the way things go." These can be very patient people, ones who deal well with difficult and temperamental individuals, who give up things to help others, especially time and energy. They would be good counselors and coordinators, confident and able to work things out slowly and smoothly. These people seem to have a destiny that cannot be rushed and so they may often be open and cheerful.

Negative Tendencies

These people can complain a lot, fret and worry much too much, are impatient and very indolent, indulgent, hedonistic (pleasure for its own sake), and debauched. Are they lazy? Very possibly, at times, while using "take it easy" or "well, why bother?" as mystic excuses. The possibility exists for such a person to be very self-centered and unmoving if they constantly worry about things not working out. They may tend toward decadence, letting things slide, and a "what, me? worry?" attitude that needs to be dealt with. They can be overwhelmed by fear and confusion if they don't take it easy and trust that things will work out.

Compatibility

The following natal hexagrams represent people you naturally tend to have a positive reaction to:

HEXAGRAM **30:** THE CLINGING FIRE
HEXAGRAM **56:** THE WANDERER
HEXAGRAM **50:** THE CAULDRON
HEXAGRAM **64:** BEFORE COMPLETION
HEXAGRAM **4:** YOUTHFUL FOLLY
HEXAGRAM **59:** DISPERSION
HEXAGRAM **6:** CONFLICT
HEXAGRAM **13:** FELLOWSHIP WITH MEN

The following natal hexagrams represent people you naturally tend to have a negative reaction to:

HEXAGRAM 6

CH'IEN

CONFLICT
(THE CONTENTIOUS ONE)

K'AN

Traits

Warrior	Tenacious
Agitator	Uphill fighter
Conqueror	Overconfident
Sets up situations	Argumentative
Schemer	Strong-willed
Combative	Tough
Of two minds	Self-doubt
Cautious or risky	Seeks guidance
Plans things	Devoted
Efficient	Deep belief
Daredevil	Powerful
Stubborn	

Life Lessons

These people need to "give peace a chance," need to learn to hold their peace more; they would benefit from some anger management.

Positive Tendencies

These people are methodical, intense, and natural rebels. They could easily be lifelong agitators and activists, people who see the natural order of things in terms of struggle and striving for what one wants. They are true warriors and, when successful, noble "conquerors." These people seize upon opportunities and are excellent at setting up situations to their advantage through careful planning. Competitive, hard-working, and very physical beings with very strong wills, they can also give in graciously when they need to. They are tough hombres who are also adept at seeing what they lack and moving quickly to fix it or get it. These people can benefit much from spiritual teachers, but they must tone down the rhetoric when one is found. Loyal and with great stamina, they love a good uphill fight and prefer relationships with a lot of activity, even some tussling and give and take. They are very fixated on origins, the beginnings of things and ideas, and they carefully reconsider things and reevaluate ideas, opinions, and beliefs when challenged, which may be often. These people often trust in others to mediate and balance things out for them and this is very wise.

Negative Tendencies

Sometimes these people can be stubborn, cantankerous, bellicose, and intemperate, and can possibly generate a lot of conflict! They may go looking for a fight, even when it's not called for. These people may at times be a touch paranoid and sometimes very borderline; here, possibly, is a temper that needs to be watched. They are sometimes bad people to cross; their retaliation might even be legendary. These are individuals who leap without looking. Though this is good in emergencies, it may be bad at more normal times. These people may have trouble giving in and/or backing down and, if not listening to the voice of reason, can be impossible to deal with. Self-doubters at times, such people have strong feelings of failure and self-dislike; depressions must be watched for at times.

Compatibility

The following natal hexagrams represent people you naturally tend to have a positive reaction to:

HEXAGRAM **2:**   THE RECEPTIVE
HEXAGRAM **24:** RETURN
HEXAGRAM **19:** APPROACH
HEXAGRAM **11:** PEACE
HEXAGRAM **34:** THE POWER OF THE GREAT
HEXAGRAM **43:** BREAKTHROUGH
HEXAGRAM **5:**   WAITING
HEXAGRAM **8:**   HOLDING TOGETHER

The following natal hexagrams represent people you naturally tend to have a negative reaction to:

HEXAGRAM **1:**   THE CREATIVE
HEXAGRAM **44:** COMING TO MEET
HEXAGRAM **33:** RETREAT
HEXAGRAM **12:** STANDSTILL
HEXAGRAM **20:** CONTEMPLATION
HEXAGRAM **23:** SPLITTING APART
HEXAGRAM **35:** PROGRESS
HEXAGRAM **14:** POSSESSION IN GREAT MEASURE

HEXAGRAM 7

K'UN

THE ARMY
(THE LEADING ONE)

K'AN

Traits

Organized	Clique-oriented
Facilitating	Group-oriented
Confused, dispersed	Go-getter
Training	Fanatic fan
Disciplined	Persistent
Conflicting emotions	Visionary
Bringing together	Noble
Crystallizing	Generous
Unstoppable when going	Audacious
Analyzing	Strong
Judging	Accommodating
Follower or leader	

Life Lessons

These people need to accept that life has many gray areas; they need to understand that there is no single truth and that they need to stay focused.

Positive Tendencies

These are the supreme organizers, everything in its place, compartmentalization of facts and the completion of projects in an organized manner being a real inherent skill. These people are the focus of collective force, of society-oriented power and influence. Whether they relish it or not, such people will be drawn to collective endeavors and naturally rise to some sort of leadership status, although there will always be those above them whose support will be vital. Training of all kinds, the acquisition of various skills and degrees, learning how to plan and execute ideas—all of these things turn these individuals on. Although they may not be disciplined, the potential is very much there to be so, as is the inner strength of will to back it up. Tests will show how strong this "backbone" is; chances are these are very brave, tough people who can succeed in almost anything. They can be very efficient and important communicators, but this must be worked at. Inner conviction, inner confidence along with being a part of the flow of society will lead to great success. These are generous people who give a lot to loved ones and have the strength of character to stick things out. These are dynamos and unstoppable when going forward on a project of one kind or another.

Negative Tendencies

Problems can arise when things are not clear-cut for these individuals. The urge to make things so may be hard to overcome, as might be a fixation on structure, dogma, and hierarchy for its own sake. Law and order, anyone? These people can be effective leaders, generals, but they can also be bossy and arrogant. They may be inclined to use force in delicate situations, which should be avoided unless absolutely necessary. Interestingly enough, a real problem here might be confusion and the dispersion of energies. When not single-minded, these people can too easily be no-minded, split, and torn in many directions, spinning their wheels in the sand, up against a wall. This can be true for emotions, which are often very confusing for them. Often the emotional life of such people will not be as clear as, say, career.

Compatibility

The following natal hexagrams represent people you naturally tend to have a positive reaction to:

HEXAGRAM **1:**   THE CREATIVE
HEXAGRAM **44:**   COMING TO MEET
HEXAGRAM **33:**   RETREAT
HEXAGRAM **12:**   STANDSTILL
HEXAGRAM **20:**   CONTEMPLATION
HEXAGRAM **23:**   SPLITTING APART
HEXAGRAM **35:**   PROGRESS
HEXAGRAM **14:**   POSSESSION IN GREAT MEASURE

The following natal hexagrams represent people you naturally tend to have a negative reaction to:

HEXAGRAM **2:**   THE RECEPTIVE

HEXAGRAM **24:** RETURN

HEXAGRAM **19:** APPROACH

HEXAGRAM **11:** PEACE

HEXAGRAM **34:** THE POWER OF THE GREAT

HEXAGRAM **43:** BREAKTHROUGH

HEXAGRAM **5:**   WAITING

HEXAGRAM **8:**   HOLDING TOGETHER

HEXAGRAM 8

KAN

HOLDING TOGETHER
(THE UNIFYING ONE)

K'UN

Traits

Gradually progressing

Uncertain

Needs reassurance

Open and caring

Receptive and insecure

Consistent if progressing

Persevering

Hesitates at wrong time

Zen-like

Inspired

Joining to others

Collective spirit

Calming

Collective energy

Difficulty discriminating

Verifies

Unsure

Confused

Mediator

Idealistic

Drawn to oracles

Very centered

Unifying or chaotic

Life Lessons

These people need to pay attention to time; they need to learn when to go and when to stay—and when to throw caution to the wind and go for it.

Positive Tendencies

These are open, caring individuals who freely give nurturing and friendship to those around them. Not one to stand out, they communicate and are creative in a sublime and subtle manner. Here are people who grow, mature, and gain all sorts of things gradually in increments, no great leaps of evolution here. The gentler aspects of things, of the world, and of cultures makes the most impression and brings the most joy to them. These people are naturally drawn to fortune-telling, oracles, and the like and may have some talent at them—they may even be psychic. They are very civic-minded and are often drawn to groups and duties that aim to better society. They are very conscientious in this way, voting, recycling, contributing to charities, and so on. If progress, however slow, is being made, then these people will be extremely consistent, supportive, and very persuasive. They are great joiners who unite others and thrive in projects that elicit a collective spirit, a movement, or creative extravaganza. These people become a center of unity in such cases and have a calming and holistic energy that helps everyone and draws everyone together. Timing is everything for these individuals, so if they pay attention, great things can be initiated.

Negative Tendencies

Put another way, these people may often miss the boat when they aren't paying attention. Lost opportunities due to caution, slowness, or inability to look ahead can be a major pitfall. Another possible problem for them is lost momentum. If these people don't see progress, they are inclined to give up too easily. Hesitation or self-doubt can kill projects, relationships, and self-confidence! These people should ignore doubts when sure of their goal; perseverance furthers! Such people may be somewhat egotistical and may try to take on leadership duties they are not fit for. They may get lost when alone, needing others too much to bolster their self-image.

Compatibility

The following natal hexagrams represent people you naturally tend to have a positive reaction to:

HEXAGRAM **30:**   THE CLINGING FIRE
HEXAGRAM **56:**   THE WANDERER
HEXAGRAM **50:**   THE CAULDRON
HEXAGRAM **64:**   BEFORE COMPLETION
HEXAGRAM **4:**   YOUTHFUL FOLLY
HEXAGRAM **59:**   DISPERSION
HEXAGRAM **6:**   CONFLICT
HEXAGRAM **13:**   FELLOWSHIP WITH MEN

The following natal hexagrams represent people you naturally tend to have a negative reaction to:

HEXAGRAM **29:**   THE ABYSMAL
HEXAGRAM **60:**   LIMITATION
HEXAGRAM **3:**   INITIAL DIFFICULTY
HEXAGRAM **63:**   AFTER COMPLETION
HEXAGRAM **49:**   REVOLUTION
HEXAGRAM **55:**   ABUNDANCE
HEXAGRAM **36:**   DARKENING OF THE LIGHT
HEXAGRAM **7:**   THE ARMY

HEXAGRAM 9

SUN

TAMING POWER OF
THE SMALL
(THE RESTRAINED ONE)

CHEN

Traits

Subtle	Depressed
Shallow	Pessimist
Long-winded	Easily frustrated
Frivolous	Gracious
Reserved	Spacey
Decorative	Patient
Skin-deep	Detail-oriented
Clever	Fussy
Witty	Picky
Subdued	Open-minded
Fickle	Positive attitude
Flexible	

Life Lessons

These people need to understand that "talking does not cook the rice," that being clever is not necessarily being smart, and that they need to learn to stick with things.

Positive Tendencies

These are clever people who can spin a tale and entertain as well as live by their wits, but they are naturally very shy and reserved. These people are very flexible and can be all things to all people. Good front men or women, here we have the natural, easygoing, go-with-the-flow type who can put a positive spin on things and show the proper face to the right people. Detail-oriented, they finish tasks in an efficient and exacting manner as well as remember small points and complex ideas. They have a good sense of decoration, of colors and decor. They are the perfect helper and creative worker. These people create tremendous atmosphere and can subtly influence others in a variety of ways. They are excellent at delicate discussions and at dealing with difficult or tense people in a calm and careful way. Never overbearing or aggressive, they are usually friendly and sweet people who keep their feelings and opinions to themselves much of the time.

Quiet and loyal good friends, they are great at keeping secrets and can often slip in and out of situations quietly and effectively.

Negative Tendencies

These people can be, at times, inconsistent, spacey, forgetful, disorganized, shallow, uncommunicative, and frivolous. Though witty, they can also be hesitant and almost closed-lipped in their social interactions, real wallflower types. Flexible can easily translate into fickle and rarely means stable. Detail-oriented can easily become picky and gossipy. These individuals can sometimes see themselves as boring, ineffectual, and powerless. This can lead to melancholy and listlessness.

Compatibility

The following natal hexagrams represent people you naturally tend to have a positive reaction to:

HEXAGRAM **51:** THE AROUSING
HEXAGRAM **16:** ENTHUSIASM
HEXAGRAM **40:** DELIVERANCE
HEXAGRAM **32:** DURATION
HEXAGRAM **46:** PUSHING UPWARD
HEXAGRAM **48:** THE WELL
HEXAGRAM **28:** PREPONDERANCE OF THE GREAT
HEXAGRAM **17:** FOLLOWING

The following natal hexagrams represent people you naturally tend to have a negative reaction to:

HEXAGRAM **57:** THE PENETRATING
HEXAGRAM **9:**   TAMING POWER OF THE SMALL
HEXAGRAM **37:** THE FAMILY
HEXAGRAM **42:** INCREASE
HEXAGRAM **25:** INNOCENCE
HEXAGRAM **21:** BITING THROUGH

HEXAGRAM 10

 CH'IEN

TREADING
(THE BALANCED ONE)

 TUI

Traits

Royal	Excellent taste
Managerial	Gourmet
Snobbish	Impractical
Organized	Popular or in trouble
Detached	Appeals to all
Keeps things separate	Charismatic
Not in touch with feelings	Ferocious
Risk-taker	Attracts disunity
Audacious	Invokes danger
Cautious—or not!	Chooses carefully
Leader	Follows instincts
Political	
Aesthete	

Life Lessons

These people need to accept that all people are equal; they need to reach out and touch others more, and they should exercise a bit more caution as well.

Positive Tendencies

Here we have true daredevils, people who seem to skate on the edge with daring-do but rarely get into trouble. These people may be intellectually brilliant and crazily aware of things others miss. Dignified persons, they are often completely accepting of others and usually "game" for interesting, unusual, or strange experiences. Natural managers, they instantly gain respect and attention: They are natural leaders who most people have no trouble following, no matter where it may lead. They are also popular people; there always seems to be an admiring aura around them that attracts all sorts of people. Such individuals can go far by following primal instincts, by going with their gut feelings. They have very elevated senses of aesthetics and good taste, expecting and enjoying the finer things of life, including the arts. These are people to whom the label "cutting edge" applies in that they are attracted to the newest, most advanced ideas, schemes, and technologies, especially if they are risky! They are able to separate things, categorize things, and in general objectively remove themselves from things. They are wild, passionate people, in romance and elsewhere. Here are people who know enough to be cautious, although they may not be wise enough to do so. Natural aristocrats, they choose everything with care.

Negative Tendencies

These people may possibly be snobs, feeling quite elevated from the masses. Communication problems, rudeness, snubbing, ignoring warning signs, and thoughtlessness are all possible here. Being detached can extend to emotions and they may in fact be the very distant sort, a kind of social loner. While craving attention and often getting it, they are at times not overly concerned with the real world and must beware of losing touch with reality. Leadership abilities can cut two ways and these people can possibly lead others astray, sometimes into serious trouble, if they are not centered. In fact, such potential daredevils may sometimes invite dangerous situations, possibly feeling above it all. These people may at times be on top of the world—or in deep trouble.

Compatibility

The following natal hexagrams represent people you naturally tend to have a positive reaction to:

HEXAGRAM **2:**   THE RECEPTIVE

HEXAGRAM **24:** RETURN

HEXAGRAM **19:** APPROACH

HEXAGRAM **11:** PEACE

HEXAGRAM **34:** THE POWER OF THE GREAT

HEXAGRAM **43:** BREAKTHROUGH

HEXAGRAM **5:**   WAITING

HEXAGRAM **8:**   HOLDING TOGETHER

The following natal hexagrams represent people you naturally tend to have a negative reaction to:

HEXAGRAM **1:**   THE CREATIVE

HEXAGRAM **44:** COMING TO MEET

HEXAGRAM **33:** RETREAT

HEXAGRAM **12:** STANDSTILL

HEXAGRAM **20:** CONTEMPLATION

HEXAGRAM **23:** SPLITTING APART

HEXAGRAM **35:** PROGRESS

HEXAGRAM **14:** POSSESSION IN GREAT MEASURE

HEXAGRAM 11

K'UN

PEACE
(THE PERVADING ONE)

CHEN

Traits

Harmonious	Picky
Plentiful	Separates things
Peaceful	Analyzes well
Confident	Of two minds
Balanced	Confused
Mediator	Great luck
Steadily growing	Lethargic
Nourishing	New beginnings
Blending Yin and Yang	Contemplative
Energetic	Open
Whiny	Fair and just
Very fortunate	

Life Lessons

These people must not lose sight of the forest for the trees; they need to learn that all things are one and that they should become a bit more forceful and stubborn.

Positive Tendencies

These are naturally wise people. They work hard to be just, value harmony, and strive to nourish all the people around them. These people have amazing bursts of new energy; they separate the old and tired from the new and prospering, encourage fruitful new growth, push projects in the right direction, regulate and control their lives, and generally create a cooperative environment. Very peaceful and relaxed, these people work on steady evolutionary growth for all people. An excellent mediator, they are very in touch with their Yin and Yang, their inner male and female selves. This unleashes great potential wisdom and understanding. Good at counseling and healing, they are adept at balancing all sorts of feelings, emotions, and deeds. They can analyze things in detail and are able to separate things into their distinct components so as to later unite them in a productive manner.

Whether working with people, paper work, ideas, or handiwork, these people have the gift of being able to weed out negative elements, reorganize the structure of something, and then renew and rebuild it so that it is better and more prosperous than it was. This can also apply to relationships, which they are great at constantly renewing and revitalizing. Contemplative and very open, these people are natural "alchemists" who, to make a long story short, can combine opposites into a harmonious whole.

Negative Tendencies

These people can get lost in analysis, dividing things up to the point of creating division instead of understanding. There is a possibility that deep understanding of duality can also lead to a kind of schizophrenia, a dividing instead of a uniting. At time open and peaceful to the point of obsequiousness, these individuals can be classic wimps, people who are limpid and lethargic with no real force. There is also a "holier than thou" attitude that may surface in these truly harmonious people; no one likes to be preached at, and any reforms or changes, no matter how necessary, can anger people when tact is ignored.

Compatibility

The following natal hexagrams represent people you naturally tend to have a positive reaction to:

HEXAGRAM **1:**   THE CREATIVE
HEXAGRAM **44:**   COMING TO MEET
HEXAGRAM **33:**   RETREAT
HEXAGRAM **12:**   STANDSTILL
HEXAGRAM **20:**   CONTEMPLATION
HEXAGRAM **23:**   SPLITTING APART
HEXAGRAM **35:**   PROGRESS
HEXAGRAM **14:**   POSSESSION IN GREAT MEASURE

The following natal hexagrams represent people you naturally tend to have a negative reaction to:

HEXAGRAM **2:**   THE RECEPTIVE

HEXAGRAM **24:**   RETURN

HEXAGRAM **19:**   APPROACH

HEXAGRAM **11:**   PEACE

HEXAGRAM **34:**   THE POWER OF THE GREAT

HEXAGRAM **43:**   BREAKTHROUGH

HEXAGRAM **5:**   WAITING

HEXAGRAM **8:**   HOLDING TOGETHER

HEXAGRAM 12

CH'IEN

STANDSTILL
(THE STILL ONE)

K'UN

Traits

Polarized	Awkward
Indecisive	Low energy
Objective	Stuffy
Able to deeply understand	Overwhelmed
Of two minds	Reserved
Distinguished	Contradictory
Separating and categorizing	Not greedy
Humble	Giving
Having inner power	Detached from possessions
Self-effacing	Fascinated
Insecure	Of two different worlds
Giving	

Life Lessons

These people need to simply do something (anything!) sometimes; they need to trust their intuition more and should seek out the strange and exciting things in life.

Positive Tendencies

Generally, these people are very balanced and persevere through all difficulties of life. They have the rare gift of being able to separate things clearly and distinctly. This means they can separate feelings, ideas, problems, and so on in order to clearly see the components of a given relationship or problem. This makes them excellent judges, very analytical as well as objective. These people may encounter many problems, but they try, and try again—persistent individuals. These are people of high moral character, people who give good advice. They never seeks the spotlight, refuse unnecessary praise or flattery, dislike scrutiny, and are naturally quiet, thoughtful, and reserved. Humble, these people don't like a lot of glory. They may do much work without getting credit for it. They can approach things from many different angles. These people are very solitary in many ways and may have very different parts of their psyche pulling them in opposite directions, but this just means that they can be very empathic, really understanding people. These people work best alone; they are often very self-disciplined, and while they may not outwardly be very powerful, this is deceiving in that inwardly they are very intense individuals. These are very nice and sweet people, as well.

Negative Tendencies

At times these people can be of two minds, and this kind of paralysis can affect many aspects of their lives; the urge to do and the urge to not do are often at war. Such people can be stuffy, vindictive, stagnant, misunderstood, unproductive, blocked, and/or mistrusted. These thoughts of others may not be their fault, but they can be perceptions. These people often get overwhelmed by choices and so don't do anything. They can sometimes be something of a nerd, a mild person who can be low-energy, maybe a little dull at times.

Compatibility

The following natal hexagrams represent people you naturally tend to have a positive reaction to:

HEXAGRAM **2:**   THE RECEPTIVE

HEXAGRAM **24:**   RETURN

HEXAGRAM **19:**   APPROACH

HEXAGRAM **11:**   PEACE

HEXAGRAM **34:**   THE POWER OF THE GREAT

HEXAGRAM **43:**   BREAKTHROUGH

HEXAGRAM **5:**   WAITING

HEXAGRAM **8:**   HOLDING TOGETHER

The following natal hexagrams represent people you naturally tend to have a negative reaction to:

HEXAGRAM **1:**   THE CREATIVE

HEXAGRAM **44:**   COMING TO MEET

HEXAGRAM **33:**   RETREAT

HEXAGRAM **12:**   STANDSTILL

HEXAGRAM **20:**   CONTEMPLATION

HEXAGRAM **23:**   SPLITTING APART

HEXAGRAM **35:**   PROGRESS

HEXAGRAM **14:**   POSSESSION IN GREAT MEASURE

HEXAGRAM 13

CH'IEN

FELLOWSHIP WITH MEN
(THE FACILITATING ONE)

LI

Traits

Organizer	Dissecting
Group leader	Secure
Facilitator	Excitable
Host	Energetic
Bully	Sublime
Controller	Holistic
Manipulator	Political
Person who reveals	Beneficent
Gossip	Selfless
Lover of all	Ego-poor
Jupiter-like	Group-dependent
Discerning judge	Focus of group work

Life Lessons

These people need to learn to chill out more, need to watch what they say to others and really learn to let go of things.

Positive Tendencies

These people are the center of the community, political people in the sense that they personify the general mood or group-mind, at that time, of their community. These people have very strong wills; they may be a bit intense, real leaders. Charismatic, these individuals can see whole patterns of things and how things work, and people listen to them. These are quietly vivacious people who often seem up and who are often persistent in the pursuit of their dreams. They are charismatic people who have the gift of helping others. Here are individuals who can have great character, a real appreciation of others, and the ability to communicate with all types of people on their own levels. These people will either be gifted leaders or superb followers, people who grasp the goals of the group and are key to making sure they come true. These are individuals who can easily have their act together, probably being motivated to watch and pursue to success health, diet, day-to-day jobs, committed relationships, and so on. Beneficent and idealistic, they are often the most important people in a group, company, or organization. They love to entertain and often get things done in the sense of getting people of different viewpoints to agree and work things out.

Negative Tendencies

These people can be too aggressive, even sometimes offensive. Words like loud, abrasive, and pushy are sometimes used to describe them. They can be natural leaders and, if motivated by negative ideals, use this to cause great harm in the community. They are skilled at facilitating but sometimes will not take no for an answer or let things drop when they should. These people may like to gossip and chat about others and often watch people. They know a lot about others but can also be manipulative and get into cliques. These people tend to adopt the views of others and might need to focus on their own ego outside of the group. Such individuals can be insecure without the tribe about them.

Compatibility

The following natal hexagrams represent people you naturally tend to have a positive reaction to:

HEXAGRAM **2:**   THE RECEPTIVE
HEXAGRAM **24:** RETURN
HEXAGRAM **19:** APPROACH
HEXAGRAM **11:** PEACE
HEXAGRAM **34:** THE POWER OF THE GREAT
HEXAGRAM **43:** BREAKTHROUGH
HEXAGRAM **5:**   WAITING
HEXAGRAM **8:**   HOLDING TOGETHER

The following natal hexagrams represent people you naturally tend to have a negative reaction to:

HEXAGRAM 14

LI

CH'IEN

POSSESSION IN GREAT
MEASURE
(THE ROYAL ONE)

Traits

Modesty leads to success	Aristocratic
Unity	Authoritative
Communing with the world soul	Center of loyalty
Spiritual fire illuminating all	Gentle
Creative	Proud
Open soul	Immodest
Power channeled gently	Despotic
Culturally giving	Illuminated
Transmitter	Arrogant
Worldly success	Gifted
Overbearing	
Smart	
Influential	

Life Lessons

These people have to be careful of getting too big for their britches; they need to focus on the divine and spirituality more and to learn to play nice—that is, do unto others. . .

Positive Tendencies

These are an extremely successful people who have quite a commanding presence, people to whom others defer, even those who are above them. They are likely to be very creative in many areas and through their diligence and mastery of various skills and subjects may be recognized in maybe more than one field. These individuals are real authorities and thus have authority, in a natural manner. In this way, if they remain modest, others will naturally see them in this light and will be very loyal. Such people are powerhouses. These very individualistic people are usually bright and often have great influence on those around them, although they may not be aware of it. They are often in the spotlight and are often being examined by those above and below them. They are often in high-profile positions. Because of this they are very aware of their own shortcomings, problems, ego, and so on, and this self-awareness is often a key to their inner balance. By suppressing their dark side they become better and thus more powerful people. These individuals are very proud of what they can do and are generally kind, gentle, and compassionate as well. They are very methodical and well-ordered in their relationships. Such individuals are lucky people and things tend to fall their way, especially in worldly affairs, in getting things done, and in making their dreams a reality.

Negative Tendencies

These people can sometimes be real SOBs—arrogant and overbearing. They can be dictatorial and paternalistic. This may happen if they get too egotistic and/or get wrapped up in success. There is potential for greed and immodesty as well. Because these people have the potential for strong spiritual beliefs, just focusing on the material world or getting power-hungry may really unbalance them.

Compatibility

The following natal hexagrams represent people you naturally tend to have a positive reaction to:

HEXAGRAM **29:**   THE ABYSMAL
HEXAGRAM **60:**   LIMITATION
HEXAGRAM **3:**   INITIAL DIFFICULTY
HEXAGRAM **63:**   AFTER COMPLETION
HEXAGRAM **49:**   REVOLUTION
HEXAGRAM **55:**   ABUNDANCE
HEXAGRAM **36:**   DARKENING OF THE LIGHT
HEXAGRAM **7:**   THE ARMY

The following natal hexagrams represent people you naturally tend to have a negative reaction to:

HEXAGRAM **30:**   THE CLINGING FIRE
HEXAGRAM **50:**   THE CAULDRON
HEXAGRAM **64:**   BEFORE COMPLETION
HEXAGRAM **4:**   YOUTHFUL FOLLY
HEXAGRAM **59:**   DISPERSION
HEXAGRAM **6:**   CONFLICT
HEXAGRAM **13:**   FELLOWSHIP WITH MEN

HEXAGRAM 15

K'UN

MODESTY
(THE MODERATE ONE)

K'EN

Traits

Equalizer	Thinks before acting
Egalitarian	Calm and calculated
Balanced	Emotionally cold
Indecisive	Meditative
Poor self-esteem	Withdrawn
Neutral	Analyst
Self-effacing	Dispenser of good
Finishes what is started	Long-lived
Great intuition	Picky
Administrator	Well-loved
Counselor	Will go far
Evenhanded	

Life Lessons

These people need to learn to snap out of bad moods, to just let some things go by without worrying about them, and to take stands more often for what they believe in.

Positive Tendencies

These are very together people in the sense of being a center of calm in even chaotic situations. They can enter a disruptive or crazy situation and just by the power of their character kind of balance things and ease stress and friction. These people have very strong senses of fair play, equality, and justice. They feel that things should be shared and they work for social justice and a more equal society. On a cosmic scale, such people see harmony and balance as spiritual goals for themselves as well as for humanity. Focusing on details, these people are warmhearted and bighearted and even-keeled. They live a relatively modest life and are not motivated or enticed to extreme excess in areas of pleasure or intoxication. These are people who know their limits and who rarely get involved with disasters or problems that they can see coming. They are classic self-actualizing people, yet they can also do quite well in the material world, especially through sincerity.

The perfect counselor or people-manager, even if this is not their profession, people will seek them out for this kind of thing. They are real people-persons who are great at settling disputes and working things out. These individuals have real insight.

Negative Tendencies

These people may be picky and a bit too politically correct. Their detail-focus might be a problem if they ignore the larger picture. These people are well-loved but can get into extreme moods and take things to conclusions that no one else might follow. They might be very cold and reserved, socially and emotionally withdrawn at times. While being insightful, they can be too evenhanded and not take a stand on one side or the other even when it is called for. These individuals may have a hard time getting angry or stating an opinion at times, even when the choice is obvious or an outrage must be addressed. This can lead to being amoral because of the lack of taking a stand, though this is not always a bad thing.

Compatibility

The following natal hexagrams represent people you naturally tend to have a positive reaction to:

HEXAGRAM **1:**   THE CREATIVE
HEXAGRAM **44:**   COMING TO MEET
HEXAGRAM **33:**   RETREAT
HEXAGRAM **12:**   STANDSTILL
HEXAGRAM **20:**   CONTEMPLATION
HEXAGRAM **23:**   SPLITTING APART
HEXAGRAM **35:**   PROGRESS
HEXAGRAM **14:**   POSSESSION IN GREAT MEASURE

The following natal hexagrams represent people you naturally tend to have a negative reaction to:

HEXAGRAM **2:**   THE RECEPTIVE

HEXAGRAM **24:**   RETURN

HEXAGRAM **19:**   APPROACH

HEXAGRAM **11:**   PEACE

HEXAGRAM **34:**   THE POWER OF THE GREAT

HEXAGRAM **43:**   BREAKTHROUGH

HEXAGRAM **5:**   WAITING

HEXAGRAM **8:**   HOLDING TOGETHER

HEXAGRAM 16

CHEN

ENTHUSIASM
(THE PROVIDING ONE)

K'UN

Traits

Enthusiastic

Effervescent

Trying

Stubborn

Terrible temper

Musically inclined

Melodic

Pattern-seeker or -weaver

Projects on others

Instigator

Mover and shaker

Uniquely organized

Political and priestly

Earthed movement

Bombastic

Harebrained

Understands trends

Scheming

Pompous

Bright

Manipulative

Social star

Exciting

Life Lessons

These people need to be more aware of their mood swings, need to keep their cool, and they should strive to be more open to others.

Positive Tendencies

These are real up people who can tap into the ideals and aspirations that underlay the culture. These are individuals who tend to outdistance others and get more work done faster. These are the kind of people who organize their entire house while others are working on one cabinet. They drive others crazy because they are efficient. They are inventive, curious, and unique individuals who not only can come up with new ideas but who are also talented at promoting and pushing those ideas into reality. Movers and shakers, they are the kind of people who are behind plans, who motivate and facilitate. Idea people, they will run with good ideas and have their own way of doing things. Though very organized, they will not be so in the usual way, having their own system that works for them. These people lecture well and really do know what they're talking about; they have a way of making others see patterns, vast ideas, and spiritual truths. These are very popular individuals, and many different types of people instantly feel comfortable with them. Social butterflies, they want to try everything and have lots of friends, but maybe not a lot of deep ones. They are a lot of fun to be with and like to go out and do stuff a lot. They are very active people who fill their schedules quickly. They probably overextend themselves, but they meet those demands. They may also have a number of unorthodox ideas and beliefs.

Negative Tendencies

These people can be very wearing and trying if they are too up, too hyper, too inventive. Sometimes they may have an awful temper that can flare up and die down quickly. It is rare, but intense. They can be stubborn when pursuing a task and may not give up even when it is clear they should. Being tenacious can be a problem when the project is not working. These people can be great at planning but they can also become too scheming, too Machiavellian with a hidden agenda. They can get a bit inflated and too concerned with their social status and also, deep down, may be extremely conservative in several ways. Such people need a bucket of water thrown on them occasionally.

Compatibility

The following natal hexagrams represent people you naturally tend to have a positive reaction to:

HEXAGRAM **57:**   THE PENETRATING

HEXAGRAM **9:**   TAMING POWER OF THE SMALL

HEXAGRAM **37:**   THE FAMILY

HEXAGRAM **42:**   INCREASE

HEXAGRAM **25:**   INNOCENCE

HEXAGRAM **21:**   BITING THROUGH

HEXAGRAM **27:**   NOURISHMENT

HEXAGRAM **18:**   WORK THAT HAS BEEN SPOILED

The following natal hexagrams represent people you naturally tend to have a negative reaction to:

HEXAGRAM **51:**   THE AROUSING

HEXAGRAM **16:**   ENTHUSIASM

HEXAGRAM **40:**   DELIVERANCE

HEXAGRAM **32:**   DURATION

HEXAGRAM **46:**   PUSHING UPWARD

HEXAGRAM **48:**   THE WELL

HEXAGRAM **28:**   PREPONDERANCE OF THE GREAT

HEXAGRAM **17:**   FOLLOWING

HEXAGRAM 17

TUI

FOLLOWING
(THE ADAPTIVE ONE)

CHEN

Traits

Relaxed	Enlightened
Retreat	Type B personality
Follower	Depressed
Well-organized	Judgmental
Prosperous	Cynical
Follows through	Submissive
Pattern-weaver	Flexible
Mimic	Narrow focus
Bland	Protective
Nice and friendly	Very prepared
Supportive	Loyal follower
Guides others	

Life Lessons

These people need to learn ways to beat the blues; they need to get more energized about things and to learn that stress can be a good and productive thing.

Positive Tendencies

These are people who are very well adjusted and competent; they take it easy and seem to effortlessly keep things going. These are low-key but friendly people. They tend to have decent jobs, good friends, be open-minded, flexible, and are all-around good friends to have. They are responsible, trustworthy people who plan well for trips, meetings, and so on. They are rock-steady, easy to have around, and natural teachers in many ways. These people are incredibly adaptable and able to fit in to many different types of situations. They are capable of clearly examining themselves and then adjusting their behavior. They are the type of people who can quit things or simply start a new hobby with an act of will. They are relaxed and kind people who take directions well, who carry through on tasks assigned to them and do an excellent job. They are very introspective people who are often lost in thought. They may have an extremely realistic and pragmatic view of the world.

Negative Tendencies

These people may sometimes suffer from depression and be down in the dumps when things are not going very well. They can sometimes be too relaxed and low-key, slack and indolent, even lazy sometimes. Such people do better with direction from outside themselves and may tend to copy or mimic others, often without meaning to. This can be irritating. These people can do well dotting the Is and crossing Ts, but they may not do well with whole visionary conceptualizing. Here-and-now people, they may not plan well for the long term. These individuals can sometimes be one-sided or prejudiced. They may hate to be pressured emotionally and may retreat from this.

Compatibility

The following natal hexagrams represent people you naturally tend to have a positive reaction to:

HEXAGRAM **52:**   KEEPING STILL

HEXAGRAM **22:**   GRACE

HEXAGRAM **26:**   TAMING POWER OF THE GREAT

HEXAGRAM **41:**   DECREASE

HEXAGRAM **38:**   OPPOSITION

HEXAGRAM **10:**   TREADING

HEXAGRAM **61:**   INNER TRUTH

HEXAGRAM **53:**   DEVELOPMENT

The following natal hexagrams represent people you naturally tend to have a negative reaction to:

HEXAGRAM **30:** THE CLINGING

HEXAGRAM **56:** THE WANDERER

HEXAGRAM **50:** THE CAULDRON

HEXAGRAM **64:** BEFORE COMPLETION

HEXAGRAM **4:** YOUTHFUL FOLLY

HEXAGRAM **59:** DISPERSION

HEXAGRAM **6:** CONFLICT

HEXAGRAM **13:** FELLOWSHIP WITH MEN

HEXAGRAM 18

K'EN

SUN

WORK THAT HAS BEEN
SPOILED
(THE REFORMING ONE)

Traits

Electric

Depressive

Feels guilt

Sympathetic

Suppresses emotions

Corrects others

Social worker

Helpful

Counselor

Stagnant

Self-absorbed

Inward-looking

Alarmist

Very stable

Reliable

Couch potato

Karmic connections

Lets things reach critical mass
    then works on them

Cyclical

Suppress or ignore...explode

Thorough

Detail-oriented

Life Lessons

These people need to not take themselves so seriously; they need to learn to say no, and they have to work hard at getting out of ruts and to pay special attention to mistakes and learn from them.

Positive Tendencies

These are people who have strong moral compasses and who like to fix things and help people with problems. They tend to be good Samaritans, the kind of people you want around in an emergency. Look to these people to help others physically, emotionally, and even financially. They are real 'fix-it' people, who can be very handy around the house as well as in counseling others. They are extremely hard workers and are strongly motivated to make things right or make things work. If in the wrong in some way or when tackling problems, the chief motivation these individuals often have is to make amends. Though naturally a bit timid, they can accomplish great tasks when rousing themselves with focus and will. They are wise people who are natural teachers or therapists; they understand intuitively how to guide or direct others in order to really help them. Such people are drawn to those who need help and will probably be very involved in a number of different causes. They flow through situations, are very reliable, and tend to step into situations to complete them or get them back on track. These are people who can catch important errors or potential problems that may not be evident to others. They have great gut feelings and are very sympathetic. These people are very conscientious in relationships and in their jobs.

Negative Tendencies

These people may be very inward-looking, but they can end up being too self-absorbed at times. They can get stuck in a rut and can seem to be spinning their wheels. They may overextend, take on the problems of too many others and too many responsibilities and so get overloaded, possibly becoming ill or having other problems because of it. They often approach things in a cyclical manner, repeating situations and getting stuck on old behaviors and experiences. They may suppress stress and problems, ignore this pressure, then explode in some way, then the cycle starts up again.

These people can need to chill out at times, but another problem can sometimes be laziness or sluggishness. Maybe they do something like watch too much TV and ignore the need for exercise.

Compatibility

The following natal hexagrams represent people you naturally tend to have a positive reaction to:

HEXAGRAM **30:**   THE CLINGING
HEXAGRAM **56:**   THE WANDERER
HEXAGRAM **50:**   THE CAULDRON
HEXAGRAM **64:**   BEFORE COMPLETION
HEXAGRAM **4:**   YOUTHFUL FOLLY
HEXAGRAM **59:**   DISPERSION
HEXAGRAM **6:**   CONFLICT
HEXAGRAM **13:**   FELLOWSHIP WITH MEN

The following natal hexagrams represent people you naturally tend to have a negative reaction to:

HEXAGRAM **52:**   KEEPING STILL
HEXAGRAM **22:**   GRACE
HEXAGRAM **26:**   TAMING POWER OF THE GREAT
HEXAGRAM **41:**   DECREASE
HEXAGRAM **38:**   OPPOSITION
HEXAGRAM **10:**   TREADING
HEXAGRAM **61:**   INNER TRUTH
HEXAGRAM **53:**   DEVELOPMENT

HEXAGRAM 19

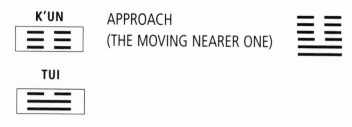

K'UN

APPROACH
(THE MOVING NEARER ONE)

TUI

Traits

High energy	High or low activity
Altruistic	Procrastinates
Positive viewpoint	Very energetic
Naive	Great stamina
Teacher-educator	Confused
Guide	Opportunistic
Salesman	Assertive
Open-minded politics	Stormy
Amoral	Great inner growth
Sanctimonious	Dynamic prosperity
Ups and downs	Self-realized

Life Lessons

These people need to work on being more level-headed, need to let their conscience be their guide, and they really need to watch their health and lead a healthy lifestyle.

Positive Tendencies

These people are natural instructors with really high energy; they'll go all out to support their friends and those they respect and admire. Dynamic, open, and outgoing people who finish an amazing number of projects, they will move up the ranks quickly through skill. They are natural entrepreneurs, talented at starting from scratch and creating a business, organization, or extended project. Self-confident, they tend to find a very deep spiritual path to work with or they create their own unique internal system of beliefs and ideas that mold their own view of the world. These people have great stamina and are competitive and a bit aggressive in a positive sense. They really take advantage of opportunities and have a knack for going with the flow. Very self-motivated, they can take a small idea and do amazing things with it, turning it into a full plan of action. They are natural salespeople who can do anything that requires charisma or charm. In relationships, they are often the instigator and like to stir things up in a fun and exciting way. They are often very prosperous, move up in a company quickly, and are real go-getters. Optimistic, positive people, they tackle things head-on and work things through. Such people may be attracted to alternative healing and different kinds of spirituality.

Negative Tendencies

These people may not have strong sets of real morals, may waffle and take the path of least resistance. They may bend the rules a bit and can have real highs and lows, being very energetic and later very run-down and burned out. They can easily get confused and disoriented and can get so hyped-up and excited that they may lose track of what's what. This high energy can sometimes be chaotic, misdirected, or even out of control. These people may need to be careful during their middle years, watch their health, and try to even out. The very peak of summer may cause them problems in life. Things in their lives escalate quickly, and they need to watch this. Small problems should not be ignored or they'll grow.

Compatibility

The following natal hexagrams represent people you naturally tend to have a positive reaction to:

HEXAGRAM **1:**   THE CREATIVE
HEXAGRAM **44:** COMING TO MEET
HEXAGRAM **33:** RETREAT
HEXAGRAM **12:** STANDSTILL
HEXAGRAM **20:** CONTEMPLATION

HEXAGRAM **23:** SPLITTING APART

HEXAGRAM **35:** PROGRESS

HEXAGRAM **14:** POSSESSION IN GREAT MEASURE

The following natal hexagrams represent people you naturally tend to have a negative reaction to:

HEXAGRAM **2:** THE RECEPTIVE

HEXAGRAM **24:** RETURN

HEXAGRAM **19:** APPROACH

HEXAGRAM **11:** PEACE

HEXAGRAM **34:** THE POWER OF THE GREAT

HEXAGRAM **43:** BREAKTHROUGH

HEXAGRAM **5:** WAITING

HEXAGRAM **8:** HOLDING TOGETHER

HEXAGRAM 20

SUN

CONTEMPLATION
(THE CLEAR ONE)

K'UN

Traits

Yoga	Relaxed
Higher spiritual disciplines	Careful
Pontifical	Slow and boring
Teaching	Trusting
Open and empathic	Con artist
Wimp	Open to new ideas
Too "white light"	Gullible

Powerful existence	Hermitlike
Shows by doing	Withdrawn
Objective	Out of touch
Instinctive	Buddha-like
Contemplative	

Life Lessons

These people need to learn to accept the bad with the good and to understand that external reality mirrors internal reality, nor should they believe everything they hear.

Positive Tendencies

These are very spiritual people who really try to bring spirituality into their daily lives. Every day is a kind of meditation to them. These people have the ability to remove themselves from a given situation and objectively examine everything about that thing or situation, and thus clearly see what will happen and/or what should be done. Many will wonder "how did he see that coming?" but it will be natural to them. These are people who give great advice. They will be open-minded and are drawn to many kinds of experiences and spiritual paths, maybe trying such things as yoga or meditation or Tai Chi. Whether following a traditional discipline or not, these people will often have some sort of spiritual practice going. These are honest and trusting people who trust their instincts about events and people, often having hunches that turn out to be correct. They are watchers, people who like observing others and keeping track of the things going on around them. Patterns of behavior fascinate these people. They are real dreamers who can easily drift into a private space inside their heads. These people will be role models; people are drawn to watching and imitating them so this is the best way for them to teach others: teaching by doing. Home is very important to these people. They are very relaxed, easygoing, and humorous.

Negative Tendencies

These people can be a bit pompous or bombastic, a bit holier than thou. These are not obviously strong people, they can appear too wimpy, too whiny, and maybe too politically correct. These people may also be finicky. They may be having trouble with the dark side of life, accepting their dark side or the negative things in others. They may only want to hear positive things and may tend to be a little too "white light." These people sometimes likes to withdraw, maybe too much, into a fantasy life. They like alone-time, which is OK, but they need to be careful or they'll become hermits. Sometimes they may be out of touch with what's going on. These people might like to play tricks sometimes, and this can be taken to extremes and end up being mean.

Compatibility

The following natal hexagrams represent people you naturally tend to have a positive reaction to:

HEXAGRAM **51:**   THE AROUSING

HEXAGRAM **16:**   ENTHUSIASM

HEXAGRAM **40:**   DELIVERANCE

HEXAGRAM **32:**   DURATION

HEXAGRAM **46:**   PUSHING UPWARD

HEXAGRAM **48:**   THE WELL

HEXAGRAM **28:**   PREPONDERANCE OF THE GREAT

HEXAGRAM **17:**   FOLLOWING

The following natal hexagrams represent people you naturally tend to have a negative reaction to:

HEXAGRAM **57:**   THE PENETRATING

HEXAGRAM **9:**   TAMING POWER OF THE SMALL

HEXAGRAM **37:**   THE FAMILY

HEXAGRAM **42:**   INCREASE

HEXAGRAM 21

BITING THROUGH
(THE PENETRATING ONE)

Traits

Loving order	Holier than thou
Strict	Decisive
Fair or unfair	Interpreter
Judgmental	Successful
Clinical-minded	Accurate
Attentive	Scientific
Conscious	Exact
Sharp	Neat
Analytical	Exasperating
Profit-oriented	Biting and sarcastic
Good decision maker	Overbearing
Dictator	Blunt and truthful

Life Lessons

These people need to learn not to be so uptight; they should be more sympathetic and supportive of others and less concerned with appearances.

Positive Tendencies

These are very moral people with clear ideas of right and wrong, not just for him or themselves but also for society. They really believe in the responsibility of the individual and of society. Duty is a key word here. These people are very fair, have sharp attentive minds, and are very analytical; they may be drawn to the sciences. They approach all things in a systematic and organized manner and gets great results. They can plan, organize, and present things well and can explain and communicate well. These are naturally just individuals and can also be very protective. They are precise people who tend to be neat and accurate. They tend to be very successful, setting goals, and following through, thus getting what they want. They have the ability to make a profit and keep track of money. Decisive people, they are also very witty and don't put up with a lot of crap. Truthseekers, they try to remain very conscious.

Negative Tendencies

They can be somewhat dictatorial, leaning toward law and order, and can be morally judgmental. They sometimes feel that things are right or wrong across the board and that is that, regardless of what other people think. These people can be exasperating, stubborn, and it is hard to change their minds at all. They may have a very hard time backing down in situations and in confrontations, even when wrong. Funny people, they can also be sarcastic and biting, even cruel. They can be moral crusaders and get a bit full of themselves. They can also take neatness and organization to real extremes, driving others crazy and stifling spontaneity and creativity.

Compatibility

The following natal hexagrams represent people you naturally tend to have a positive reaction to:

HEXAGRAM **29:** THE ABYSMAL

HEXAGRAM **60:** LIMITATION

HEXAGRAM **3:** INITIAL DIFFICULTY

HEXAGRAM **63:** AFTER COMPLETION

HEXAGRAM **49:**   REVOLUTION

HEXAGRAM **55:**   ABUNDANCE

HEXAGRAM **36:**   DARKENING OF THE LIGHT

HEXAGRAM **7:**   THE ARMY

The following natal hexagrams represent people you naturally tend to have a negative reaction to:

HEXAGRAM **30:**   THE CLINGING FIRE

HEXAGRAM **56:**   THE WANDERER

HEXAGRAM **50:**   THE CAULDRON

HEXAGRAM **64:**   BEFORE COMPLETION

HEXAGRAM **4:**   YOUTHFUL FOLLY

HEXAGRAM **59:**   DISPERSION

HEXAGRAM **6:**   CONFLICT

HEXAGRAM **13:**   FELLOWSHIP WITH MEN

HEXAGRAM 22

K'EN

GRACE
(THE ADORNED ONE)

LI

Traits

Beautiful	Mannered
Shallow	Do limited projects well
Lovely	Meticulous
Gracious	Suppressed temper
Calm	Narrow view
Poised	Detail-oriented

Designer or artistic	Clueless
Clear-minded	Forceful
Planner	Strong-willed
Step-by-step person	Short attention span
No big plans	Easy to be with
Petty	

Life Lessons

These people need to pay more attention to the things that go on around them; they need to be more aware of things and of the effects of their actions; these people also need to stop judging things and people by surface appearances.

Positive Tendencies

These are very beautiful people, whether physically so or not; they are quite attractive to many people on several different levels. They are the kind of people who stop conversation when they enter a room. Well-groomed, graceful, and well-mannered, they tend to have pleasant vocal tones and can easily fit in anywhere. These people do well in careers in or near the arts, in retail, or in areas where personal relations are important. Strong-willed, they get their way and succeed in small tasks, step by step. They would usually do better as members of a team than as coordinator or boss. Such people like sequential thinking, logic, and tasks. They are very detail-oriented, doing a great job on well-defined tasks. They tend to be very artistic and creative and are often very nice and enjoyable to be with.

Negative Tendencies

These people sometimes do not do well with large projects, being unable to grasp the big picture or make leaps in ideas. They can be meticulous but can also be picky and petty. Though strong-willed, such individuals can also be clueless, sometimes like a bull in a china shop. They might have trouble sticking with things and may flit from relationship to relationship or job to job. They sometimes love things that are not long-term, but commitment can be a real difficulty. They can also be very easy come, easy go and will avoid problems or difficult things.

Compatibility

The following natal hexagrams represent people you naturally tend to have a positive reaction to:

HEXAGRAM **30**:   THE CLINGING

HEXAGRAM **56**:   THE WANDERER

HEXAGRAM **50**:   THE CAULDRON

HEXAGRAM **64**:   BEFORE COMPLETION

HEXAGRAM **4**:   YOUTHFUL FOLLY

HEXAGRAM **59**:   DISPERSION

HEXAGRAM **6**:   CONFLICT

HEXAGRAM **13**:   FELLOWSHIP WITH MEN

The following natal hexagrams represent people you naturally tend to have a negative reaction to:

HEXAGRAM **52**:   KEEPING STILL

HEXAGRAM **22**:   GRACE

HEXAGRAM **26**:   TAMING POWER OF THE GREAT

HEXAGRAM **41**:   DECREASE

HEXAGRAM **38**:   OPPOSITION

HEXAGRAM **10**:   TREADING

HEXAGRAM **61**:   INNER TRUTH

HEXAGRAM **53**:   DEVELOPMENT

HEXAGRAM   23:

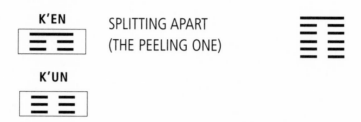

K'EN

SPLITTING APART
(THE PEELING ONE)

K'UN

Traits

Unbalanced	Erupting temper
Insightful	Learns through radical change
Divided	Radical shifts
Empathic	Delicate health
Stubborn	Compartmentalizes
Bigoted	Placid
Pretentious	Jinx
Overbearing	Things just happen
Snobbish	Catalyst
Generous	Critic
Bighearted and giving	Analyst
Accepts things as they are	

Life Lessons

These people need to aim for balance more; they should try to avoid trouble more, to not sweat the small stuff in life, and they need to take care of their bodies more.

Positive Tendencies

These people often don't have the easiest life, but they grow from adversity and become strong. They are very nice, kind, and like to give of themselves. The more they concentrate on altruistic things, on helping others, the less the chaos of life will bother them. These people are very empathic and they identify with others, so they are wonderful to have around; they sympathize and lend a shoulder all the time. These are individuals who take things as they come, are very live-and-let-live. They are very meditative, roll with the punches, and have a knack for doing a lot with a little, making things work out. Such people have an inner peace and are often seen as the calm in the center of a storm. They love change, especially rapid change. They are comfortable with shifts in internal or external reality, very shamanic in that sense, and they tend to grow from radical shocks. These people might go bungee jumping, for example, or fly off to Italy on a whim. They are very analytical and can review, summarize, and evaluate things. They often approach things in this manner and learn a lot.

Negative Tendencies

These people can be something of a jinx; stuff just constantly seems to happen to them. It sometimes seems as if they're lightning rods for all sorts of trouble, usually through no fault of their own. They are often the catalyst, and this is not always positive. Such individuals may not be the most balanced of people, flipping from extreme to extreme. Very "Jekyll-and-Hyde." They can at times be very opinionated, critical, one-sided, and often have a terrible temper.

Compatibility

The following natal hexagrams represent people you naturally tend to have a positive reaction to:

HEXAGRAM **30:**   THE CLINGING
HEXAGRAM **56:**   THE WANDERER
HEXAGRAM **50:**   THE CAULDRON
HEXAGRAM **64:**   BEFORE COMPLETION
HEXAGRAM **4:**   YOUTHFUL FOLLY
HEXAGRAM **59:**   DISPERSION
HEXAGRAM **6:**   CONFLICT
HEXAGRAM **13:**   FELLOWSHIP WITH MEN

The following natal hexagrams represent people you naturally tend to have a negative reaction to:

HEXAGRAM **52:** KEEPING STILL

HEXAGRAM **22:** GRACE

HEXAGRAM **26:** TAMING POWER OF THE GREAT

HEXAGRAM **41:** DECREASE

HEXAGRAM **38:** OPPOSITION

HEXAGRAM **10:** TREADING

HEXAGRAM **61:** INNER TRUTH

HEXAGRAM **53:** DEVELOPMENT

HEXAGRAM 24

K'UN

RETURN
(THE REMEMBERING ONE)

CHEN

Traits

Deep thunder	Giving of self
Introverted	Repetitive
Indecisive or decisive	Nostalgic
Many helping friends	Receptive to others
Feels apart	Fosters new beginnings
Quiet decision maker	Pushy
Deep power	Impatient
Founder	Cautious
Corrector	Keeper of traditions
Historian; past-finder	Focused on cycles
Understands patterns and cycles	Openhanded
Growth by returning to roots	Inner strength

Life Lessons

These people should not doubt themselves so much, should have faith that things do get better, and should look more to the future and cheer up.

Positive Tendencies

They are very intense people, very heavy thinkers. They have powerful and complex inner lives unfolding and this is evident to others. They are deep contemplators and are seen to have a lot of personal power, even though they may often be very quiet and low-key. They can be very subtle but influential. These individuals attract many friends and are fascinated with the past and with historical cycles. They may be drawn to history, anthropology, and the like. They have an instinctual grasp of patterns, traditions, and behaviors. They work very well with people, people organizations, and evolving groups. These people believe in personal growth through discovering root skills, deep ideas within the inner mind. They are nostalgic and very helpful and openhearted. Great starters of new projects, these people really get the ball rolling. For these cautious, tradition-minded people, cycles are the key to life. Opportunities will often come back around if they just have patience.

Negative Tendencies

These are people who can be very indecisive, who sometimes feel alienated and excluded. They can be very impatient and overbearing, especially if they feel that the cycle is on the downswing, that things aren't breaking fast enough. Such individuals can be a bit aggressive and sometimes repetitive. They must beware of being maudlin and on focusing on the past as opposed to the future. They also may tend to live "in the mind," maybe too much so.

Compatibility

The following natal hexagrams represent people you naturally tend to have a positive reaction to:

HEXAGRAM **1:**   THE CREATIVE

HEXAGRAM **44:**   COMING TO MEET

HEXAGRAM **33:**   RETREAT

HEXAGRAM **12:**   STANDSTILL

HEXAGRAM **20:**   CONTEMPLATION

HEXAGRAM **23:**   SPLITTING APART

HEXAGRAM **35:**   PROGRESS

HEXAGRAM **14:**   POSSESSION IN GREAT MEASURE

The following natal hexagrams represent people you naturally tend to have a negative reaction to:

HEXAGRAM **2:**   THE RECEPTIVE

HEXAGRAM **24:**   RETURN

HEXAGRAM **19:**   APPROACH

HEXAGRAM **11:**   PEACE

HEXAGRAM **34:**   THE POWER OF THE GREAT

HEXAGRAM **43:**   BREAKTHROUGH

HEXAGRAM **5:**   WAITING

HEXAGRAM **8:**   HOLDING TOGETHER

HEXAGRAM 25

CH'IEN

INNOCENCE
(THE REMOVED ONE)

CHEN

Traits

Primal	Easily swayed
Naive	When dishonest are failures
Deep-rooted	Animalistic
Dull	Extremely single-minded
Easily corruptible	All-natural
Salt of the Earth	Oriented or disoriented
Good person	Virtuous
Successful	Unpredictable
Moral	Spontaneous
Clueless	Primitive
Unsophisticated	Loyal
Honest	

Life Lessons

These people need to think for themselves more; they should ponder decisions more carefully before acting and be careful who they hang out with.

Positive Tendencies

These people are very natural, very primal, very down to earth. Nature-lovers, they are very innocent and tend not to value the strictures and restrictions of society, morality, and law. The natural order, the way things are in real life, is their real focus. These are very good, sincere, loving people who have clear and unsophisticated views of the world. Often having many friends, they are very spontaneous and easily swayed by spontaneous feelings into, for example, throwing a party with no notice or going skinny dipping. They are very influenced by the natural world on all levels of life and look to it for guidance. Virtuous, these individuals often have few long-term goals and that's fine; they do well following instinct, noblesse oblige.

Negative Tendencies

These people can be very easily influenced and swayed by others. They may sometimes be somewhat naive and so can easily fall victim to slick, immoral, aggressive people. These people are very loyal, which is good, unless the loyalty is misplaced—and this can happen. They can be corrupted if they get in with the wrong crowds. Such people may have a real chance to become dishonest and degraded if so influenced by others, and if this happens it will lead to failure. Sometimes clueless, these people may need to question things more; they can be the classic mark for con artists. They can be very spaced out and can leap before looking, something that might be hard on a relationship or an employer.

Compatibility

The following natal hexagrams represent people you naturally tend to have a positive reaction to:

HEXAGRAM **2:**   THE RECEPTIVE
HEXAGRAM **24:**   RETURN
HEXAGRAM **19:**   APPROACH
HEXAGRAM **11:**   PEACE
HEXAGRAM **34:**   THE POWER OF THE GREAT
HEXAGRAM **43:**   BREAKTHROUGH
HEXAGRAM **5:**   WAITING
HEXAGRAM **8:**   HOLDING TOGETHER

The following natal hexagrams represent people you naturally tend to have a negative reaction to:

HEXAGRAM **1:**   THE CREATIVE
HEXAGRAM **44:**   COMING TO MEET
HEXAGRAM **33:**   RETREAT
HEXAGRAM **12:**   STANDSTILL
HEXAGRAM **20:**   CONTEMPLATION

HEXAGRAM 26

K'EN

THE TAMING POWER
OF THE GREAT
(THE ACCUMULATING ONE)

CH'IEN

Traits

Inner strength	Centered
Great character	Organizer or coordinator
Firm	Instructor
Disciplined	Mediator or politician
Reserved	Spreads inner teachings
Stubborn	Emotionally cold
Conservative	Powerful
Thick	Immovable
Scholar of ancient wisdom	Inflexible
Bookworm	Stable
Persistent	Controlling
Humanitarian	

Life Lessons

These people should be less of a stick-in-the-mud; they need to try new things, needs to let go more, and should learn to say "I'm wrong" more often.

Positive Tendencies

These are people who are often stable, strong, and well-rounded. They have wonderful characters and know a lot. They are steadfast and tend to study quite a bit and amass significant wisdom both from books and from others. Very centered, they are really clear about goals, about self, and about their place in the universe. Like a brick, these individuals are dependable and organized; they manage, facilitate, teach, and/or counsel very well. They bring gravity to any situation, a serious and deep viewpoint. They are respected and have natural authority and tend to gain power. Such people would do well in politics or something that requires real responsibility. They also like to plan things and keep them under control. These are disciplined people as well.

Negative Tendencies

These people can be very stubborn and conservative. They may dislike trying new things, preferring to stick with the tried and true. They can use past events to determine future actions and this can get very restrictive. They can be very controlling and are not very flexible. Such people may feel that everyone should be as disciplined as they are and thus can be too regimented. These people can also be very bombastic, a bit boring, and sometimes a little dense. They may simply not "get" what someone is saying if it is contrary to what they believe.

Compatibility

The following natal hexagrams represent people you naturally tend to have a positive reaction to:

HEXAGRAM **30:**   THE CLINGING
HEXAGRAM **56:**   THE WANDERER
HEXAGRAM **50:**   THE CAULDRON
HEXAGRAM **64:**   BEFORE COMPLETION
HEXAGRAM **4:**   YOUTHFUL FOLLY
HEXAGRAM **59:**   DISPERSION
HEXAGRAM **6:**   CONFLICT
HEXAGRAM **13:**   FELLOWSHIP WITH MEN

The following natal hexagrams represent people you naturally tend to have a negative reaction to:

HEXAGRAM **52:**   KEEPING STILL

HEXAGRAM **22:**   GRACE

HEXAGRAM **26:**   TAMING POWER OF THE GREAT

HEXAGRAM **41:**   DECREASE

HEXAGRAM **38:**   OPPOSITION

HEXAGRAM **10:**   TREADING

HEXAGRAM **61:**   INNER TRUTH

HEXAGRAM **53:**   DEVELOPMENT

HEXAGRAM 27

K'EN

PROVIDING NOURISHMENT
(THE FEEDING ONE)

CHEN

Traits

Nourishing and giving	Sociable
Sharing and open	Unsophisticated
Caregiver	Spacey
Healer	Optimist
Provider	Bigmouthed
Teacher	Gullible
Condescending	Gives it all away
Paternal	Altruistic
Simplistic	Liberal-minded
Loving	Compassionate
Nonjudgmental	Idealistic
Initiate beginnings	Meddlesome

Life Lessons

These people need to mind their own business more; they need to be quiet at times, to be more pragmatic, and to organize things better.

Positive Tendencies

These are your classic openhearted, optimistic, loving, nourishing, paternal or maternal, caring people. Givers and healers, they are always helping others and will almost certainly enter a field of work where some of these qualities can shine through. These people are wonderful friends who will always be supportive. They are also very selfless, don't look for a reward, and truly care for those less fortunate. Compassionate beings, these people might be seen as the classic nice guy. They are fun to be around, very social, and do not have many complex ideas or feelings; they tend to see things in black and white—bad things being things that are bad for people. Viewing things often in a loving, nonjudgmental way, they are very people-motivated and optimistic.

Negative Tendencies

These people can be too idealistic, tending to use words like "should" a lot. They may aim for perfection, but they don't cope with the "real" world very well at times. These people can often be busybodies and can meddle. These can be, at times, disorganized people who space out things and events and have trouble keeping track of appointments. They can be very condescending and a bit haughty or even parental with people who are not heeding their sage advice. Such people can sometimes take to extremes things involving the greater good—like banning all smoking on the planet.

Compatibility

The following natal hexagrams represent people you naturally tend to have a positive reaction to:

HEXAGRAM **30:**   THE CLINGING
HEXAGRAM **56:**   THE WANDERER

HEXAGRAM **50:**   THE CAULDRON

HEXAGRAM **64:**   BEFORE COMPLETION

HEXAGRAM **4:**   YOUTHFUL FOLLY

HEXAGRAM **59:**   DISPERSION

HEXAGRAM **6:**   CONFLICT

HEXAGRAM **13:**   FELLOWSHIP WITH MEN

The following natal hexagrams represent people you naturally tend to have a negative reaction to:

HEXAGRAM **52:**   KEEPING STILL

HEXAGRAM **22:**   GRACE

HEXAGRAM **26:**   TAMING POWER OF THE GREAT

HEXAGRAM **41:**   DECREASE

HEXAGRAM **38:**   OPPOSITION

HEXAGRAM **10:**   TREADING

HEXAGRAM **61:**   INNER TRUTH

HEXAGRAM **53:**   DEVELOPMENT

HEXAGRAM 28

TUI

PREPONDERANCE
OF THE GREAT
(THE EXCEEDING ONE)

SUN

Traits

Great pressures	Decision maker
Incredible moments	Active
Breaking point	Fearless
Breakthrough	Fulcrum
Introverted	Intense life
Forced to be alone	Focus of fate
Tenacious	Suffers great extremes
A tree in the wind	Drought or flood patterns
Independent	Pivotal roles
Withdrawn	Catalyst
Flexible	Survivor
Momentous	

Life Lessons

These people need to learn to face their fears squarely; they need to learn to deal with crises and attach less importance to things.

Positive Tendencies

These are often wild individuals who live for peak experiences. They do very well under great pressure, and if not actually seeking out such situations, they will create them in order to get things done and to reach a high pitch of performance. They want to be the best. These are people who are often fearless, who leap wholeheartedly into the center of life. They measure things in terms of intensity: intense emotions, experiences, ideas, and so on. Not relaxing people, they bring out the best in others. Very independent, such individuals bend in the wind and survive even the most insane situations; in fact, they often emerge better, stronger, and more prosperous. They are real sparks; they get things moving, get decisions made, make projects accelerate, and so on.

Negative Tendencies

Extreme changes may swirl around these people—feast or famine, floods or draughts, loud noise or silence. This can be unnerving; they can be hard to be around. These people may sometimes be severely introverted, though you'd think the opposite. They may simply withdraw at key moments and this may shock others. Such individuals can sometimes be too much the maverick and may like to take things to the brink, to the breaking point. They sometimes like to push things as far as possible as a way of understanding what's what. They are not usually boring, but look out.

Compatibility

The following natal hexagrams represent people you naturally tend to have a positive reaction to:

HEXAGRAM **52:** KEEPING STILL

HEXAGRAM **22:** GRACE

HEXAGRAM **26:** TAMING POWER OF THE GREAT

HEXAGRAM **41:** DECREASE

HEXAGRAM **38:** OPPOSITION

HEXAGRAM **10:** TREADING

HEXAGRAM **61:** INNER TRUTH

HEXAGRAM **53:** DEVELOPMENT

The following natal hexagrams represent people you naturally tend to have a negative reaction to:

HEXAGRAM **30:** THE CLINGING

HEXAGRAM **56:** THE WANDERER

HEXAGRAM **50:** THE CAULDRON

HEXAGRAM **64:** BEFORE COMPLETION

HEXAGRAM **4:**   YOUTHFUL FOLLY

HEXAGRAM **59:** DISPERSION
HEXAGRAM **6:**   CONFLICT
HEXAGRAM **13:** FELLOWSHIP WITH MEN

HEXAGRAM 29

K'AN

THE ABYSMAL
(THE DEEP ONE)

K'AN

Traits

Hidden currents	Virtuous
Manic or depressed	Educator
Hard life	Ethical
Learns from dangers	Changing
Daredevil	Amorphous
OK when steady / wild when volatile	Hidden life
	Special instructor
Slowly persistent	Kind and giving
Access to the unconscious	Slow steady success
Accustoms to situations	Hard worker
Adaptable	Trials
Self-confident	Patience and care

Life Lessons

These people need to learn limits, what is and is not realistic; they also need to learn to mellow out more.

Positive Tendencies

These people tend to have a difficult life but are excellent at pushing themselves and succeeding. They learn best from problems, often seeing them as opportunities to learn, and are often very adaptable as well. Success is slow but steady for these people; they may have to work harder than others, but they will reach their goals with more maturity than many. Such individuals have a lot of patience and are very caring; they have firm moral characters and are very ethical and loving in a deep way. They work through problems methodically and are excellent people for crisis resolution or mediating. The fact that they may actually experience many difficulties firsthand makes them more sympathetic and understanding of others. These people really work hard to earn the loyalty of others, are somewhat hidden thrill-seekers and are not always open about their inner life, which makes up a very rich part of their personality.

Negative Tendencies

These people can have real highs and real lows. They can be volatile and, if pushed at the wrong time, can get a bit crazy. They may have very strong connections with the unconscious, which could be good or bad if it overwhelms them. They may have to be very careful to keep fantasy and reality clearly separate. These people might be prone to obsession, and this may be part of their hidden lives. Such people tend to have harder lives than others, yet they develop great character, though this may not be much consolation at times. If these people don't follow their higher spiritual voice, there can be real dangers. Consciousness is very important.

Compatibility

The following natal hexagrams represent people you naturally tend to have a positive reaction to:

HEXAGRAM **30:**   THE CLINGING FIRE
HEXAGRAM **56:**   THE WANDERER
HEXAGRAM **50:**   THE CAULDRON
HEXAGRAM **64:**   BEFORE COMPLETION
HEXAGRAM **4:**   YOUTHFUL FOLLY
HEXAGRAM **59:**   DISPERSION

HEXAGRAM **6**:   CONFLICT

HEXAGRAM **3**:   FELLOWSHIP WITH MEN

The following natal hexagrams represent people you naturally tend to have a negative reaction to:

HEXAGRAM **29**:   THE ABYSMAL

HEXAGRAM **60**:   LIMITATION

HEXAGRAM **3**:   INITIAL DIFFICULTY

HEXAGRAM **63**:   AFTER COMPLETION

HEXAGRAM **49**:   REVOLUTION

HEXAGRAM **55**:   ABUNDANCE

HEXAGRAM **36**:   DARKENING OF THE LIGHT

HEXAGRAM **7**:   THE ARMY

HEXAGRAM 30

LI

THE CLINGING FIRE
(THE RADIANT ONE)

LI

Traits

Clarity	Deep spirituality
Openness	Irrepressible
Intense	Decisive
Fanatic	Egotistic
Devoted	Bright
Emanates energy	Idealistic
Essence of nature	Caregiver
Naturalistic	Children-oriented

Humanitarian
Paternal
Altruistic
Illuminating

Witty
Good-natured
Ascetic

Life Lessons

These people need to learn when to quit; they also need to take more time off and empathize more with others.

Positive Tendencies

These individuals are very clear, bright, and exciting. They are very funny at times, witty and intelligent. They are great party people, and can work a room and leave everyone amused, thoughtful, or entertained. They have many different skills and a seemingly infinite number of interests that are always growing. Probably voracious readers, these people also live for social discourse and will chat with almost anyone. They are true seekers, on many levels. They probably check out all kinds of spiritual paths, clubs, schools, types of software, and so on. These people are often deeply spiritual. They have very strong urges to enlighten others, either by teaching, showing, negotiating, selling, writing, or whatever. They are socially adept and probably have many different kinds of friends, people from completely different walks of life. These people are fascinated with communication and ideas, a natural Internet or computer lover, but never a techno-nerd. They love and work well in groups, often emerging as the soul of a group. They are very exciting lovers as well, with all kinds of flashy ideas.

Negative Tendencies

These people can be really trying, very insistent, and sometimes simply be too much to take, like an out-of-control party guest who won't leave. They can be very egotistical, overbearing, and snobbish at times. These people often burn the candle at both ends and can simply burn out. Overdoing it can be a problem. They know a little about a great many things but may not be well-versed on specific topics. Relationships can be superficial and they can be fickle. Such people can be catty, gossipy, with a bit of backbiting, but usually not for long. Though very enthusiastic, these people can really overdo it trying to hook others into their new consuming passion (which changes).

Compatibility

The following natal hexagrams represent people you naturally tend to have a positive reaction to:

HEXAGRAM **29:** THE ABYSMAL
HEXAGRAM **60:** LIMITATION
HEXAGRAM **3:** INITIAL DIFFICULTY
HEXAGRAM **63:** AFTER COMPLETION
HEXAGRAM **49:** REVOLUTION
HEXAGRAM **55:** ABUNDANCE
HEXAGRAM **36:** DARKENING OF THE LIGHT
HEXAGRAM **7:** THE ARMY

The following natal hexagrams represent people you naturally tend to have a negative reaction to:

HEXAGRAM **30:** THE CLINGING FIRE
HEXAGRAM **56:** THE WANDERER
HEXAGRAM **50:** THE CAULDRON
HEXAGRAM **64:** BEFORE COMPLETION
HEXAGRAM **4:**   YOUTHFUL FOLLY
HEXAGRAM **59:** DISPERSION
HEXAGRAM **6:** CONFLICT
HEXAGRAM **13:** FELLOWSHIP WITH MEN

HEXAGRAM 31

TUI

INFLUENCE
(THE JOINING ONE)

K'EN

Traits

Bighearted	Great listener
Trusting	Steady and dependable
Innocent	Loyal friend
Patient	Gossip
Influential	Nonconfrontational
Slow	Manager
Subtle manipulator	Climbs any ladder
Influences	Like a rock
Not active	Good influence
Not a mover and shaker	Slacker
Good parent	Accepting of others
Good community member	

Life Lessons

These people need to get more inner strength, more stubbornness of character; they also need to learn to say no both to others and to their impulses; these people should never be a patsy for another.

Positive Tendencies

These are very attractive people who draw things and others to them. They are very influential, even though they may not be aware of the effect they have on their surroundings. Very bighearted people, they are somewhat slow, quiet, and gentle. They move and motivate things and people in subtle ways that are not always obvious, very behind the scenes. These are, potentially, very good parents, people who give a lot of pleasant stabilizing energy to whatever they do. Very community-minded people, they are fun in a steady and enjoyable way. Mysterious and enigmatic, such individuals have some very intense aspects to their being. People are drawn to them, though they may not know why. These people are strongly drawn to people and things, the type who fall in love at first sight. They can dedicate themselves wholeheartedly to projects and hobbies very quickly and they are often shaped and influenced by these ideas or projects, thus they often clearly know what they want to do in life.

Negative Tendencies

These people can be very slack, sluggish, and nonconfrontational. They may like to hide their head in the sand and not deal with things. Such people can be timid, not liking to rock the boat. They may gain weight easily because of not liking exercise and not being super energetic. They can be very trusting and somewhat innocent and this can lead to trouble. They sometimes don't see past the surface of things and they can be too subservient, a sycophant, and so on. The sudden infatuations to which these people can be subject can also be very negative. An object of desire may not feel the same way and it may be difficult for such people to break obsessions.

Compatibility

The following natal hexagrams represent people you naturally tend to have a positive reaction to:

HEXAGRAM **52:** KEEPING STILL
HEXAGRAM **22:** GRACE
HEXAGRAM **26:** TAMING POWER OF THE GREAT
HEXAGRAM **41:** DECREASE
HEXAGRAM **38:** OPPOSITION
HEXAGRAM **10:** TREADING
HEXAGRAM **61:** INNER TRUTH
HEXAGRAM **53:** DEVELOPMENT

The following natal hexagrams represent people you naturally tend to have a negative reaction to:

HEXAGRAM **30:**   THE CLINGING

HEXAGRAM **56:**   THE WANDERER

HEXAGRAM **50:**   THE CAULDRON

HEXAGRAM **64:**   BEFORE COMPLETION

HEXAGRAM **4:**   YOUTHFUL FOLLY

HEXAGRAM **59:**   DISPERSION

HEXAGRAM **6:**   CONFLICT

HEXAGRAM **13:**   FELLOWSHIP WITH MEN

HEXAGRAM 32

CHEN

DURATION
(THE PERSEVERING ONE)

SUN

Traits

Committed

Stubborn

Durable

Slow but sure growth

Strong-willed

Devoted

Slow-moving

Orderly

Restrictive

Laid back

Successful

Windbag

Likes ritual

Strives for successes

Fruitful

Traditional and historical

Aims for a great work

Artistic

Intellectual

Tough person

Firm and consistent

Directed

Open to natural cycles

Life Lessons

These people need to learn to not care so much about details and small things; they need to choose their battles carefully and to be open to new things more.

Positive Tendencies

These are people who have strong commitments to lasting values, to established social tradition. They love to set goals and to follow—slowly but steadily—plans to achieve them. They are constantly reinventing themselves, crafting new personalities to fit new situations. Following their instincts is the key to great success for these people; it brings constant and repetitive successes. These are not radical or shocking people; they are classic step-by-step, climb-the-ladder-of-success types. These people are very firm and stable; once committed, they will always follow through and actually love to do this. Loyal friends, these people will stay with you. They are very good at cutting through slack morals, believing in real basic ideals of good and bad. Fundamental traditions are important to them. They can take a traditional company, job, or relationship and make it better, more workable, more organized, and more successful. They tend to value a harmonious and orderly lifestyle. These people often like daily ritual and routine and a nice homelife. They are often a very artistic people, too.

Negative Tendencies

These can be very stubborn people who can be very restrictive; they like to set limits for others. They sometimes fixate on minutiae, counting pennies and being very picky. They can have a real problem altering plans or routines. Such individuals may have a real lack of spontaneity at times. These can be very tough people, both in a good and in a bad way, even at times tending toward mean. They can sometimes be windbags, babbling on and on about good habits or what people should do and so on. These people can be classic anal-retentive stick-in-the-muds who impose their set of fundamental values on others who may or may not share them.

Compatibility

The following natal hexagrams represent people you naturally tend to
have a positive reaction to:

HEXAGRAM **57**: THE PENETRATING

HEXAGRAM **9**:   TAMING POWER OF THE SMALL

HEXAGRAM **37**: THE FAMILY

HEXAGRAM **42**: INCREASE

HEXAGRAM **25**: INNOCENCE

HEXAGRAM **21**: BITING THROUGH

HEXAGRAM **27**: NOURISHMENT

HEXAGRAM **18**: WORK THAT HAS BEEN SPOILED

The following natal hexagrams represent people you naturally tend to
have a negative reaction to:

HEXAGRAM **51**: THE AROUSING

HEXAGRAM **16**: ENTHUSIASM

HEXAGRAM **40**: DELIVERANCE

HEXAGRAM **32**: DURATION

HEXAGRAM **46**: PUSHING UPWARD

HEXAGRAM **48**: THE WELL

HEXAGRAM **28**: PREPONDERANCE OF THE GREAT

HEXAGRAM **17**: FOLLOWING

HEXAGRAM 33

CH'IEN

RETREAT
(THE RETIRING ONE)

K'EN

Traits

Introvert	Works well alone
Successful in small endeavors	Prefers mental work
Meek and mild	Few close friends
Dignified	Snobbish
Shy	Agoraphobic
Divinely protected	Very concentrated
Conserves strength	Snobbish
Reserved	Internalizes all
Envied	Suppresses emotions
Blends in easily	Hides thoughts
Inward-seeking	Shaman
Spiritual hermit	

Life Lessons

These people need to learn that it is OK to show their emotions (it's even healthy!); they need to remember that everyone has something to teach and that it is OK to be a complete fool sometimes.

Positive Tendencies

These are very nice people who are often drawn to the interior life and may be introverted. They have vivid, strong, creative, and exciting inner lives. These people are often very mild, quiet, and polite. They value harmony and peace and often smooth things over when there are problems. A great front-line person with the public, they are very patient and understanding and they keep things flowing and work things out. These are still-waters-run-deep people who are much more intense than others may realize. They can lower the energy level in a room in a positive way and they have very strong spiritual auras, almost seemingly protected by divine energy. They blend in easily in social situations and they work very well independently; in fact, they work best if left alone. Not great group people, they tend to fade away in a crowd, often they are not even remembered from a class, and this is what they like. These are very mental, bright people who work out most things in their heads. They don't have tons of friends, but the ones they have are very close. Very focused, these people could, if it was their bent, be the classic shaman in that they could easily follow a magical or mystical path, journeying inward into the inner mind.

Negative Tendencies

These people can be too meek and too mild. They can be passive-aggressive and can get upset or angry at times, but no one would know it because they don't communicate it. They suppress emotions a lot and they are sometimes very misunderstood. On the other side, people can envy or be angry with such individuals and they would be clueless about it. They are focused too inwardly at times. People can transfer strange things onto these people and sometimes they won't fight back, so you may have difficult situations arising. These people can hate large spaces as well as crowds, huge cities, and the like. These people can be snobbish, sometimes being critical and secretly seeing themselves as superior. They can be too formal and this puts people off. They sometimes do not communicate emotions well and do poorly in confrontations. They may even have a suppressed temper that explodes at times.

Compatibility

The following natal hexagrams represent people you naturally tend to have a positive reaction to:

HEXAGRAM **2:**   THE RECEPTIVE

HEXAGRAM **24:**   RETURN

HEXAGRAM **19:**   APPROACH

HEXAGRAM **11:**   PEACE

HEXAGRAM **34:**   THE POWER OF THE GREAT

HEXAGRAM **43:**   BREAKTHROUGH

HEXAGRAM **5:**   WAITING

HEXAGRAM **8:**   HOLDING TOGETHER

The following natal hexagrams represent people you naturally tend to have a negative reaction to:

HEXAGRAM **1:**   THE CREATIVE

HEXAGRAM **44:**   COMING TO MEET

HEXAGRAM **33:**   RETREAT

HEXAGRAM **12:**   STANDSTILL

HEXAGRAM **20:**   CONTEMPLATION

HEXAGRAM **23:**   SPLITTING APART

HEXAGRAM **35:**   PROGRESS

HEXAGRAM **14:**   POSSESSION IN GREAT MEASURE

HEXAGRAM 34

CHEN

THE POWER OF THE GREAT
(THE INVIGORATING ONE)

CH'IEN

Traits

Strength	Be careful!
Big temper	Erupting
Personal power	Directed
Intensity	Very accomplished
Lots of movement	A true ruler
Motivated	Passionate
Tyrannical	Respected
Occasionally destructive	Conventional
Loud and rambunctious	Center of attention
Wild	Conservative and traditional
Forceful	Mighty
Occasionally out of control	

Life Lessons

These people need to learn to be nicer, to not throw their weight around so much, to be gentler, and to own up to things more.

Positive Tendencies

These are very powerful people who are strong of character and, maybe later in life, also politically or economically powerful. Acquiring power is easy for these people; it is an innate skill. They are very charismatic people who are often not aware of it. They are very intense and often strongly influence others without knowing it. They can be very motivated, directed, accomplished, and often accumulate impressive skills and rise quickly in their professions. These people are go-getters, very respected and very passionate as well. They appear almost as royalty in an abstract way. Often the center of attention, they crave this and need a lot of love to feel good. They can be very conservative and forceful, but they can also be wildly fun and boisterous. These people can get a lot done, accomplishing really amazing things for themselves and for society.

Negative Tendencies

They can do some really terrible things sometimes; a lot depends on their moral compass, the direction they take, the goals they choose, and so on. They can be spectacularly self-destructive sometimes, maybe even criminal, if they become too self-centered. These people can be loud and rambunctious, occasionally even destructive and bullying. Sometimes tyrannical, they have terrible tempers and must be careful of emotionally harming others because they simply don't realize the effect their personality has on others. Not accepting responsibility for their power can be very destructive.

Compatibility

The following natal hexagrams represent people you naturally tend to have a positive reaction to:

HEXAGRAM **57**: THE PENETRATING

HEXAGRAM **9**:   TAMING POWER OF THE SMALL

HEXAGRAM **37**: THE FAMILY

HEXAGRAM **42**: INCREASE

HEXAGRAM **25**: INNOCENCE

HEXAGRAM **21**: BITING THROUGH

HEXAGRAM **27**: NOURISHMENT

HEXAGRAM **18**: WORK THAT HAS BEEN SPOILED

The following natal hexagrams represent people you naturally tend to have a negative reaction to:

HEXAGRAM **51**: THE AROUSING

HEXAGRAM **16**: ENTHUSIASM

HEXAGRAM **40**: DELIVERANCE

HEXAGRAM **32**: DURATION

HEXAGRAM **46**: PUSHING UPWARD

HEXAGRAM **48**:   THE WELL

HEXAGRAM **28**: PREPONDERANCE OF THE GREAT

HEXAGRAM **17**: FOLLOWING

HEXAGRAM 35

LI

PROGRESS
(THE PROSPEROUS ONE)

K'UN

Traits

Great leader	Comfortable
Successful	Self-centered
Joyful	Visionary
Things come easy	Sometimes shallow
Positions of power	Not sympathetic
Tempted by corruption	Wealthy
Tends toward laziness	Easily promoted
Indolent	Unchallenged
Golden boy or girl	Well-off
Admired	High-minded
Giving much good to others	Intelligent
Conceited	

Life Lessons

These people need to walk in the shoes of others, to see their points of view; they need to avoid procrastinating and should always strive to do things that are challenging or difficult.

Positive Tendencies

These people are natural leaders who are joyful, enlightened, and progressive. They often slip into positions of power; their bosses view them as capable, self-directed, and hardworking and so they move up. They have the classic golden touch; things just always seem to come their way or fall into their lap. They are born lucky, it seems, and they have the knack of gathering wealth (of all kinds) if they follow their natural instincts and enhance their natural skills. These people are often admired by others. They are sure-witted, great communicators, and very loyal as well. Powerful individuals often gather people like this around them because of their skills, intelligence, and loyalty as well as their flexibility of thought. They can easily be very altruistic, and if so, they really shine in that giving to others and helping others is a natural part of their being. They can do amazing good in the world. These are dedicated, thoughtful spouses, lovers, and friends. They tend to be successful people who are great to have around.

Negative Tendencies

These people can be indolent. They like pleasure but can easily get lost in it and lose track of things. These people can also be conceited and very self-centered if they are not careful. Sometimes they are very shallow and don't have very deep emotions; things can go easily for them so they do not always sympathize with those less fortunate. They have trouble empathizing at times and can get wrapped up in material goods. These people may not be challenged enough and so can get arrogant about their skills, becoming a bit mentally lazy. They slide and avoid; they need to be challenged more. Such individuals can be dismissive of other people's needs and problems, and they can be corrupted fairly easily, doing things not good for their health.

Compatibility

The following natal hexagrams represent people you naturally tend to have a positive reaction to:

HEXAGRAM **29:**   THE ABYSMAL
HEXAGRAM **60:**   LIMITATION
HEXAGRAM **3:**   INITIAL DIFFICULTY
HEXAGRAM **63:**   AFTER COMPLETION
HEXAGRAM **49:**   REVOLUTION
HEXAGRAM **55:**   ABUNDANCE
HEXAGRAM **36:**   DARKENING OF THE LIGHT
HEXAGRAM **7:**   THE ARMY

The following natal hexagrams represent people you naturally tend to have a negative reaction to:

HEXAGRAM **30:**   THE CLINGING FIRE
HEXAGRAM **56:**   THE WANDERER

HEXAGRAM 36

K'UN

DARKENING OF THE LIGHT
(THE INNER-BRIGHT ONE)

LI

Traits

Inferior position	Cautious
Hides the light	Concealed intelligence
Hides true nature	Volcanic
Encounters obstacles	Physically strong
Needs to be humble	Melancholy
Strong dark side	Easily tricked
Persevering	Needs alone-time
Things don't come easy	Unaware
Needs to push	Creative
Inner strength	Good-hearted
Strong Yin energy	Works in shadows
Reserved	

Life Lessons

These people need to learn how to enjoy life more, to worry less about things, to let bygones be bygones, and move on after things change.

Positive Tendencies

These people are natural fighters, quickly developing thick skins and strong wills that will see them through almost anything. They hide true feelings and are very strategic, quickly learning circumspection and when—and when not—to talk. Brilliant tacticians, they are very persevering. When setting a goal, these people will stick to it through thick or thin. They have a lot of inner strength and are very strong inside—often bodily strong as well. Naturally cautious, these people are often handy to have around, especially in security situations, something they are often drawn to in the sense of helping and protecting others. They are bright and have great common sense, but they are often misjudged because of their blunt style of communicating. Not always refined, they are innately wise and can cut to the heart of issues. These people can be very body conscious and so are often healthy; they also enjoy periods of solitude, which they need to keep centered. These individuals are naturally drawn to hidden spiritual paths, secret societies, sects, and such in the search for obscure hidden wisdom. They can be very good-hearted, though a bit gruff, and they like to stay out of the spotlight, a bit slyly so. They are much deeper than they let on.

Negative Tendencies

These people may be drawn to the shadowy side of life, to the darker parts of their psyche and to the shadows of reality in general. These people can be very stubborn. They can be pessimistic, cynical, and even paranoid sometimes. They can at times be fatalistic or feel "'why bother?" They may find themselves in subordinate positions and chafe at this, though they are great workers when they put a mind to it. They tend not to lead well, being very volcanic, and their temper tantrums are sometimes legendary. They can also be melancholy, depressed, and somewhat clueless at times. Others sometimes mistakenly take these people for dim and slow, but this just means they were not paying attention. These people can be drawn into very self-destructive behavior.

Compatibility

The following natal hexagrams represent people you naturally tend to have a positive reaction to:

HEXAGRAM **1:**   THE CREATIVE

HEXAGRAM **44:**   COMING TO MEET

HEXAGRAM **33:**   RETREAT

HEXAGRAM **12:**   STANDSTILL

HEXAGRAM **20:**   CONTEMPLATION

HEXAGRAM **23:**   SPLITTING APART

HEXAGRAM **35:**   PROGRESS

HEXAGRAM **14:**   POSSESSION IN GREAT MEASURE

The following natal hexagrams represent people you naturally tend to have a negative reaction to:

HEXAGRAM **2:**   THE RECEPTIVE

HEXAGRAM **24:**   RETURN

HEXAGRAM **19:**   APPROACH

HEXAGRAM **11:**   PEACE

HEXAGRAM **34:**   THE POWER OF THE GREAT

HEXAGRAM **43:**   BREAKTHROUGH

HEXAGRAM **5:**   WAITING

HEXAGRAM **8:**   HOLDING TOGETHER

HEXAGRAM 37

SUN

LI

THE FAMILY
(THE CLAN-CENTERED ONE)

Traits

Tribe-oriented

Social nexus

Focus of social order

Authority figure

Holder of traditions

Status-oriented

Opportunist = success

Politically oriented

Mediator

In-betweener

Imitative

Community-oriented

Leader of groups

High motivations

Empathic

Great endurance

Great writer or speaker

Affectionate

Informal

Faithful

Loyal

Obedient

Impulsive and insightful

Life Lessons

These people need to be alone more and to learn to do more things independently of others; they should keep their feelings hidden a bit more and strive to be original in thought and deed.

Positive Tendencies

These are very group-oriented people who like to be right in the middle of social situations and "tribal" gatherings. They are natural authority figures within familial-like groups, tend to enjoy bringing groups together, and are affectionate, empathic, and loyal. These people are excellent facilitators for work groups or organizational projects; they are natural mediators, reconcilers, and great at helping people find a common cause or "group will." These are very spiritual people who want to share and communicate spiritual ideas and truths to others. When not the center of the group or the leader, such individuals are excellent at following others and helping the group attain its goal. The flexibility of leading and following well is very rare and a key to the success of these people. They also follow through and like traditions, festivals, fairs, seasonal gatherings, and things of this sort. Very family-oriented, they tend to view others and even the world in terms of family, and they are very respectful of progressive social causes and functions. Very one-for-all-and-all-for-one, these people are concerned with such things as solving social problems.

Negative Tendencies

These people can be very status-oriented and become very lost without a group to validate them. They can be very ego-poor in this way. They are often relaxed and informal and sometimes they can do this inappropriately and excessively. They can be too touchy-feely as well as being too impulsive, blurting out rude things or being wacky when it is not appropriate to do so. They sometimes excessively imitate others, even down to copying ideas, and this can upset people. They can be excessively paternal or maternal and may use traditional situations and holidays as a way to critique or manipulate others. They can be opportunistic, which can be a bit much at times, and they sometimes like to grab the limelight. These people can be overly dependent, indecisive, and clingy.

Compatibility

The following natal hexagrams represent people you naturally tend to have a positive reaction to:

HEXAGRAM **51:** THE AROUSING
HEXAGRAM **16:** ENTHUSIASM
HEXAGRAM **40:** DELIVERANCE
HEXAGRAM **32:** DURATION
HEXAGRAM **46:** PUSHING UPWARD
HEXAGRAM **48:** THE WELL
HEXAGRAM **28:** PREPONDERANCE OF THE GREAT
HEXAGRAM **17:** FOLLOWING

The following natal hexagrams represent people you naturally tend to have a negative reaction to:

HEXAGRAM **57**: THE PENETRATING

HEXAGRAM **9**:   TAMING POWER OF THE SMALL

HEXAGRAM **37**: THE FAMILY

HEXAGRAM **42**: INCREASE

HEXAGRAM **25**:   INNOCENCE

HEXAGRAM **21**: BITING THROUGH

HEXAGRAM **27**:   NOURISHMENT

HEXAGRAM **18**: WORK THAT HAS BEEN SPOILED

HEXAGRAM 38

LI

OPPOSITION
(THE POLARIZING ONE)

TUI

Traits

Tenacious	Charge builds . . . builds . . . boom!
Brave	Sees life as a battle
Contrary	Independent
Split	Individualistic
A bit paranoid	Contrary
Going in two directions at once	Not subservient
Causes great friction	A bit anarchistic
Alienated	Strong-willed
Success step by step	True warrior
Sees things in black and white	Great pal
Grows through overcoming trials	
Breaker of barriers	
Risk-taker	

Life Lessons

These people need to learn to bend to the will of the majority at times, to socialize more, and they need to learn to synthesize things and ideas, bringing them together.

Positive Tendencies

These are brave people who really stick to their guns. Tenacious, these social critics love to intelligently argue and criticize, but by being such analyzers they learn a lot. Insightful, these people can often see problems and angles on situations that others cannot, also giving advice to boot. They are likely very independent to an extreme degree and individualistic with their own unique point of view. "Life, liberty and the pursuit of happiness" could be their motto. They are almost allergic to authority and do not place themselves under any particular philosophy or -ism and can be somewhat anarchistic. Having a very strong will, these people are excellent buddies, lovers, or comrades, loyal to the end and unsparingly honest. They are very adventurous, often following in the "warrior" tradition of embracing all the joys and conflicts of life with a grand style, almost heroically. Such individuals overcome obstacles with gusto, like to take risks, and tend to succeed better at small short-term projects and goals in that things shift often for them. They really are unique.

Negative Tendencies

These people can be hypercritical, even cruelly so, and may have inherent contradictions in their character that can drive others crazy. They can be devil's advocates, but this can be taken too far. They may be a bit paranoid at times and they can polarize things very quickly, sometimes seeing issues as black and white. These people can cause a lot of friction and chaos in group situations because they are such lone wolves that they sometimes have a very hard time working with others, especially in terms of compromising. They may hold things in emotionally, then explode, and this can be a pattern. These people can be too combative and almost self-destructive in some of the foolish risks they take. They can also be nihilistic and naysayers just to do so.

Compatibility

The following natal hexagrams represent people you naturally tend to have a positive reaction to:

HEXAGRAM **29:**   THE ABYSMAL

HEXAGRAM **60:**   LIMITATION

HEXAGRAM **3:**   INITIAL DIFFICULTY

HEXAGRAM **63:**   AFTER COMPLETION

HEXAGRAM **49:**   REVOLUTION

HEXAGRAM **55:**   ABUNDANCE

HEXAGRAM **36:**   DARKENING OF THE LIGHT

HEXAGRAM **7:**   THE ARMY

The following natal hexagrams represent people you naturally tend to have a negative reaction to:

HEXAGRAM **30:**   THE CLINGING FIRE

HEXAGRAM **56:**   THE WANDERER

HEXAGRAM **50:**   THE CAULDRON

HEXAGRAM **64:**   BEFORE COMPLETION

HEXAGRAM **4:**   YOUTHFUL FOLLY

HEXAGRAM **59:**   DISPERSION

HEXAGRAM **6:**   CONFLICT

HEXAGRAM **13:**   FELLOWSHIP WITH MEN

HEXAGRAM 39

K'AN

OBSTRUCTION
(THE PERSEVERING ONE)

K'EN

Traits

Overcomes problems	Works on karma
Able to reassess	Deep thinker
Good at self-examination	Meditation is important
The key is within	Impetuous
Can transfer and blame others	Look before you leap!
Stubborn	Perfectionist
Loyal	Works best with others
Troublemaker	Conscientious
Able to leap over chasms	Self-critical
Problem solver	Timing is everything
Strategic	Persevering
Tactician	

Life Lessons

These people need to lighten up on themselves; they need to learn to move through and past problems but also to simply screw off and be irresponsible sometimes.

Positive Tendencies

These are very conscientious, self-critical, deep-thinking people who are very good at deeply understanding situations and people's problems. Problem solvers, they are good at puzzles, often figuring out complex, tangled plots; they are also great at finding solutions for the most complex mess. Such individuals are very strategic and have a great understanding of the many factors that make up something. They are very holistic in their viewpoint. They are probably drawn to some form of meditation, whether it be active or passive, and this is important to them. Very persevering, these people are probably very involved with figuring out their psychology, problems, blockages, hidden talents, and inner strengths. These people are very involved in self-growth and they are successful at finding positive paths of evolving. They often respond best to things as opposed to initiating them. These people have a lot of life-obstacles and they see them as opportunities to grow, to overcome, and to get better and this is very positive. They are loyal to a fault and will do everything to save a love or a friendship. Such people can be impetuous and have a good sense of timing; things can fall out of the blue into their lives and be just right.

Negative Tendencies

These people can be much too hard on themselves, too self-critical, and can be too harsh on others as well. They can get stuck on problems, obsessing on them to the exclusion of other things, even those problems that time will solve. They may sometimes have trouble letting go of things. They can get hung up on processing and on working things out, and this is not always a good thing. They can get too abstract and idealistic sometimes and forget about real people and real emotions, using a lot of shoulds and woulds. These people sometimes do not think things through and can jump to negative conclusions or jump into bad situations without a lot of forethought. They can be very picky and hard to please. These people are not great independent workers because they can fixate on one part. They can be perfectionists and stubborn and can blame others for things that go wrong.

Compatibility

The following natal hexagrams represent people you naturally tend to have a positive reaction to:

HEXAGRAM **30:** THE CLINGING FIRE

HEXAGRAM **56:** THE WANDERER

HEXAGRAM **50:** THE CAULDRON

HEXAGRAM **64:** BEFORE COMPLETION

HEXAGRAM **4:** YOUTHFUL FOLLY

HEXAGRAM **59:** DISPERSION

HEXAGRAM **6:** CONFLICT

HEXAGRAM **13:** FELLOWSHIP WITH MEN

The following natal hexagrams represent people you naturally tend to have a negative reaction to:

HEXAGRAM **29:** THE ABYSMAL

HEXAGRAM **60:** LIMITATION

HEXAGRAM **3:**   INITIAL DIFFICULTY

HEXAGRAM **63:** AFTER COMPLETION

HEXAGRAM **49:** REVOLUTION

HEXAGRAM **55:** ABUNDANCE

HEXAGRAM **36:** DARKENING OF THE LIGHT

HEXAGRAM **7:**   THE ARMY

HEXAGRAM 40

CHEN

DELIVERANCE
(THE LIBERATING ONE)

K'AN

Traits

Wild	Enthusiastic
Stormlike	Bighearted
Has cycles of tension and release	Emotive
Catalyst in a big way	Powerful
Electric	Changer and renewer
Ties up loose ends	Revitalizer
Always seeking normalcy	Life of the party
Conscious of patterns	Rude
Volcanic	Extreme
Chatty Kathy	Obnoxious
Into the business of business	Unforgettable
Needs to watch the details	

Life Lessons

These people need to learn to take aggressive action at times; they also need to remember their manners and to accept unexpected opportunities.

Positive Tendencies

These are wild people who are catalysts in a big way and great at resolving things. They are natural therapists, natural healers who can help others get unstuck. Real motivators, these people can get things moving, both in work and in relationships, and they can also help others find their real gifts. They are very electric individuals who can be very charismatic; others see them as helpers and they are talented at unleashing all kinds of energy in a variety of professional and personal situations. Good at reorganizing and removing dead wood, these people are revitalizers and very aware of patterns. They may be attracted to things like business or science and love intricate information. People-oriented, these emotive, enthusiastic people are very much the life of the party and can be very unforgettable. Their relationships are often quite intense and rarely boring, always involved in change. These people are rarely caught in a rut. They are probably very nice as well as bighearted and forgiving; they can often see everyone's good side.

Negative Tendencies

These can be stormy people, rarely mellow or relaxed, often very intense and "on," which can be a trial at times for others. Such people can get out of control and be chatterboxes and gossipers. They can tend to lecture. They sometimes like to shake things up just to do it, and they change things radically at times without a lot of forethought or consideration. These people often let everyone know what they are feeling, and this isn't always such a good idea; they are often too emotive sometimes as well. They can be rude and even obnoxious, and they tend toward extremes. Things are often very wild around them. This can be too much at times.

Compatibility

The following natal hexagrams represent people you naturally tend to have a positive reaction to:

HEXAGRAM **57:** THE PENETRATING

HEXAGRAM **9:**   TAMING POWER OF THE SMALL

HEXAGRAM **37:** THE FAMILY

HEXAGRAM **42:** INCREASE

HEXAGRAM **25:** INNOCENCE

HEXAGRAM **21:** BITING THROUGH

HEXAGRAM **27:** NOURISHMENT

HEXAGRAM **18:** WORK THAT HAS BEEN SPOILED

The following natal hexagrams represent people you naturally tend to have a negative reaction to:

HEXAGRAM **51:** THE AROUSING

HEXAGRAM **16:** ENTHUSIASM

HEXAGRAM **40:** DELIVERANCE

HEXAGRAM **32:** DURATION

HEXAGRAM **46:** PUSHING UPWARD

HEXAGRAM **48:** THE WELL

HEXAGRAM **28:** PREPONDERANCE OF THE GREAT

HEXAGRAM **17:** FOLLOWING

HEXAGRAM 41

K'EN

DECREASE
(THE DIMINISHING ONE)

TUI

Traits

One who sacrifices	Tends toward stability
Selfless	Too serious
Altruistic	Greedy
Simplistic	Self-centered
Rising	Overshadows others
Destroys shadows	Confidence brings prosperity
Psychoanalyst	Dominator
Works things out	Does for others
Controls emotional highs and lows	Social worker
	Victim or martyr
Balance	Dissipating
Moderate	Banisher of ill will

Life Lessons

These people need to not be so overconfident and to accept loss gracefully; they also need to be more positive in their outlook and dealings with others.

Positive Tendencies

These are people who like to live simply, who like to get rid of excess things, who honor austerity, and who don't attach much to things and status. These are very selfless people who tend to devote themselves to the good of others in many ways. They are good at managing resources—people, things, business resources, or whatever. They are very attuned to the cosmos and are usually strong vital beings. These people love to analyze the inner workings of things and mentally take them apart to understand them. They probably have real strong personal highs and lows, but in these times they are ironically good at moderating and balancing things out. They are good at calming others down and are very low-key; they like a mellow atmosphere. Such people love to get rid of bad feelings, to work things out, and so on; they really turn negative vibes to positive ones and are great at economizing. They are into keeping things going. These people will probably never be rich, but they'll lead a good, comfortable life help-ing others and making the world a better place.

Negative Tendencies

These people can be down, depressed, or maudlin sometimes. They tend to break problems down into aspects that are too simplistic, too sim-ple. They can be pessimistic. They sometimes dislike extreme emotions or intense bonds. They can be very dominating, but they are also sometimes drawn to being a martyr with a victim-script. They are sometimes very low-energy, even lazy at times, and they can waste a lot of time.

Compatibility

The following natal hexagrams represent people you naturally tend to have a positive reaction to:

HEXAGRAM **30:**   THE CLINGING

HEXAGRAM **56:**   THE WANDERER

HEXAGRAM **50:**   THE CAULDRON

HEXAGRAM **64:**   BEFORE COMPLETION

HEXAGRAM **4:**   YOUTHFUL FOLLY

HEXAGRAM **59:**   DISPERSION

HEXAGRAM **6:**   CONFLICT

HEXAGRAM **13:**   FELLOWSHIP WITH MEN

The following natal hexagrams represent people you naturally tend to have a negative reaction to:

HEXAGRAM **52:**   KEEPING STILL

HEXAGRAM **22:**   GRACE

HEXAGRAM **26:**   TAMING POWER OF THE GREAT

HEXAGRAM **41:**   DECREASE

HEXAGRAM **38:**   OPPOSITION

HEXAGRAM **10:**   TREADING

HEXAGRAM **61:** INNER TRUTH

HEXAGRAM **53:** DEVELOPMENT

HEXAGRAM 42

SUN

INCREASE
(THE AUGMENTING ONE)

CHEN

Traits

Spiritually open	Builds upon other things
Either on or off	Lucky
Very aware	Spreads the wealth
Chameleonlike	High highs, low lows
Successful in big projects	Benevolent
Attracts things	Turns negative to positive
Easily swayed by surroundings	Goal-oriented
Materialistic	Generous
Joy in serving others	Self-improving
Yuppie	Fortuitous
Needs to focus on spirit	Self-aware
Prosperous	

Life Lessons

These people need to be humbler with others; they must learn more from errors as well as be more materially generous to others.

Positive Tendencies

These are pragmatic, energetic people who bring exceptional enthusiasm and skill to jobs, problems, and relationships. These are very persevering and goal-oriented people who do best when their goals focus on bettering others and not just themselves. They are very successful, natural leaders who often end up managing and directing things into harmonious wholes and then propelling them into reality. Very generous, these people are flashy and born idealists, entrepreneurs, or even politicians. They are very supportive and intense people with tremendous character and positive energy. These people's investments naturally return to them many times over, both emotionally and financially. They are very focused on self-improvement as well as helping those around them improve. These people really enhance all situations with focus and energy. They can be very disciplined and self-aware and do a lot of good in the world.

Negative Tendencies

These people are the classic yuppies in the sense of sometimes tending toward being materialistic, self-centered, egotistic, arrogant, overbearing, and so on. These people are often very prosperous but it can bend them into being too focused on stuff and not on relationships. These lucky people sometimes take things for granted and can develop a bad attitude toward those beneath them socially or economically. These people can be either very hot or very cold, either very on or very off, and these swings can be a problem for others.

Compatibility

The following natal hexagrams represent people you naturally tend to have a positive reaction to:

HEXAGRAM **51:**   THE AROUSING
HEXAGRAM **16:**   ENTHUSIASM
HEXAGRAM **40:**   DELIVERANCE
HEXAGRAM **32:**   DURATION
HEXAGRAM **46:**   PUSHING UPWARD
HEXAGRAM **48:**   THE WELL
HEXAGRAM **28:**   PREPONDERANCE OF THE GREAT
HEXAGRAM **17:**   FOLLOWING

The following natal hexagrams represent people you naturally tend to have a negative reaction to:

HEXAGRAM **57:** THE PENETRATING

HEXAGRAM **9:** TAMING POWER OF THE SMALL

HEXAGRAM **37:** THE FAMILY

HEXAGRAM **42:** INCREASE

HEXAGRAM **25:** INNOCENCE

HEXAGRAM **21:** BITING THROUGH

HEXAGRAM **27:** NOURISHMENT

HEXAGRAM **18:** WORK THAT HAS BEEN SPOILED

HEXAGRAM 43

TUI

BREAKTHROUGH
(THE ACTIVE ONE)

CH'IEN

Traits

Resolute	Radical actions
Decisive	Honest
Adventurous	Focused on justice
Doer	Bridge-builder
Action-oriented	Confrontational
Needs meditation	Modest
Tense . . . relaxed . . . tense	Forceful
Intense	Warrior of the heart
A patron	Uncompromising
Frank	Righteous
Capricious	Proud
Problem solver	

Life Lessons

These people need to learn to be more moderate in their activities and habits; they need to be nicer to others as well as to bend and not break in turbulent times.

Positive Tendencies

These people are very concerned with justice, truth, honesty, and openness. They tend to focus on these values in day-to-day life as a general rule. They are often drawn to jobs based on these ideals, such as law enforcement, mediation, guarding, or even conflict resolution. Social work may be a way of life for these people; they actively seek problems to fix. They are real doers, people who get out into the world and try to make a difference. These people can pursue these things in small or large ways, and they exemplify the idea of the "spiritual warrior" in that they are confronting things and events that make them cope, make them excel and grow, and do not allow them to cop out. Decisive, these people are always compelled to move forward and be true to their feelings and ideals. They can be very blunt and can communicate well, problem-solve, and synthesize things that may be contradictory and make them work. These people are very constructive, pragmatic, and practical. Though idealistic, they are not interested in theory but in the practice of ideals. They can be forceful and probably make good role models, very good at turning others around. These people can be strict and disciplined as well.

Negative Tendencies

These people can go too far, can butt into other people's business, can be rude and self-righteous, and can sometimes be too politically correct. These people tend to be meddlesome and go through extreme cycles of tension or hyperactivity and slackness or indolence. They can be capricious and hop from one thing to another. Such individuals can take things to the extreme, be too radical. They can take idealistic confrontation too far and become dogmatic and uncompromising. As these people go through life, their code of morals is the key to who they are, so if they become corrupt, if they turn against these ideals, they can become very nasty and self-destructive.

Compatibility

The following natal hexagrams represent people you naturally tend to have a positive reaction to:

HEXAGRAM **52:** KEEPING STILL

HEXAGRAM **22:** GRACE

HEXAGRAM **26:** TAMING POWER OF THE GREAT

HEXAGRAM **41:** DECREASE

HEXAGRAM **38:** OPPOSITION

HEXAGRAM **10:**   TREADING

HEXAGRAM **61:** INNER TRUTH

HEXAGRAM **53:** DEVELOPMENT

The following natal hexagrams represent people you naturally tend to have a negative reaction to:

HEXAGRAM **30:** THE CLINGING

HEXAGRAM **56:** THE WANDERER

HEXAGRAM **50:** THE CAULDRON

HEXAGRAM **64:** BEFORE COMPLETION

HEXAGRAM **4:**   YOUTHFUL FOLLY

HEXAGRAM **59:** DISPERSION

HEXAGRAM **6:**   CONFLICT

HEXAGRAM **13:** FELLOWSHIP WITH MEN

HEXAGRAM 44

CH'IEN

SUN

COMING TO MEET
(THE SEDUCTIVE ONE)

Traits

Swift	Artistic
Commanding	Fascinated with occult (hidden)
Passive	Scholar
Corruptible	Tightrope walker
Bitchy	Powerful
Corner-cutter	Indulges
Tends toward pacifying	Chaotic
Attracts troubles	Guarded
Hidden mover	Confronts weakness
Resolves problems by	Self-disciplined
confronting them	Strict
Strong shadow; uses it	Too many expectations
Manager	

Life Lessons

These people need to learn to be more respectful of others, to think twice before rushing into things (and relationships), and to avoid taking shortcuts in life.

Positive Tendencies

These are people who intuitively understand others and can grasp underlying feelings, ideas, and thoughts. They tend to openly express feelings, thoughts, desires, and creativity. These people can be very good at pacifying others and can take a rough situation and smooth things out.

They tend to do well when focused and self-disciplined; when they confront situations and challenge them directly, they have much success. These are artistic individuals who may also be fascinated with the occult or hidden things and knowledge as well as all manner of psychology. They tend toward deep, dramatic, and mysterious love relationships. They are real risk-takers in that they'll push limits between what is enjoyed and what is harmful to themselves. They like to go out, have a good time, and be social; they are also behind-the-scenes people, who like to motivate and manage others. They can be a little strict toward others and often have a very commanding presence.

Negative Tendencies

These people can be led (or lead others) down the wrong path, be pulled into vices and negative behaviors, and this can become a real problem. They can be bitchy, much too passive, and sometimes look for short-cuts due to laziness. These people tend to be chaotic and very guarded or cold. They look for the easy way out too often and have very strong dark sides or shadows to their personality. With no self-discipline, these people can get out of control and lose perspective. They can be back-stabbing, offensive, and even mean. They need to be aware of substance abuse and, most important, must be aware of running from problems or uncomfortable situations.

Compatibility

The following natal hexagrams represent people you naturally tend to have a positive reaction to:

HEXAGRAM **2:**   THE RECEPTIVE
HEXAGRAM **24:**   RETURN
HEXAGRAM **19:**   APPROACH
HEXAGRAM **11:**   PEACE
HEXAGRAM **34:**   THE POWER OF THE GREAT
HEXAGRAM **43:**   BREAKTHROUGH
HEXAGRAM **5:**   WAITING
HEXAGRAM **8:**   HOLDING TOGETHER

The following natal hexagrams represent people you naturally tend to have a negative reaction to:

HEXAGRAM **1:**   THE CREATIVE

HEXAGRAM **44:**   COMING TO MEET

HEXAGRAM **33:**   RETREAT

HEXAGRAM **12:**   STANDSTILL

HEXAGRAM **20:**   CONTEMPLATION

HEXAGRAM **23:**   SPLITTING APART

HEXAGRAM **35:**   PROGRESS

HEXAGRAM **14:**   POSSESSION IN GREAT MEASURE

HEXAGRAM 45

TUI

GATHERING TOGETHER
(THE CLUSTERING ONE)

K'UN

Traits

Center of the collective	Paranoid
Group leader	Sacrifices for others
Lost in one's head	Guide
Facilitator	Selfless
Center of creativity	Avoids strife
Unexpected problems	Politically correct
Unexpected gifts	Influenced by others
Expects the unexpected	People person
Generous	Social
Loves sudden challenges	Demagogue or follower
Coordinator	Voice of sanity
Counselor	

Life Lessons

These people need to learn to let fear pass through and go away; they need to learn to be more self-observant and to pay attention to timing in all things.

Positive Tendencies

These people are excellent centers of power, great leaders, and natural centers of collective action. These people are always among others, real people persons; they like to live, play, work, and so on with others. Receptive, these individuals persist in correct action and work hard at it. Very active mentally, they have many unusual skills that fit together remarkably well and so lead them into relationships and professional situations that are interesting. Natural facilitators and coordinators, these people like challenges and can succeed at them. They can be selfless, altruistic, idealistic, and goal-oriented. Unity and character are important to such individuals and they are great at self-criticism and self-examination. Interested in social causes, they often sacrifice time, energy, and such to make things better and to just do quality work. Generous to a fault, these are very creative people with good taste.

Negative Tendencies

These people can hide in their heads and be very standoffish and reserved. Arrogant at times, they also sometimes drift into paranoia if not careful. These people can have very powerful defenses and can be touchy and thin-skinned at times, not taking criticism well. They are group-oriented but can also feel detached and separated from others. These people are prone to be real "BS artists," can be very deceiving if they're not moral, and also power-hungry. Such people can at times be too fanatical, either as a follower or leader, and at times are somewhat unlucky. They can attract odd problems and situations that are often no one's fault.

Compatibility

The following natal hexagrams represent people you naturally tend to have a positive reaction to:

HEXAGRAM **52:** KEEPING STILL

HEXAGRAM **22:** GRACE

HEXAGRAM **26:** TAMING POWER OF THE GREAT

HEXAGRAM **41:** DECREASE

HEXAGRAM **38:** OPPOSITION

HEXAGRAM **10:** TREADING

HEXAGRAM **61:** INNER TRUTH

HEXAGRAM **53:** DEVELOPMENT

The following natal hexagrams represent people you naturally tend to have a negative reaction to:

HEXAGRAM **30:** THE CLINGING

HEXAGRAM **56:** THE WANDERER

HEXAGRAM **50:** THE CAULDRON

HEXAGRAM **64:** BEFORE COMPLETION

HEXAGRAM **4:** YOUTHFUL FOLLY

HEXAGRAM **59:** DISPERSION

HEXAGRAM **6:** CONFLICT

HEXAGRAM **13:** FELLOWSHIP WITH MEN

HEXAGRAM 46

K'UN

PUSHING UPWARD
(THE ASCENDING ONE)

SUN

Traits

Goes with the flow	Picky
Indolent	Slow and thorough
Good karma	Very neat or very messy
Easy progress	Easygoing
Hardworking or lazy	Natural person
Devout	Like a tree
Attracts spiritual teachers	Evolving
Impatient	Accumulates energy and things
Curious	Adaptable
Strives for progress	Psychic
Nosy	Spiritual questing
Lively	

Life Lessons

These people need to learn patience and how to adapt quickly to changing situations; they need to discover how to find balance in all sorts of situations.

Positive Tendencies

These people will combine a constant search for spirituality with a dedication to material success. In politics, business, relationships, and so on, there will be unexpected gains. They will do best by just letting things flow, and so will find natural success almost without conscious effort. They are very drawn to the earth, to nature, and like immersing themselves in the natural world—this is very important for them. Such individuals are very brave and can get involved in risky undertakings but seem always to emerge unhurt. Exceptional progress will be found if these people approach projects without grasping or getting greedy; just by being relaxed, calm, and centered they will do well. They tend to influence those in power and should keep this in mind. They seem to have a truthful and knowledgeable aura. Though not very attached to material things, these people do enjoy them and the active life and seem to collect stuff as well as information. These people tend to create positive space, relationships, and such around themselves, being great at communicating and almost everything else! They tend to do best by just naturally doing what they're drawn to; many might say these people have great karma. They also do very well with gurus and spiritual teachers.

Negative Tendencies

These people can be either very hardworking or incredibly lazy and may seesaw between the two. Sometimes impatient, they can sabotage themselves by not letting things mature, not letting things get to the right time before doing things. Sometimes they don't complete projects. Being pushy, picky, jumping the gun—these are all possible problems. These people can be critical, sometimes to the point of absurdity, and this can hurt others. They tend to accumulate things and may have too much junk. Their houses can be cluttered and not very organized. These people can be spiritually or psychically chaotic and even self-damaging; they need discipline at times, a set path or at least some organization in their spiritual growth.

Compatibility

The following natal hexagrams represent people you naturally tend to have a positive reaction to:

HEXAGRAM **1:** THE CREATIVE
HEXAGRAM **44:** COMING TO MEET
HEXAGRAM **33:** RETREAT
HEXAGRAM **12:** STANDSTILL
HEXAGRAM **20:** CONTEMPLATION
HEXAGRAM **23:** SPLITTING APART
HEXAGRAM **35:** PROGRESS
HEXAGRAM **14:** POSSESSION IN GREAT MEASURE

The following natal hexagrams represent people you naturally tend to have a negative reaction to:

HEXAGRAM **2:**   THE RECEPTIVE
HEXAGRAM **24:** RETURN
HEXAGRAM **19:** APPROACH
HEXAGRAM **11:** PEACE
HEXAGRAM **34:** THE POWER OF THE GREAT
HEXAGRAM **43:** BREAKTHROUGH
HEXAGRAM **5:**   WAITING
HEXAGRAM **8:**   HOLDING TOGETHER

HEXAGRAM 47

TUI

EXHAUSTION
(THE CONFINING ONE)

K'AN

Traits

Strong-willed	Ever-growing
Stamina	Dedicated
Tough life	Courageous
Overcomes obstacles	Misunderstood
Flexible	Takes risks
Sense of humor	Born fighter
Adversity brings strength	Great stamina
Whiner and doomsayer	Insecure
Must follow will	Exhausted
Learns from problems	Confused
Sets up real successes	Determined
Depressed at times	

Life Lessons

These people need to be strong and not bow down in the face of adversity; they must work at not becoming hard people and need to find joy in may things in life.

Positive Tendencies

This is actually a good natal hexagram, though it may not seem so at first. These people are very strong, courageous, and brave when necessary. They have exceptionally good character and are good leaders in the sense of a battle commander; they organize and lead others in stressful situations. They will not have the easiest life—the prime way they grow is by overcoming problems and challenges. These people have very strong wills and are good people in general. Not big talkers, these people are the strong but silent types who'd rather do something, take action, than discuss it. Somewhat stoic, they may not be geniuses, but they have strong minds and bodies. They may in fact be very strong physically and may be drawn to things like the martial arts. These people have to approach success in a very tactical, point-by-point manner, never leaving things to chance or just letting things happen. They must make things happen and stay with them all the way. Dedicated people, they are often misunderstood and need to take care when communicating. Relationships may be a little rocky because they are not easy people, but they are committed, loyal, dedicated, and very devoted. They can be optimistic and develop inwardly quite a bit—very centered people.

Negative Tendencies

These can be tough people who attract a lot of adversity; to them, life may be a struggle at times. They can get depressed, have a lot of trouble relaxing and enjoying things, may focus too much on the negative, may be overly harsh and judgmental, and may even be something of a bully. They can be gloomy as well as insecure and confused. Such people may push the limits too much mentally and physically, and though they have great stamina, they may injure themselves or even burn out. They may drive others in a similar way, forgetting that not everyone has the same strength.

Compatibility

The following natal hexagrams represent people you naturally tend to have a positive reaction to:

HEXAGRAM **52:** KEEPING STILL

HEXAGRAM **22:** GRACE

HEXAGRAM **26:** TAMING POWER OF THE GREAT

HEXAGRAM **41:** DECREASE

HEXAGRAM **38:** OPPOSITION

HEXAGRAM **10:** TREADING

HEXAGRAM **61:** INNER TRUTH

HEXAGRAM **53:** DEVELOPMENT

The following natal hexagrams represent people you naturally tend to have a negative reaction to:

HEXAGRAM **30:** THE CLINGING

HEXAGRAM **56:** THE WANDERER

HEXAGRAM **50:** THE CAULDRON

HEXAGRAM **64:** BEFORE COMPLETION

HEXAGRAM **4:**   YOUTHFUL FOLLY

HEXAGRAM **59:** DISPERSION

HEXAGRAM **6:**   CONFLICT

HEXAGRAM **13:** FELLOWSHIP WITH MEN

HEXAGRAM 48

K'AN

THE WELL
(THE FLOWING ONE)

SUN

Traits

Good-natured

Deep character

Taps the source of being

Understands human nature

Depth psychologist

Thinks of the common good

Kinglike

Superficial

Independent

Deep and creative

Somewhat educated

BS artist

Encouraging

Unconventional

Connects with others

Powerful spirit

Cultivates evolution

Shallow-seeming

Independent

Quick

Contemplative

Aimless

Helpful

Life Lessons

These people need to keep their feet on the ground more; they need to listen more to others as well and spread the spiritual gifts they have to others.

Positive Tendencies

These are exceptionally deep and spiritual people. They could easily become priests, priestesses, monks, or some sort of holy person. These people are naturally tuned in to the Tao as the Source, the essence behind all creation and being, and can communicate this sense of awe and wonder to others. Good-natured souls, they often have lots of friends and loved ones. Very apt at grasping gestalts, inner truth, and patterns behind things, these people really understand what is going on in situations and so should be listened to, having great advice for others. These people will for sure be involved in counseling, teaching, and/or will in some way be helping others reach their full potential, their true wills. In this, they will succeed and grow. These people understand human nature and would make natural psychologists, being gifted at getting to the roots of things. They are regal, somewhat aristocratic, very independent, and often drawn to art or aesthetics. Blessed with quick intellects, these people can come to decisions or ideas very swiftly and are often correct right off the bat. Very helpful, they tend to be well-educated and drawn to learning.

Negative Tendencies

These people can be somewhat shallow, judgmental, can drift into egotism, and may even be a bit spiritually arrogant. These people are also somewhat bohemian and unconventional at times, and this may throw others off. They can be master con artists and can talk about almost anything or nothing. They sometimes love to chat and can go off on all subjects. They can be very spaced-out, out of touch with the real world, and at times be unconcerned about practical things like bills, rent, and so on.

Compatibility

The following natal hexagrams represent people you naturally tend to have a positive reaction to:

HEXAGRAM **30:**   THE CLINGING FIRE
HEXAGRAM **56:**   THE WANDERER
HEXAGRAM **50:**   THE CAULDRON
HEXAGRAM **64:**   BEFORE COMPLETION
HEXAGRAM **4:**   YOUTHFUL FOLLY
HEXAGRAM **59:**   DISPERSION
HEXAGRAM **6:**   CONFLICT
HEXAGRAM **13:**   FELLOWSHIP WITH MEN

The following natal hexagrams represent people you naturally tend to have a negative reaction to:

HEXAGRAM **29:**   THE ABYSMAL
HEXAGRAM **60:**   LIMITATION
HEXAGRAM **3:**   INITIAL DIFFICULTY
HEXAGRAM **63:**   AFTER COMPLETION

HEXAGRAM **49:** REVOLUTION

HEXAGRAM **55:** ABUNDANCE

HEXAGRAM **36:** DARKENING OF THE LIGHT

HEXAGRAM **7:** THE ARMY

HEXAGRAM 49

TUI

REVOLUTION
(THE TRANSFORMING ONE)

LI

Traits

Mover and shaker	Grow and change or ruination
Evolving	Molder
Moving	Shedder of old skins
Changing for sake of change	Shape-shifter
Radical shifting	Internal or external conflicts
Transformation	Fire and ice
Machiavellian	Harmonizes with the past
Instigator	Opportunistic
Contradictory	Know-it-all
Catalyst	Successful through rebellion
Pure and selfless motives	Insightful
Knight in shining armor	

Life Lessons

These people need to work at finding inner peace and calm; they need to simply be still more often as well as to think of others more.

Positive Tendencies

These are very energetic people who never seem to rest, who are physically always in motion, who are often throwing off many ideas and thoughts, and who seem to have endless stores of energy! They see life in terms of changes and growth through changes in lifestyle, ideas, living place, projects, jobs, and in ideas. Change and transformation are the keys to their creativity and joy of life; they probably like the image of a snake shedding its skin every so often. They are fascinated with new places, new ideas, new clothes, people, toys, and so on. There are natural travelers, people who hunger for new images, feelings, tastes, ideas, customs, music, and art; they internalize and blend them together into a very unique and personal aesthetic and sense of taste. These people are movers and shakers and on-task completers of projects. They play just as hard. A classic systems person, they approach things from several angles and probably have a number of very different kinds of friends and/or lovers as well. These are people who like meeting an amazing variety of people—even people with whom they have nothing in common. These people are catalysts who often change the dynamics of a party, a project, or a relationship. Very opportunistic, they are hot on new trends and styles and often are at the right place at the right time. Very future-oriented, they are probably into new technologies and have real insights about the future. These can be fun, interesting, transformative people who are never boring.

Negative Tendencies

These people sometimes drive others nuts because they are rarely still; many times they don't contemplate things, have trouble relaxing, and even have trouble just being quiet. They can be into change just for the sake of it, not always a good idea. These people can have trouble staying with things, projects, and relationships, and so they sometimes hurt others and even possibly damage their own careers. At times something of a know-it-all, these people can learn a little and expound a lot on almost anything. They can be hot or cold; they are often either on or totally off, passionately in love or completely indifferent, and this comes and goes, sometimes quickly. At times they may reject or resist change, which can really cause serious problems since change is vital to them. These can be scheming, plotting, manipulative people at times, too.

Compatibility

The following natal hexagrams represent people you naturally tend to have a positive reaction to:

HEXAGRAM **52:** KEEPING STILL

HEXAGRAM **22:** GRACE

HEXAGRAM **26:** TAMING POWER OF THE GREAT

HEXAGRAM **41:** DECREASE

HEXAGRAM **38:** OPPOSITION

HEXAGRAM **10:** TREADING

HEXAGRAM **61:** INNER TRUTH

HEXAGRAM **53:** DEVELOPMENT

The following natal hexagrams represent people you naturally tend to have a negative reaction to:

HEXAGRAM **30:** THE CLINGING

HEXAGRAM **56:** THE WANDERER

HEXAGRAM **50:** THE CAULDRON

HEXAGRAM **64:** BEFORE COMPLETION

HEXAGRAM **4:** YOUTHFUL FOLLY

HEXAGRAM **59:** DISPERSION

HEXAGRAM **6:** CONFLICT

HEXAGRAM **13:** FELLOWSHIP WITH MEN

HEXAGRAM 50

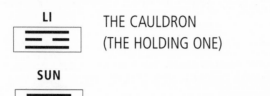

LI

THE CAULDRON
(THE HOLDING ONE)

SUN

Traits

Very successful

Touch of Midas

Supremely lucky

Fortunate

Great karma

Good disposition

Very religious

Fanatical

Self-confident

Egomaniac

Nourishing personality

Generous

Manifestor of great spirituality

Easy connection with inner self

Indolent and lazy

Selfish

Wise

Perceptive

Needs to harmonize

Insightful

Energetic

Incredible potential

Possibly truly great

Life Lessons

These people needs to be less controlling and to learn to be wise teachers; they should also strive for greatness and not settle for mediocrity.

Positive Tendencies

These are very successful people, a-silver-spoon-in-the-mouth types who are very self-confident, very generous, and very driven to succeed in whatever they focus on—if they even need to work! These are lucky people who are very nurturing, helpful, and loving with friends and lovers. They are energetic and can get a lot of things done. A key for these people in getting success and in helping others is using relatives and a wide network of loyal friends. Relationships are key for them in focusing energy to make things better on all levels. They can be real leaders, presidents of companies, governors, or whatever. The potential is there. These are harmonious people, ones who naturally bring their reality together, who know their true worth. Classic well-rounded people, they are accepted by others and like organized things; in fact, they are good at taking chaotic situations and organizing them. These would be good people for stream-lining or making more efficient an agency or department. These are natural moneymakers who can be very ambitious setting and achieving goals.

Negative Tendencies

These can be very overbearing people, at times something of a dicta-tor, at times a bit fanatical and patriarchal. They can be indolent, selfish, and a bit self-centered at times. They can have great insight and influence on others, but can sometimes use that to dominate and use them. These people sometimes have great luck and charisma but use it for selfish, negative ends; power corrupts, as they say. These people can be very successful and leave a great mark on the world, but they can also be lazy and blow it all.

Compatibility

The following natal hexagrams represent people you naturally tend to have a positive reaction to:

HEXAGRAM **29:** THE ABYSMAL

HEXAGRAM **60:** LIMITATION

HEXAGRAM **3:**   INITIAL DIFFICULTY

HEXAGRAM **63:** AFTER COMPLETION

HEXAGRAM **49:** REVOLUTION

HEXAGRAM **55:** ABUNDANCE

HEXAGRAM **36:** DARKENING OF THE LIGHT

HEXAGRAM **7:**   THE ARMY

The following natal hexagrams represent people you naturally tend to have a negative reaction to:

HEXAGRAM **30:** THE CLINGING FIRE

HEXAGRAM **56:** THE WANDERER

HEXAGRAM **50:** THE CAULDRON

HEXAGRAM **64:** BEFORE COMPLETION

HEXAGRAM **4:**   YOUTHFUL FOLLY

HEXAGRAM **59:** DISPERSION

HEXAGRAM **6:**   CONFLICT

HEXAGRAM **13:** FELLOWSHIP WITH MEN

HEXAGRAM 51

CHEN

THE AROUSING
(THE SHOCKING ONE)

CHEN

Traits

Powerful	Loves danger
Spontaneous	Seeks truth
Shocking	Impatient
Iconoclast	Radical learner or teacher
Responsible or irresponsible	Thrill-seeker
Wild child	Tends to panic
Uncontrollable	Vision quester
Grows in spurts	Adaptable
Zen-awakening (illuminations)	Frenetic
Revelation of Self	Very sensitive
Possibly hurtful	Inspired
Deals with fear issues	

Life Lessons

These people need to learn when to turn it down and when to be wild; they could be a bit more conservative at times and learn to respect traditions.

Positive Tendencies

These are very powerful, spontaneous, and sometimes wild people. Willfully independent, these people are classic rebels. Often going against the grain, they like to shake things up; they also have tremendous senses of humor. These people accept their foolishness and are respected for their alternative values and ideas. Real radical types, they rarely like to play it safe, follow tradition, or be middle-of-the-road. Eccentric and iconoclastic, these people are natural teachers who really get through to others by using almost shocking techniques and skills. Very creative, they are thrill-seekers and often love wild entertainment. Full of frantic energy, they can get a lot done and devote much energy to causes or ideas. Probably keeping odd hours, these people deeply analyze themselves and really understand what makes them tick. They are a lot of fun, tending to be witty, bright, argumentative, aware, interesting, humorous, great hosts, and good entertainment planners. Innovative and inventive, these joyful, adaptable people can come up with amazing ideas.

Negative Tendencies

These people can act seriously crazy and over the top, wild and uncontrollable occasionally. They can be catty, sarcastic, and even mean to others. "Going too far" applies to them at times, as do (at times) the terms dangerous sports, death wish, and daredevil. These people like to challenge everything and everyone and sometimes push the limits to a breaking point. They can get overwrought, tend to panic, can get wacked out if things get chaotic, and sometimes leap into things without thinking. These people can be influenced by everything intensely and sometimes forget the past very quickly when leaping to a new thing. These can be irresponsible people.

Compatibility

The following natal hexagrams represent people you naturally tend to have a positive reaction to:

HEXAGRAM **57:** THE PENETRATING

HEXAGRAM **9:**   TAMING POWER OF THE SMALL

HEXAGRAM **37:** THE FAMILY

HEXAGRAM **42:** INCREASE

HEXAGRAM **25:** I NNOCENCE

HEXAGRAM **21:** BITING THROUGH

HEXAGRAM **27:** NOURISHMENT

HEXAGRAM **18:** WORK THAT HAS BEEN SPOILED

The following natal hexagrams represent people you naturally tend to have a negative reaction to:

HEXAGRAM **51:** THE AROUSING

HEXAGRAM **16:** ENTHUSIASM

HEXAGRAM **40:** DELIVERANCE

HEXAGRAM **32:** DURATION

HEXAGRAM **46:** PUSHING UPWARD

HEXAGRAM **48:** THE WELL

HEXAGRAM **28:** PREPONDERANCE OF THE GREAT

HEXAGRAM **17:** FOLLOWING

HEXAGRAM 52

K'EN

KEEPING STILL
(THE CONTEMPLATIVE ONE)

K'EN

Traits

Yogi	Unnoticed
Still waters run deep	Basic and essential
Rugged	Ignores others
Still	Self-centered
Comforting	Stubborn
Slow	Careful
Thoughtful	Slow to change
Peaceful warrior	Connected with traditions and
Lets go of ego easily	history
Stable and solid	Easy mediator
Projects onto others	Takes all to heart
Lives day-to-day	Supportive

Life Lessons

These people need to learn to "stay real" (practical) and also need to learn that attachments to some things and people are OK; they should also take time to enjoy popular junk culture occasionally.

Positive Tendencies

These are very calm, centered, self-reliant people who often live life internally. They can be very quiet and are natural mediators who may or may not be drawn to various meditational disciplines. They probably spend a lot of time thinking, processing, and contemplating things, especially the big questions. These people have the natural inner stillness most people lack, a great gift to have and attractive to others. Natural and quietly spiritual people, their devotion to the cosmic power is seen as a very personal thing. They really believe in peace both as a personal ideal and as a political goal. These people often believe very strongly in harmony and try to practice it in real ways. They are amazingly open to new ideas, people, and concepts and have remarkably few prejudices, being accepting and appropriate and respectful toward others. These people live for the moment and don't set great store by history, past events, or even future goals. They live for today and find great joy in simple things. They are very selfless people who may seek and join progressive movements. Such people have very strong fantasy and visionary lives and are drawn to this kind of art and music. They not only love fantastic art but also love nature and often find strength and centeredness by going to nature.

Negative Tendencies

These people can be too passive, can just let things drift by, and can anger others by their lack of caring, attachment, or motivation. They may have trouble holding relationships for the same reason—just too passive, too open, too "zen" to make that effort or commitment. They sometimes ignore others and at times don't think of them, but mostly out of innocent disregard. These can be stubborn people who fixate on things and at times don't like to bend. They can go unnoticed, can slip through school, parties, jobs, and just not be noticed. These are people who can easily detach from their egos, which is good at times but can also lead to ego-poor individuals who can be lonely because they have not made an impression or been noticed. These people can get lost in their internal world and have trouble planning for the future. They can be "too politically correct."

Compatibility

The following natal hexagrams represent people you naturally tend to have a positive reaction to:

HEXAGRAM **30:** THE CLINGING

HEXAGRAM **56:** THE WANDERER

HEXAGRAM **50:** THE CAULDRON

HEXAGRAM **64:** BEFORE COMPLETION

HEXAGRAM **4:**   YOUTHFUL FOLLY

HEXAGRAM **59:** DISPERSION

HEXAGRAM **6:**   CONFLICT

HEXAGRAM **13:** FELLOWSHIP WITH MEN

The following natal hexagrams represent people you naturally tend to have a negative reaction to:

HEXAGRAM **52:** KEEPING STILL

HEXAGRAM **22:** GRACE

HEXAGRAM **26:** TAMING POWER OF THE GREAT

HEXAGRAM **41:** DECREASE

HEXAGRAM **38:** OPPOSITION

HEXAGRAM **10:** TREADING

HEXAGRAM **61:** INNER TRUTH

HEXAGRAM **53:** DEVELOPMENT

HEXAGRAM 53

SUN

DEVELOPMENT
(THE INFILTRATING ONE)

K'EN

Traits

Onward and upward . . . slowly	Four-square
Slow-acting	Stuffy
Quiet	Like a tree
Slow-moving	Reliable
Peaceful	Friendly
Calm	Boring
Persevering	Regular fellow
Avoids hasty action	Well-mannered
Sluggish	Careful planner
Unmotivated	Moral
Stable	Dutiful
Honorable	

Life Lessons

These people need to stand up for their beliefs more often—a change that is not only good but inescapable; they should learn to make life more exciting and adventurous.

Positive Tendencies

These are relaxed, easygoing people who enjoy slow-but-steady progress and who work their way through life, take care of essentials, are calm, good-natured, and not particularly extreme. They are naturally very conservative, do not like to change established routines, revere traditions and like to continue them. These people carefully build a foundation for their lives before they build a good and solid life upon it. They are very methodical with firm inner visions of how things should go and can manifest that vision as well. These people are comfortable with established social mores and institutions like engagement, marriage, family unity, a traditional faith, and so on. They believe in courtesy and like a comfortable environment and are good at making that a reality. These people are usually well-mannered, plan carefully, hate rushing through things, are responsible and methodical, very detail-oriented, great at eliminating errors, and very fair. They have a steady inner calm and a sense of duty and morality; providing for others and being very maternal or paternal are often key traits.

Negative Tendencies

These people tend to be very slow and sluggish, slow starters, and are at times not that exciting. These people can be overly moral, too preachy, and too subjective from a conservative point of view. They can be too formal and stuffy. They can be so middle-of-the-road as to be almost devoid of passionate beliefs. This person can be a bit unmotivated, especially once a comfortable status quo has been established. They sometimes dislike people with different ideas or thoughts and can dislike anything that rocks the boat. They sometimes don't like spontaneity, rapid change, or changing their views.

Compatibility

The following natal hexagrams represent people you naturally tend to have a positive reaction to:

HEXAGRAM **51**: THE AROUSING

HEXAGRAM **16**: ENTHUSIASM

HEXAGRAM **40**: DELIVERANCE

HEXAGRAM **32**: DURATION

HEXAGRAM **46**: PUSHING UPWARD

HEXAGRAM **48**: THE WELL

HEXAGRAM **28**: PREPONDERANCE OF THE GREAT

HEXAGRAM **17**: FOLLOWING

The following natal hexagrams represent people you naturally tend to have a negative reaction to:

HEXAGRAM **57**: THE PENETRATING

HEXAGRAM **9**:   TAMING POWER OF THE SMALL

HEXAGRAM **37**: THE FAMILY

HEXAGRAM **42**: INCREASE

HEXAGRAM **25**: INNOCENCE

HEXAGRAM **21**: BITING THROUGH

HEXAGRAM **27**: NOURISHMENT

HEXAGRAM **18**: WORK THAT HAS BEEN SPOILED

HEXAGRAM 54:

CHEN

TUI

THE MARRYING MAIDEN
(THE ACCEPTING ONE)

Traits

People who attract many things	Soft
Pushiness brings problems	Obsequious
Humble	Gentle and sweet
Circumspect	Mystical
Focused on relationships	Sacrifices for others
Submissive	Falls into victim-scripts
Intuitive	Seeks guidance from gurus
The marrying kind	Follows the light into Spirit
Loyal	Gullible and earnest
Strong emotional bonds	Trusting and innocent
Loving	
Weak	

Life Lessons

These people need to learn to lead others and to become a bit tougher; they should strive to be more independent as well.

Positive Tendencies

These are very humble people who are very much mirrors of their surroundings; through gentle, persistent efforts they can achieve great rewards. These are gentle, sweet people who are loyal and honest and who see things through to their completion in a steadfast manner. They work well for others and hold important, responsible positions. These are often indispensable individuals who may not be very flashy but who are key players. They often have very clear long-range plans, which are the key to their success. Slow, steady advancement following a master plan without a lot of fanfare will give these people success. They tend not to be loud or pushy, like long-term relationships, thrive on mutually helpful and/or dependent loving relationships, and need others (and others need them). These are proper people who tend to maintain good outward personas and so build consensus and compromise a lot. These intuitive people understand a lot, are talented communicators, are empathic, and identify with the pain and joy of others. These are trusting people who can be attracted to the mystical, the poetic, and the artistic.

Negative Tendencies

These people can be too submissive, too dependent, too weak, too soft, and too gullible. They can be a victim, a brown noser, a yes-man (or woman). These people are often naturally quiet, but they can become almost zombielike at times. They can also throw tantrums and be oddly loud or shrill when things don't go right. These people can be something of a nerd who loses track of the real world.

Compatibility

The following natal hexagrams represent people you naturally tend to have a positive reaction to:

HEXAGRAM **57:** THE PENETRATING
HEXAGRAM **9:**   TAMING POWER OF THE SMALL
HEXAGRAM **37:** THE FAMILY
HEXAGRAM **42:** INCREASE
HEXAGRAM **25:** INNOCENCE
HEXAGRAM **21:** BITING THROUGH
HEXAGRAM **27:** NOURISHMENT
HEXAGRAM **18:** WORK THAT HAS BEEN SPOILED

The following natal hexagrams represent people you naturally tend to have a negative reaction to:

HEXAGRAM **51:** THE AROUSING
HEXAGRAM **16:** ENTHUSIASM
HEXAGRAM **40:** DELIVERANCE
HEXAGRAM **32:** DURATION
HEXAGRAM **46:** PUSHING UPWARD
HEXAGRAM **48:** THE WELL

HEXAGRAM **28:** PREPONDERANCE OF THE GREAT
HEXAGRAM **17:** FOLLOWING

HEXAGRAM 55

CHEN

ABUNDANCE
(THE ABOUNDING ONE)

LI

Traits

Ruler	Great organizer
Powerful	Magician
Great person	Ambitious
Strong-willed	Intense
Role model	Overly aggressive
Administrator	Overwhelming
Judge other men/women	Shoulders great responsibility
Arrogant	Mature
Above the law	Guardian
Lucky	Paternal
Aristocratic	Dictator
Target of jealousy	

Life Lessons

These people need to learn to be more spontaneously loving and more modest; they must also accept that chaos is part of life—sometimes a very necessary part.

Positive Tendencies

These are people who are often in top mental and physical form, or at least try to be. The classic golden boy or girl, the sun always seems to shine on them and they have real presence. They often have charisma, are naturally aristocratic, and tend to attract abundance in great measure. These are genuinely lucky people. Such individuals like the good life and have the today-is-the-first-day-of-the-rest-of-my-life optimistic attitude. They are always seeking that peak performance, that peak thrill or experience. These people feel great satisfaction with their jobs, relationships, and life in general. They are really natural leaders and easily granted positions of power, wealth, or leadership, sometimes by inheriting it. These people are natural businesspeople but could be successful in almost any field. They are somewhat principled and, if following a set of moral principles, will benefit society and do a lot of good. They often have a lot of responsibility and an almost guardianlike aura for those who look up to them. These people often end up judging others and so must work hard at being true to themselves. These people are often meticulous planners and are often fascinated with self-discovery (and it is very important that this inner work never stop). These are intense people who can organize well and are great role models.

Negative Tendencies

These people can be too strong-willed, too haughty, and may even see themselves as above the law, outside the masses who are beneath them. These people can also be too un-giving, too tightly wound, too overly organized. They can also be too bossy and too aggressive at times, even physically. They often do not like to be contradicted and can have fits if someone says no to them. These people are sometimes not emotionally spontaneous and can be overbearing about their needs and wants. They can be very selfish people at times who, if they lose their way, can do bad things.

Compatibility

The following natal hexagrams represent people you naturally tend to have a positive reaction to:

HEXAGRAM **57:** THE PENETRATING

HEXAGRAM **9:** TAMING POWER OF THE SMALL

HEXAGRAM **37:** THE FAMILY

HEXAGRAM **42:** INCREASE

HEXAGRAM **25:** INNOCENCE

HEXAGRAM **21:** BITING THROUGH

HEXAGRAM **27:** NOURISHMENT

HEXAGRAM **18:** WORK THAT HAS BEEN SPOILED

The following natal hexagrams represent people you naturally tend to have a negative reaction to:

HEXAGRAM **51:** THE AROUSING

HEXAGRAM **16:** ENTHUSIASM

HEXAGRAM **40:** DELIVERANCE

HEXAGRAM **32:** DURATION

HEXAGRAM **46:** PUSHING UPWARD

HEXAGRAM **48:** THE WELL

HEXAGRAM **28:** PREPONDERANCE OF THE GREAT

HEXAGRAM **17:** FOLLOWING

HEXAGRAM 56

LI

THE WANDERER
(THE SOJOURNING ONE)

K'EN

Traits

Visitor and wanderer	Kind
Always moving	Extroverted
Driven	Nips things in the bud
Hyper	Tends to quarrel
Interesting	Decisive
Amusing	Deals with things fast
Frenetic	Cautious (paranoid?)
Fascinating	Open-minded
Studies many cultures	Intelligent
Easily detoured	Quick-tempered
Spontaneous	Mystic
Looks before leaping	

Life Lessons

These people need to learn to be more sensitive and more appropriate ("when in Rome . . ."); they also need to learn to resolve disputes better and to be more helpful and a bit more humble.

Positive Tendencies

These are restless and adventurous people with large intellectual appetites. They go in many different directions, sometimes at once, and can achieve a number of significant goals that may be very different from one another. They love travel and new things—cultures, places, and people. These people crave new experiences, are always experimenting, and are almost radically open-minded. Generally intelligent, these people are often extroverted, interesting, and tell fascinating tales. They could be talented artists, writers, teachers, and/or students. They can set up programs as well as flexible and multipurpose situations, classes, jobs, and so on. Flexible is a key word here, but these people do best with modest goals and targets, not big sweeping changes or projects. These people will always be seeking and sampling different traditions, cultures, foods, and maybe even philosophies and religions. Similarly, they have a wide variety of friends and are always on the go, never feeling that there is enough time. Spontaneous, they have a bit of the "Indiana Jones" adventurer in them. They love to debate and argue all the time, but rarely stupidly. Passionate, these chameleon-like people are always moving one way or another. Though people think them changeable, they actually have a strong, solid core of beliefs and morals.

Negative Tendencies

These people can be a bit crazed and frenetic; they are sometimes easily detoured and distracted and sometimes jump before looking into all the ramifications. These people may quarrel, may be argumentative, may be picky, and may at times think others can't do things as well they can. Sometimes hard to please, these people can have quick tempers and be very impractical. These people can be too restless, sometimes not settling down or completing things, sometimes avoiding long-term commitments, and sometimes bolting when things get heavy. They can feel at loose ends, rootless, and have few ties or possessions. They can have a big mouth and it gets them into trouble.

Compatibility

The following natal hexagrams represent people you naturally tend to have a positive reaction to:

HEXAGRAM **29:** THE ABYSMAL
HEXAGRAM **60:** LIMITATION
HEXAGRAM **3:**   INITIAL DIFFICULTY
HEXAGRAM **63:** AFTER COMPLETION
HEXAGRAM **49:** REVOLUTION
HEXAGRAM **55:** ABUNDANCE
HEXAGRAM **36:** DARKENING OF THE LIGHT
HEXAGRAM **7:**   THE ARMY

The following natal hexagrams represent people you naturally tend to have a negative reaction to:

HEXAGRAM **30:**   THE CLINGING FIRE

HEXAGRAM **56:**   THE WANDERER

HEXAGRAM **50:**   THE CAULDRON

HEXAGRAM **64:**   BEFORE COMPLETION

HEXAGRAM **4:**   YOUTHFUL FOLLY

HEXAGRAM **59:**   DISPERSION

HEXAGRAM **6:**   CONFLICT

HEXAGRAM **13:**   FELLOWSHIP WITH MEN

HEXAGRAM 57

SUN

THE GENTLE
(THE PENETRATING ONE)

SUN

Traits

Absorbing	Specialized
Open to influence	Unobtrusive
Intuitive	Tasteful
Gentle	Polite and urbane
Slow and steady movement	Unassuming
Cerebral	Influenced by long-term, forces
Slowly influences others	Giver of great advice
Quietly creative	Frustrated
Great helper	Airhead
Devotee and ardent student	Forgetful
Excellent with small projects	Nice
Detail-oriented	

Life Lessons

These people need to find ways to avoid frustrating situations; they need to learn to ask for and accept help from others and also to learn that sometimes procrastinating is OK.

Positive Tendencies

These are very gentle but insistent people who are steadfast and who maintain a sense of purpose without losing sight of their goals. They are very graceful and nonintrusive, but very effective in a quiet, smooth sort of way. Very insightful, these people understand the spirit or inner essence of things, people, and objects and can relate on a subtle level with their environment. They are therefore intuitive and know how to change, help, or influence situations and people very well. Long-term friendships and relationships are a hallmark of these people; they do not befriend others or fall in love suddenly but slowly, gradually, and completely. These people often have very good aesthetics, great style, and a deep understanding of art as well as a clear understanding of their destiny. They are very open to new influences and tend to interpret the world in terms of movements, forces, patterns, and ideals. These are very detail-oriented people who are great at following through and completing things, especially long-term tasks. Very polite, these people are consummate hosts, give great advice, and have clever ideas.

Negative Tendencies

These people can be too open; they sometimes take almost everything at face value and can be naive. They often parrot things and can repeat opinions or gossip that is not very nice. These people are often not good at defending themselves, making quick decisions, taking aggressive action, or arguing their points well. They can be wishy-washy and have trouble taking a stand on things. These people may be very frustrated at times because they sometimes do not get enough time to process things, something they need to do. They like to be slow and methodical but sometimes things do not go that way. When that happens they can get irritable and overloaded and then may shut down or retreat. They can be snobbish at times, dismissive of uncultured things, be too narrow in their focus, too picky, and sometimes be something of an airhead.

Compatibility

The following natal hexagrams represent people you naturally tend to have a positive reaction to:

HEXAGRAM **51:**   THE AROUSING

HEXAGRAM **16:**   ENTHUSIASM

HEXAGRAM **40:**   DELIVERANCE

HEXAGRAM **32:**   DURATION

HEXAGRAM **46:**   PUSHING UPWARD

HEXAGRAM **48:**   THE WELL

HEXAGRAM **28:**   PREPONDERANCE OF THE GREAT

HEXAGRAM **17:**   FOLLOWING

The following natal hexagrams represent people you naturally tend to have a negative reaction to:

HEXAGRAM **57:**   THE PENETRATING

HEXAGRAM **9:**   TAMING POWER OF THE SMALL

HEXAGRAM **37:**   THE FAMILY

HEXAGRAM **42:**   INCREASE

HEXAGRAM **25:**   INNOCENCE

HEXAGRAM **21:**   BITING THROUGH

HEXAGRAM **27:**   NOURISHMENT

HEXAGRAM **18:**   WORK THAT HAS BEEN SPOILED

HEXAGRAM 58

TUI

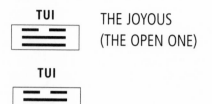

THE JOYOUS
(THE OPEN ONE)

TUI

Traits

Happy	Great teacher
Carefree	Collectivizes
Fun and wild	Facilitator
Immature	Social climber
Entertainer	Super-nice person
Life of the party	Frivolous
Gentle	Positive influence
Joyous	More than meets the eye
Optimistic	Party animal
Too good to be true	Great vibes
Shallow	Disruptive
Insincere	Talkative

Life Lessons

These people need to learn ways to face problems head-on and to accept more responsibility for their lives; they also need to learn to be a bit more serious about things.

Positive Tendencies

These are very happy and up people who are kind, often generous, usually pleasant, cooperative, and they get along with others. They can be really fun and very social, the life-of-the-party type. Here are people who like to get along, who are easygoing and want to please others. They are the perfect entertainer, love to give and attend social events, and can mix with almost anyone anywhere. They are great dates and often use friendship and kindness to achieve significant goals. Very loyal, these people also invoke loyalty in others. They are pleasure-seekers, very hedonistic. They are also great managers, good bosses who inspire their employees to work hard. They take a lot of pleasure in helping others and in doing good work. Very caring people, they would be good people to have a relationship with; they are extremely encouraging, helpful, and great at communicating things, especially feelings.

Negative Tendencies

These people can be immature at times, sometimes too giddy, and too happy; they can see the world through rose-colored glasses. They avoid problems and may sometimes avoid the dark side of life, especially ugly or problematic things. They can have trouble facing up to difficult things. These people can be shallow at times, sometimes bend the truth, be insincere, flatter too much, and be frivolous with money too easily. They can be social butterflies and disruptive because they love to chat, interrupt, babble on and on, and gossip.

Compatibility

The following natal hexagrams represent people you naturally tend to have a positive reaction to:

HEXAGRAM **52:** KEEPING STILL

HEXAGRAM **22:** GRACE

HEXAGRAM **26:** TAMING POWER OF THE GREAT

HEXAGRAM **41:** DECREASE

HEXAGRAM **38:** OPPOSITION

HEXAGRAM **10:** TREADING

HEXAGRAM **61:** INNER TRUTH

HEXAGRAM **53:** DEVELOPMENT

The following natal hexagrams represent people you naturally tend to have a negative reaction to:

HEXAGRAM **30:**   THE CLINGING
HEXAGRAM **56:**   THE WANDERER
HEXAGRAM **50:**   THE CAULDRON
HEXAGRAM **64:**   BEFORE COMPLETION
HEXAGRAM **4:**   YOUTHFUL FOLLY
HEXAGRAM **59:**   DISPERSION
HEXAGRAM **6:**   CONFLICT
HEXAGRAM **13:**   FELLOWSHIP WITH MEN

HEXAGRAM 59

SUN

DISSOLUTION
(THE DISPERSING ONE)

K'AN

Traits

Alchemist

Flips between extremes

Breaks through

Tight or release

Shake-up kind of person

Removes blockages

Knight slaying the dragons

Energetic

Reinvents self

Egocentric . . . but selfless

Artistic and creative

Synthesizer/banisher

Stirs up the psyche

Cynical

Analytical

Changing

Reviving

Group-oriented

Devoted to causes

Renewing

Passionate

Confusing and confused

Illuminated

Life Lessons

These people need to accept limitations better and to understand what can and cannot be done; they need to learn ways to wholeheartedly join with others and also learn to communicate more clearly.

Positive Tendencies

These people are very much like the classic magician or alchemist in that they bring different things together to create something new and more wondrous. This constant process is the key to these people. These are significant people who have great insight into the patterns and flows of history and of the society around them—these are very profound things. Strongly motivated by feelings of social responsibility and destiny, these individuals are focused on helping the world and on making something of themselves. These are artistic people who excel at bringing people together. These people do not put up with BS, are efficient and very directed, get things done, and always have an overall plan. They don't mince words and do not waste a lot of time on chitchat or social niceties. Very passionate people, they are very spiritual but see this in terms of doing, not talking or wishing. They are crusaders and like to go out and get things done. These people will be at the center of causes or even consciousness, more a focus of events or projects than the leader, though they are good leaders when it is necessary. They will often be found on the cutting edge of something—art, politics, whatever—always in the center of things.

Negative Tendencies

These can be very cynical people who stir things up just to see what will happen. They can be impatient and even brutal in their methods for getting things done. These people can be great synthesizers, though sometimes this simply can't be done—some things simply cannot go together, and these people have trouble seeing that and may get irate. They can get carried away and be a bit fanatical, too idealistic. They can be confused and sometimes confuse others with their visions about the future, about how things should be. Thus, people may become alienated.

They can sometimes make enemies trying to reform things or by pushing a social cause.

Compatibility

The following natal hexagrams represent people you naturally tend to have a positive reaction to:

HEXAGRAM **51:** THE AROUSING

HEXAGRAM **16:** ENTHUSIASM

HEXAGRAM **40:** DELIVERANCE

HEXAGRAM **32:** DURATION

HEXAGRAM **46:** PUSHING UPWARD

HEXAGRAM **48:** THE WELL

HEXAGRAM **28:** PREPONDERANCE OF THE GREAT

HEXAGRAM **17:** FOLLOWING

The following natal hexagrams represent people you naturally tend to have a negative reaction to:

HEXAGRAM **57:** THE PENETRATING

HEXAGRAM **9:** TAMING POWER OF THE SMALL

HEXAGRAM **37:** THE FAMILY

HEXAGRAM **42:** INCREASE

HEXAGRAM **25:** INNOCENCE

HEXAGRAM **21:** BITING THROUGH

HEXAGRAM **27:** NOURISHMENT

HEXAGRAM **18:** WORK THAT HAS BEEN SPOILED

HEXAGRAM 60

K'AN

LIMITATION
(THE ARTICULATING ONE)

TUI

Traits

Strict

Moral

Ethical

Consistent

Dependable

Logical

Linear in action

Very analytical

Sets and observes laws

Succeeds best within limits

Lives by patterns

Self-critical

Critical of all

Perfectionist

Organized and clean

Principled

Thrifty

Excellent planner

Super businessperson

Scientific or legal mind

Defines

Shortsighted

Scholar

Life Lessons

These people need to be more lenient and more forgiving; they should find ways to loosen up more, and they need to understand that many things cannot be logically analyzed.

Positive Tendencies

These are very disciplined, self-motivated individuals who set their own agenda and can follow it easily. These people don't need or desire much guidance from others and excel at all aspects of life without help. These are clearly very independent people. They have a very strong ethical and moral code, rarely lie, and are often bluntly truthful. Such people are great believers in civilization, law, manners, customs, an orderly society, and a purposeful universe. They are very likely involved in structured careers, something to do with organization, laws, enforcement, regulations, or the like. They are great at organizing others, information, or ideas, and they set limits, goals, and/or plans of action. They respond well to set programs, diets, classes, exercise regimens, and so on. If they set borders and limitations, they will really do well, especially in terms of creative work. These people are consistent, reliable, truthful, and analytical. They mentally examine and take apart things to really understand them, and once they have, they are great at communicating what they have learned. These people are often good at saving money, budgeting, and almost anything requiring exact facts or ideas like science, business, or law. These are often very smart, scholarly people.

Negative Tendencies

These people can be very critical, both of others and of themselves. They can be too strict and may set limits and expectations that are extreme. At times these people can be haughty, controlling, and overly moral, to the point of wanting others to follow the same moral code they do. These are, sometimes, perfectionists who at times feel that those who are looser in their methods and ideals are "sloppy." They can be very shortsighted, sometimes focusing on the immediate and not good at seeing the big picture. These people can be too robotic, too cold, too distant, and may try to set standards and rules for others.

Compatibility

The following natal hexagrams represent people you naturally tend to have a positive reaction to:

HEXAGRAM **30:** THE CLINGING FIRE
HEXAGRAM **56:** THE WANDERER
HEXAGRAM **50:** THE CAULDRON
HEXAGRAM **64:** BEFORE COMPLETION
HEXAGRAM **4:** YOUTHFUL FOLLY

HEXAGRAM **59:** DISPERSION

HEXAGRAM **6:** CONFLICT

HEXAGRAM **13:** FELLOWSHIP WITH MEN

The following natal hexagrams represent people you naturally tend to have a negative reaction to:

HEXAGRAM **29:** THE ABYSMAL

HEXAGRAM **60:** LIMITATION

HEXAGRAM **3:** INITIAL DIFFICULTY

HEXAGRAM **63:** AFTER COMPLETION

HEXAGRAM **49:** REVOLUTION

HEXAGRAM **55:** ABUNDANCE

HEXAGRAM **36:** DARKENING OF THE LIGHT

HEXAGRAM **7:** THE ARMY

HEXAGRAM 61

SUN

INNER TRUTH
(THE CENTERED ONE)

TUI

Traits

Balanced	Holier than thou
Seeks inner truth	Spiritually arrogant
Keyed-in to justice	Misunderstood
Sympathetic	Very spiritual
Empathic	Strong inner connection
Cares for all	Intellectual
Altruistic	Always challenging self

Traits

Blunt	Progressive
Social critic	Fanatical
Activist	Judgmental
Teacher	Extremely truthful
Believes in freedom	

Life Lessons

These people need to keep balanced when teaching others; they need to accept that all views are relative and that not everyone needs to hear the truth. These people also need to relax more!

Positive Tendencies

These are people who really do understand others and are empathic, sympathetic, and drawn to helping others. They are very instinctual, very in touch with their most primal being, almost genetic in their focus. These people often do well in life, are often fortunate or just plain lucky, and they understand this. They are great at moderating disputes, at finding common ground for sparring people or in group situations. A real agreement-builder, they feel out a given situation and instinctively know how best to proceed to get a consensus, often to the astonishment of those who are approaching things more intellectually. These are very open people who often see all sides of a situation; they are very penetrating and can see through the BS to the core of what a problem or situation really is, right to the heart of the matter. They are excellent counselors, therapists, social workers, teachers, parents, and/or activists. They have a great balanced humanistic sense of good and bad, right and wrong. They usually seek the underlying truth in any situation. These people really believe in personal freedom and personal responsibility, and they are always looking for something better, something higher, something more evolved, and much of their lives, relationships, goods, and so on are seen as a means to this end. They have strong inner visions and they often either go outward trying to better others and the world, or they turn inward to develop their own spirituality and grasp of the divine.

Negative Tendencies

They can be subjective, blunt, and unkind in their messages, and they can sometimes be very misunderstood. As they try to guide or instruct others, they can be seen as critical or pushy. They can be too spiritual to the point of being a bit crazy with it, even sometimes pushing it on others to help them. At times very intellectual, they can become too brainy and sometimes are not pragmatic. He or she can be too idealistic, too pie-in-the-sky, and they may sometimes be accused of not living in the real world. These people can be fussy and can make a mountain out of a molehill. They can be too moralistic and may sometimes have trouble just relaxing and enjoying life.

Compatibility

The following natal hexagrams represent people you naturally tend to have a positive reaction to:

HEXAGRAM **51**: THE AROUSING

HEXAGRAM **16**: ENTHUSIASM

HEXAGRAM **40**: DELIVERANCE

HEXAGRAM **32**: DURATION

HEXAGRAM **46**: PUSHING UPWARD

HEXAGRAM **48**: THE WELL

HEXAGRAM **28**: PREPONDERANCE OF THE GREAT

HEXAGRAM **17**: FOLLOWING

The following natal hexagrams represent people you naturally tend to have a negative reaction to:

HEXAGRAM **57**: THE PENETRATING

HEXAGRAM **9**:   TAMING POWER OF THE SMALL

HEXAGRAM **37**: THE FAMILY

HEXAGRAM **42**: INCREASE

HEXAGRAM **25**: INNOCENCE

HEXAGRAM **21:** BITING THROUGH

HEXAGRAM **27:** NOURISHMENT

HEXAGRAM **18:** WORK THAT HAS BEEN SPOILED

HEXAGRAM 62

CHEN

PREPONDERANCE
OF THE SMALL
(THE CONSCIENTIOUS ONE)

K'EN

Traits

Homebody	Success is modest but lasting
Subservient	Small moments of depression
Honest	Seeks to improve the world
Excellent parent	Volunteer
Caring	Kind
Nurturing	Friendly
Small-minded	Conservative
Banal	Nondescript
Doesn't rock the boat	Entrepreneur
Routine lover	Society-oriented
Modest	Hard worker
Indecisive	

Life Lessons

These people need to learn not to bite off more than they can chew; they need to loosen up and to spend their money more generously.

Positive Tendencies

These are very respectful people who are self-controlled, directed, and spell out where they are going. They can be meticulous, noticing even minute details in life that others miss. They are very observant and keep track of all sorts of things, have a great sense of duty (though they can be rebellious, too), and have great memories. Independent, they gain great fortune following the path of responsibility and duty. These people are honest and very domestic in that they probably love being at home, focusing on their family, working in a garden or workshop, and so on. They like to be constructive and tend to be financially conservative, having a knack for saving and investing money. These people could be real entrepreneurs who can make an investment venture really work. Life and work are best approached by them in small steps. These people have a lot of dignity and pride and are very conscious of how they look, act, and so on. They like to make good impressions, pay attention to what others think, and can be very successful financially and commercially. These are very stable, prepared individuals, not wild or flamboyant. They are regular guys, the kind of people everyone wants for a neighbor or co-worker, who don't stand out too much. They like things steady, work very hard, and usually believe in a work ethic. They like routine and ritual in the sense of things done every day in the same way—these things are important to them. These are conscientious people who are often great lovers, spouses, or friends.

Negative Tendencies

These people can be very boring and somewhat subservient. They may dislike being the leader and may be somewhat conservative, often disliking anything really new or radical. They can be small-minded at times and maybe even a bit prejudiced against certain people or ideas. They can have somewhat narrow interests and may tend to like the same things (food, movies, TV shows) over and over. These people may be big on returning to past values, which can either be good or repressive depending on their intentions. They can be nondescript at times, sometimes something of a wallflower. Such individuals often play it safe too much.

Compatibility

The following natal hexagrams represent people you naturally tend to have a positive reaction to:

HEXAGRAM **57**: THE PENETRATING

HEXAGRAM **9**:   TAMING POWER OF THE SMALL

HEXAGRAM **37**: THE FAMILY

HEXAGRAM **42**: INCREASE

HEXAGRAM **25**: INNOCENCE

HEXAGRAM **21**: BITING THROUGH

HEXAGRAM **27**: NOURISHMENT

HEXAGRAM **18**: WORK THAT HAS BEEN SPOILED

The following natal hexagrams represent people you naturally tend to have a negative reaction to:

HEXAGRAM **51**: THE AROUSING

HEXAGRAM **16**: ENTHUSIASM

HEXAGRAM **40**: DELIVERANCE

HEXAGRAM **32**: DURATION

HEXAGRAM **46**: PUSHING UPWARD

HEXAGRAM **48**: THE WELL

HEXAGRAM **28**: PREPONDERANCE OF THE GREAT

HEXAGRAM **17**: FOLLOWING

HEXAGRAM 63

K'AN

AFTER COMPLETION
(THE FINISHING ONE)

LI

Traits

Lucky	Easy life
Gifted	Often inconvenienced
Very well-off	Easily enters situations . . .
Talented	harder getting out
Successful	Works on awareness
Stable	Procrastinator
Lazy or ambitious	Indolent
Persevere!	Pleasure-lover
Step by step	Two sides, two-faced
Constantly watchful is key	Inventive
Easily distracted	Important ideas
Confused	Centered

Life Lessons

These people need to remain conscious of things and should work at becoming more aware; they should not put things off so much and should be more prepared for difficulties in life.

Positive Tendencies

The possibility of being very successful is very real for these people, but in small incremental ways. These are very aware and prepared people; they like to plan carefully. Being balanced is very important to these individuals and they are very good at being very still, at meditation, at instinctively finding that balance point between Yin and Yang, Positive and Negative, Sleep and Wakefulness. They are great at solving problems, talented at nipping things in the bud, and have an inner alarm that lets them know when difficult or problematic things are coming up. People should listen to them carefully. They are great at protecting or guarding others and are realistic, see things as they are, pragmatic, and have little use for idealism. These are very detail-oriented people who get things done and can unravel and straighten out the most complex mess. Very stable, these people have strong wills and persevere even under trying situations, which these people may encounter quite a bit in life. Things will rarely go easily for these individuals, but they grow through their trials and will not only overcome them but will also sharpen their psychic and intuitive abilities. These people are fun and like pleasure but may not appear jolly or cheerful on the surface, yet deep down they are not gloomy—in fact, they have a steady inner peace and equilibrium that they can share with others. These are inventive people with lots of original talent and ideals, and they may have a number of extreme life-changes that will bring a lot of knowledge and self-awareness.

Negative Tendencies

These people can be very ambitious and/or extremely lazy, or both at the same time. They can have great success, then blow it by not paying attention. Sometimes big projects, plans, and/or events are not good for these individuals; they'd often do better with small, sequential projects and small changes. These people can be very slothful and indolent, sometimes liking to lay around a lot and letting things drift by. They may be terrible procrastinators, and, if so, small problems can easily become big ones. They can be two-faced, sometimes backbiters, and at times may drift mentally and physically. They may need to watch their weight, health, drinking, and so forth in that there could be a tendency toward decline if they are not active.

Compatibility

The following natal hexagrams represent people you naturally tend to have a positive reaction to:

HEXAGRAM **30:** THE CLINGING FIRE
HEXAGRAM **56:** THE WANDERER
HEXAGRAM **50:** THE CAULDRON
HEXAGRAM **64:** BEFORE COMPLETION
HEXAGRAM **4:**   YOUTHFUL FOLLY
HEXAGRAM **59:** DISPERSION
HEXAGRAM **6:**   CONFLICT
HEXAGRAM **13:** FELLOWSHIP WITH MEN

The following natal hexagrams represent people you naturally tend to have a negative reaction to:

HEXAGRAM **29:** THE ABYSMAL
HEXAGRAM **60:** LIMITATION
HEXAGRAM **3:** INITIAL DIFFICULTY
HEXAGRAM **63:** AFTER COMPLETION
HEXAGRAM **49:** REVOLUTION
HEXAGRAM **55:** ABUNDANCE
HEXAGRAM **36:** DARKENING OF THE LIGHT
HEXAGRAM **7:** THE ARMY

HEXAGRAM 64

LI

K'AN

BEFORE COMPLETION
(THE PREPARED ONE)

Traits

Cautious	Plodding planner
Brings order from chaos	Cold and calculating
Amazing	Magician
Juggler	Syzygy
Avaricious	Dissecting mind
Careful	Heart and head separate
Many irons in the fire	Compartmentalizes
Finishes and completes	Discriminating
Slow but sure	Wary
Observer	Prepared
Rash actions lead to danger	Creator

Life Lessons

These people need to pay attention to details more as well as plan ahead more; they need to learn that timing is everything when bringing order out of chaos and that every ending is also a new beginning.

Positive Tendencies

These people are classic tightrope walkers or jugglers. They are extremely creative and brilliant in many ways, classic artists or actor types who are always juggling a million things at once. The key to these people is that they bring order out of chaos and can take ugliness or strangeness and bring forth beauty or usefulness. They are quite the observers, like to be objective, and are great at collecting information. They are very careful, look before leaping, discriminating people who have specific tastes and ideas and articulate them well. They may be very wise people with insight into the psyche, capable of helping others. These are the kind of people who can affect the psychology of groups, who can understand group dynamics and change them. There is a real feeling of renewal or rebirth to these people; they tend to cycle through great life changes, rising, peaking, and then shifting to something completely different, a new phase of life. These people are somewhat wary, a bit protective of themselves, but they can also be very brave, resourceful, and adventurous when it is called for. They are very conscious of certain overall high-level life goals, certain watermarks that will lead to some kind of transcendent success, but not in the usual sense. These people often reach these goals and they love to gather wisdom and information like gold. At key moments of transformation, they often use this accumulated knowledge to positively further that transformation. These people are often fascinating, seeming to have lived several different lives in one. They can be good at helping others transform, renew, or revive their lives, interests, and/or talents. They are very slow and sure people who actually complete the many projects they have going. These people probably have very exciting relationships but are not really domesticated.

Negative Tendencies

These people can sometimes be too rash and can sabotage projects by rushing to the end carelessly. These people can be hard to satisfy. They sometimes have great experiences or finish great works and then are unhappy once the quest is over. They can be very much the observer and so can sometimes be seen as cold and distant. They may hide their emotions at times. They sometimes compartmentalize things; sometimes heart and head are in different places and this can be a regular problem. These people can be too slow at times and be wrongly seen as uninteresting. They can be greedy and grasping as well. They can be dishonest at times and may borrow ideas, images, or phrases without realizing it. They can be real creators of chaos as well as makers of order; they can be like a juggler. If they trip it could affect others; chaos could result. This is not always bad, but might not be good.

Compatibility

The following natal hexagrams represent people you naturally tend to have a positive reaction to:

HEXAGRAM **29:** THE ABYSMAL

HEXAGRAM **60:** LIMITATION

HEXAGRAM **3:** INITIAL DIFFICULTY

HEXAGRAM **63:** AFTER COMPLETION

HEXAGRAM **49:** REVOLUTION

HEXAGRAM **55:** ABUNDANCE

HEXAGRAM **36:** DARKENING OF THE LIGHT

HEXAGRAM **7:** THE ARMY

The following natal hexagrams represent people you naturally tend to have a negative reaction to:

HEXAGRAM **30:** THE CLINGING FIRE

HEXAGRAM **56:** THE WANDERER

HEXAGRAM **50:** THE CAULDRON

HEXAGRAM **64:** BEFORE COMPLETION

HEXAGRAM **4:**   YOUTHFUL FOLLY

HEXAGRAM **59:** DISPERSION

HEXAGRAM **6:**   CONFLICT

HEXAGRAM **13:** FELLOWSHIP WITH MEN

Improving Your Life with Natal Hexagrams

In this section of the book you will learn how to use your natal hexagram to improve your body, your mind, and your spirit through practical study and to analyze your Self and your life through the power of your natal hexagram. You will also learn how to improve your interpersonal relationships: with people you love, people you dislike, and people you just have to deal with in your day-to-day life.

There is nothing mysterious about the exercises introduced here. They only require an open and alert mind, a notebook, a pencil, this book, and a little time. Combined, they can transform your life and the way you live it. These exercises have produced real, practical improvement in the lives of many people. With them you, too, can transform yourself and the world around you in a positive way.

The first part of this section is an explanation of the Taoist view of the world and how we can best live life. It focuses on key concepts that will make the journey of self-discovery and evolution on which you are about to embark easier and more interesting.

You will read how these ideas are expressed and how people like you have used the power of their natal hexagrams to unlock their creative potential and increase their happiness and prosperity. Then, step-by-step directions will be given on how to do the same for yourself and further use natal hexagrams to improve your relationships with all sorts of people in your life.

An orthodox Taoist priest may be somewhat shocked at some of the casual explanations made here, but then this book isn't written for him! The view of Taoism, and how you can use it to improve your life, presented here is from my point of view, though I have the words of the Sages behind me. I make no claim that this book defines Taoism—that was never the intent. This book exists to help you find the path that makes you happy—that is the most important goal in this universe. If you are living a joyful and creative life, then you will prosper.

So, what are you waiting for? Pour a cup of jasmine tea and let's get started!

The Path

Let me first generally, then specifically, explain in my own way what Taoists consider the root of troubles and unhappiness and how they apply to people today. By understanding how "losing your way" comes about, you can better understand how to "find your way" again and so manage your life in such a manner as to be happier and more successful than you can possibly imagine. And it is all very simple!

First, a few terms need to be discussed. These words and the ideas they represent may take on definitions different from what you have always thought. I ask that you open your mind to new ways of thinking in order for this Taoist vision of the Way Things Are to become clear to you. Once you understand the basic ideas, then the positive uses of the natal hexagram in bettering your life will become more apparent.

Self and Ego

As I mentioned earlier in this book, Taoists consider nothing good or bad in and of itself. All is relative, and something we consider terrible might be necessary in the right place and time. Yet there are tendencies and things (like death, for instance) that lend themselves to the Shadow and others (like love) that lend themselves to the light. Yet both death and love are necessary. All things are a blend of Yin and Yang. Accepting this simple idea changes everything. Keeping this in mind, we can look at the Ego and the Self (or Spirit) in different ways.

Just as all existence can be divided into Heaven and Earth, Yang and Yin, Conscious and Unconscious, so, too, can we see these two aspects of the Tao manifesting in our psyche as Ego/Shadow and Self/Spirit. Neither is good or bad in and of themselves. Both are necessary.

The Ego is a primary manifestation of Yin because it manifests and deals with the Lower aspects of physical life, or Earth. Our Egos are created here on Earth—by our environment, our parents, our society, and so on. The Ego is a conglomerate entity that we refer to as Me or I because it is made up of all those reflections and ideas and feelings which we have come to believe make up "this person who I am." The Ego is a necessary thing in that we would not be able to function without it. People who have lost their Ego or who are unable to form one can be high spiritual Yogis; they may also be lost in their unconscious and so be labeled insane.

The Ego is our anchor on Earth, meaning this physical world. As humans, our Ego is the key to our survival and our interrelationship with society. A sense of I is necessary to carry on a conversation, work, have a relationship, or become part of society. We refer to this as "Yin" or being in an "Inferior position" because the physical world is the lower aspect of the Tao. This does not mean lesser! It means it simply is the denser or lower vibration of reality. The higher level or vibration is referred to by Taoists as "Heaven" or "Yang." This simply means that it represents the nonphysical energetic vibrational reality behind all things, the Spirit that moves through matter. Just as "the 10,000 things" (Earth/Yin) are a manifestation of the Tao, so, too, the Creative (Heaven/Yang) is the Spirit behind this manifestation. One cannot exist without the other.

The Ego is a necessary part of this equation and it keeps us rooted in the here and now, with our feet on the Earth and with a healthy self-interest that urges us to do better and to accomplish tasks that mean something and that give us satisfaction. It is the Ego that is the barometer of the Spirit; it acts out and has tantrums when something is amiss. It urges us to overeat or sabotage a job or relationship when we are unhappy. In fact, the Ego clearly shows us on the physical plane the state of our spirit, the way the Tao is manifesting through us here and now. The Ego's home is the conscious mind and its reflection is the physical body. Without it we would not be well-rooted in either and would not be able to do our True Will, the reason we exist in this life.

The Self is the twin to the Ego. Some call it Spirit or Soul. Is it something we are born with? Does it supersede death? Taoists (and Carl Jung, the well-known psychoanalyst) believe that we are born with the seed of Self but that it is up to us, by following the Path of our True Will, to individualize or to nurture and expand the Self through spiritual (or psychological) development. The way to do this is by following the Way that the Tao has manifested for each of us individually.

The "Inferior" and "Superior"

Before we can discuss the practical applications of the natal I Ching in dealing with others and with the troubles in our lives, two often mentioned concepts that are deeply rooted within the philosophy of the I Ching must be discussed and understood.

According to the I Ching, there are two types of people, things, experiences, and so on: the "Inferior" and the "Superior." It is clear from reading the *I Ching* and its auxiliary commentaries that we are not separating humanity into good or bad people when we use these terms to type people or their actions. In fact, the highly ingrained concept of duality with which most Westerners view the world must be quietly set aside here.

In the Taoist universe of the I Ching there is no good or bad, no absolute right or wrong, and therefore no wholly good or bad people. What a Taoist would consider good is harmony. In a family, it means all the members working together. In terms of you, it means all the parts of your persona working together toward a single life-path that is in line with the flow of the Tao. This will manifest in your happiness, or at least general contentment. Therefore, a Taoist interpretation of Inferior is the placing of an attribute (or person, thing, idea, etc.) so as to cause disharmony—that is, the situation or combination of elements within your life or within your persona that is manifesting in such a way so as to cause conflicts, negative feelings, and general unhappiness or discontent. In short, it means something or someone is in the wrong place at the wrong time, the words place and time here being very open in meaning! It then follows that something or someone is Superior when it is in its proper place and each is doing what it or he ought to do. Of course, this is always variable and that is the trick to being in a Superior place, being in line with what should be. How does one accomplish this? Read on!

In the I Ching, certain placements of Yin or Yang lines are referred to as Superior or Inferior in that they are or are not in an auspicious or positive place. This changes moment by moment, and to be in a situation where Inferior elements dominate may not be your fault at all. (Just think of work!) Now, how you deal with a situation presented to you, how you relate to a given situation, this makes you what the I Ching refers to as a "Superior Person" or an "Inferior Person." This relates to, of course, both men and women, and it refers to how well and how appropriately you cope. Are you graceful under pressure? Are you kind but detached? Compassionate but not controlling? Are you ardently following your True Will but also being flexible and open? Then you are following the path of the Superior person. Each of us, deep down, knows when we are following this path. It is marked by a deep feeling that you are doing what is right and that you feel balanced, no matter what the outcome is.

Harmony and Disharmony

The universe is one vast combination, or dance, of Yin and Yang elements, as we have discussed earlier. You are a perfect combination of these two elements and this is represented by your unique natal hexagram, which reflects the larger cosmos about you. There is an old saying : "That which is Within is like unto that which is Without and that which is Without is like that which is Within." In other words, the universe is wholly and completely reflected within the tiniest atom and, for our purposes, within each person's Spirit or Self.

It is therefore no surprise that when the parts of our being, both conscious and unconscious, are in harmony, then our world is in harmony. Everyone has had certain perfect days when everything seemed to go right. Your attitude was good, everything fell into line, you accomplished a number of things you didn't think you could, and the whole experience was one of sailing with the wind or floating down a stream. It is almost effortlessly pleasant. This is called "moving with the Tao" and reflects the joining of both inner and outer harmony. If one is in harmony, even the rainiest day is seen as beautiful, even the most mundane task flows by with little pain.

Conversely, we have all had days when nothing, nothing went right. It felt as if you were bucking the wind or rowing against a strong river current and all your work seemed to just blow away. The smallest task seemed onerous, and what might have been a minor annoyance suddenly became unbearable. This is known as "fighting the Tao," and the *Tao Teh Ching* reminds us that those who fight the Tao on a regular basis do not live very long!

Now, in the first instance, when you had Harmony, this was called Superior. In the second, when you had Disharmony, this was known as Inferior. As you can see, each of us lives as both the Inferior and Superior! How can this be? Because we are constantly focused on our Ego, on Me and I, terms that are rarely used in many Asian languages, especially when beginning a sentence. Though we need Ego to survive, the I Ching teaches us to let go of the idea that the world revolves only around us, for how can any of us prosper if we each think that everything should be to our benefit? By thinking this way, we invite disharmony when things do not go our way. In fact, the first lesson must be to accept that there is only the Way— that is, the Tao—and that how we flow through life is up to how we approach this Way and the people, things, and events it presents to us daily.

The Tao cannot be forced or extorted or blackmailed into giving us what our Ego desires. We must learn to abandon our constant demanding and wanting, because, if you truly think about it, getting what you want rarely brings happiness for more than a few fleeting moments, and it certainly does not bring lasting contentment. But receiving (notice that verb!) what you need brings sure contentment, like a good meal when you're hungry.

So, when we "force our way" in the world, we have bowed to and become a part of mundane forces that are not bad in and of themselves but that form the Inferior. Why? Because maybe we are pushing when we should be waiting, or yelling when we should be quiet. If we hold to the inner light, the intuition and inner knowing of what the right way is, then we become the Superior, we choose to let what our inner mind knows rule the Inferior aspects of our personality, and we detach from demanding and wanting things we don't really need, which are not necessary for our particular Path. Suddenly, we find ourselves content and happy, even when difficulties arise, because we are holding to what is true and letting the negative or incorrect (for us) aspects of ourselves, or of our surroundings, sail past.

How does one do this? By meditating, by returning to nature, and by being silent. The most important way to accomplish this is by listening to the inner voice after quieting the ego.

The "Head Guiding the Feet" and the Self

The written character in Chinese that means Tao shows a foot that is guided by a head. This is the perfect analogy for the Way to approach living a positive life. The foot can be seen as those forces or characteristics that lead us to attach to things, those parts of us that reach and grab and want and move and do. The Ego is chief of these. These are all necessary and good things and processes if they are controlled by the True Will (your Path) and not the other way around. Those parts of you or of your life that should be the vehicle or the method the Self uses to go forward and grow must be ordered and commanded by your True Will, your Inner Self, not the other way around. For example, when desire or nurturing or sadness are natural expressions of the growth or evolution of your spirit, they are positive and form the functioning of the Superior, but if they take control, if the tail wags the dog, as it were, if your desires bend you (or bankrupt you) or your nurturing instincts smother a loved one, then the feet (Yin) have taken over the position of the head (Yang) and disharmony occurs. This is an Inferior situation.

The way to prevent this from happening is simple. Constant vigilance and rigorous self-examination as well as something that is simply not taught in our society: an abiding respect for the intuition and the spiritual essence within all things.

When I use the term Self, as you know by now, I am not referring to the Ego at all but to something rarer and far more important. This is the unfolding spirit within each of us that must be nurtured, meditated upon, and, most important, listened to. Some call it the voice of intuition. By paying close attention to our inner Self (a Western analogy might be the Guardian Angel), the personified essence of our True Will or Way, we instinctively know what is right and what is not. This Self, according to Taoism, manifests as the head we have been referring to, and its expression is constantly referred to in the *I Ching* as "The Creative" or the essence of Heaven.

The Creative

It is no mistake that the *I Ching* begins with the hexagram Heaven over Heaven, The Creative—also called the Dragon Power. This is the beginning of everything, it is the source of all wisdom and the perfect lens of the Tao in our world. We can refer to it as God or Spirit if we wish, but it is, in fact, far more open in meaning than these words imply.

We shall simply refer to it as the Taoists do, as The Creative. Think of The Creative as that spark which causes you to create, to be kind, to be loving and helpful. It is the source of all great art and music and advancement. It is the spirit of evolution that pushes you to be better than you are, to improve your life and the lives of your offspring, family, friends, and loved ones. It naturally manifests with no conscious effort when there is clarity and harmony, stillness and awareness. When we are doing things like running, sailing, or skiing without conscious thought, merely doing what we Will to do, without Ego-consciousness, then we approach The Creative.

Here are a few analogies. All the parts of our skis or our sailboat are in working order. Our muscles and reactions are prepared and working in sync with the flashing synapses of our mind. Desire is silent, ego is stilled, and we glide. Maybe we glide on skis, easily threading our way down a difficult course, our mind and body one, filled with joy and almost no conscious thought. Or we are sailing on a windblown lake, tacking, coming about, and weaving about difficult areas. One with the boat and the wind, we are exhilarated, without conscious thought, just becoming one with the experience.

Moments like this can be found in your life almost every day: performing a piece of music, creating a drawing, initializing some software, trading stock. Whatever it may be, people in whatever field often refer to those moments as going with the flow or having a peak experience. In fact, they are experiencing the perfect alignment of Yin and Yang, of Head and Feet, of Inner and Outer, and so they experienced the harmony of being a

Superior Person. If you think about it, you have had many of these experiences, often without realizing it, and that is, of course, the whole point!

The Superior reflects the ultimate creative expression of all the positive parts of your personality. It is said that one can only see the bottom of a pond when the muddy waters become still, when the silt settles to the bottom. This only happens when there is stillness and harmony. In this way, the Yin (silt-Earth) and Yang (water-Heaven) become clear to each other and we are restored to our original state of Harmony, of being a Superior person. This is a very important point; we are simply seeking to return to our original state of being, our original harmony, the place we would be if we lived completely open and natural lives. Taoists often refer to this state as "being like an infant." We instinctively know this and often feel smothered by the products and pulls of our own culture, which mostly disrupt this "returning" process and thus cause disharmony. Striving for this kind of awareness leads to the Superior. Some of the most common attributes of the Superior person are innocence, modesty, honesty, openness, clarity, and kindness, things we still value today, personally, but which are often not valued by our culture or by some of the people we work or live with!

These are all natural and spontaneous expressions of human beings and they are all furthered by the Creative force of the universe. We strive toward these ideals, or as the *I Ching* says, we persevere, and this determines how well we live our lives.

Think about how you were as a small child. When you saw a sick animal, you felt kindness and sympathy. You were, for the most part, open, honest, and in awe of everything. You found beauty and joy in simple things: clouds, rainbows, a cool drink. The Taoists often call for us to return to a childlike innocence in order to find harmony and fulfillment, and even Jesus said that one had to be as children to enter Heaven. Yet to simply return to this natural primal state of innocence and openness is not enough, even if it were possible. As adults, the last part of the equation, perseverance, must be developed and honed in order for us to stick to these Superior ways of being.

Perseverance means cultivating a dedication to your True Will, or Path, and not giving up. The stamina and determination to follow your own path in life is very difficult to master, but it can be accomplished if you know yourself. We are born with perseverance in the form of instincts, but for humans this is only the beginning. Instincts must be nurtured, trained, and pushed. In the inner world, they grow to become intuition and inner consciousness. We develop this by listening to our inner voice and by not discounting or ignoring it. On the outer, we do this by adhering to the Yang principles of right and good and the Yin qualities of nurturing and accepting, things that are even more difficult to master if the society in which we live does not support tolerance and the practice of ethical and spiritual perseverance. Yet this is what we need to do to follow our own unique Paths, and, deep down, we all know this.

The Superior and Inferior and the Natal Hexagram

You are now probably thinking: How does my natal hexagram come into play here? In fact, your natal hexagram is your game plan or template for becoming a Superior person. It is the ideogram or symbol of your natural self, your root. The first part of this book described what your natal hexagram is, what it means, and how it can be interpreted. Here we would like to go a step farther. Rather than be happy with a simple interpretation of who you are and what your strengths, weaknesses, and things to work on are, your natal hexagram can also point you toward your Life-Path and help you make changes and adjustments so that you can lead a Superior life. This is far more important than simply learning a bit about yourself.

Before exploring this in depth, we must resolve what "your Path" really means. This personal Way is a very important key. One's Way is the "Way of the Superior Person," the Way of your head guiding your feet; it is the Way of returning to your original state of clarity, of following your True Will, and it is the very unique and specific-to-you Way for you to manifest the Creative on this Earth during your life. There is a name for this personal Way in Chinese: It is called Teh.

Teh

"Teh, often translated as power or virtue, refers to the power to realize Tao in action, to become what you are meant to be."
—Rudolph Ritsema and Stephen Karcher, *I Ching*

Teh can, in modern language, be referred to as True Will—that is, the orbit your star (Self) must make as you are born, live, and die. It is what you are here to do, your great work or personal unfolding of the Tao. What all this fancy philosophy means is that all your genetic and environmental influences, as well as your innately unique Spirit or Self, combine to create a very important and special being, one who has special talents, needs, and ways of expressing the Creative here on this Earth.

No one can tell you what your Path is; only you can discover this. Like all physical things, each of us is a manifestation of Tao, but the way each of us lives our lives is called Teh. Your very individual being brings forth "the Creative" here on this planet as a life well lived. This balancing in each person of World and Self is symbolized in every I Ching hexagram by the fact that the upper hexagram is Heaven (Tao), the lower hexagram is Earth (Teh), and Humanity (you) is what is balanced in the center. Thus we each must Balance the Divine (the creative power) and our own unfolding life (our personal expression of this power—Teh) as we live. You may feel powerless at times and you may also feel controlled by forces beyond yourself, but you always have access to the power of the cosmos in the form of your Teh, though it is easy to forget this. In common psycho-speak we talk of "giving our personal power away" or of "recovering our personal power," and these comments strike at the heart of what Teh means.

In fact, you cannot really give away or recover your personal power, or Teh; it is always a part of you as your Way, or Path. Your Teh, the prime manifestation of that personal power, always lies potentially before you. It is, however, possible to lose your Way. You may let others guide you or push you in directions you know are not right, and therefore you may fall into depression, anger, cruelty, suffering, or simply ill-health—all, in the Taoist view of things, symptoms of disharmony. In short, ignoring your Teh, or wandering off the Path of your Teh, causes your inferior elements to assume a dominant position and so you will become the Inferior, even if only for a short time. The "remembering" (which literally means "putting back together") of your Teh and the perseverance to follow it will, in all cases, correct this state of affairs. As soon as you fall into your natural state, or groove, and follow the one true Path that is correct for you, you will rediscover harmony and happiness.

This is not a difficult or arcane idea to master and requires no mystic or psychological feats. As Lao Tzu, the author of the *Tao Teh Ching*, said, "How do I know these things are true? By observing Nature!" And so a period of simple observation will show you the truth of Teh.

First, in the animal kingdom, the most obvious teacher of Teh is the nearest ecosystem. Through a combination of instinct and training from a parent or parents, most animals fall into their Way and live within the limits of their evolutionary niche. In this way they function as part of a much larger web of life that depends on them and upon which they depend. Remove that animal from that system and the entire system unravels. Move that animal (consciously or by mistake) to another ecosystem within which it was not meant to function and either it will die or it will damage the ecosystem within which it is an alien.

Swallows taking over New York City, box squirrels destroying native species in New York State, imported medflies destroying apple crops, all of these show what happens when one meddles with complex and interwoven ecosystems.

Fine and good, but what does this have to do with Teh and with you? The lesson is this: If you are following your Way, then you are an aware part of the cosmos and are going with the grain as it were, living within the flow of Tao. You are functioning as an integral part of the cosmic ecosystem. In this way, as the Taoists say, the entire universe supports you and you succeed without trying. Why? Because this is the nature of things as observed in the flow of the Tao in the world. However, if you insist on being something that you are not, or on striving for things that are not right for you, then you are fighting against not only your own Way but also against the very Way of the universe—you are fighting against the Tao and the natural flow of things.

This does not mean that you shouldn't strive for the things you desire or to reach your goals! It does not mean that you should be a passive observer of your own life or to just let others make decisions for you. In fact, it means the exact opposite. It means that your Teh is your most precious possession, it is the path of your creative life and the source of your long-lasting contentment and happiness. Because of this, it is your primary responsibility in this life to make sure you are following your true Path or, as Joseph Campbell said, "Follow your bliss." Therefore, our primary goal in life should be to discover what our True Will is and to follow it, no matter what others may say or feel.

You not only have a right to follow your own Way, but a duty to do so, just as the hawk has a duty to hunt mice and rabbits that would otherwise overpopulate, or as a tree has a duty to produce oxygen for us. By following your Way you are living in accord with the universe and with your fellow human beings. If you follow your Way, you will find that it helps everyone around you. It helps hold society together and it helps weave the Tao throughout the span of your life in a productive way.

If we exist to channel the Creative in our lives and to be happy, then the only way to do this is to follow our Teh. Of course, the obverse is true as well. If you are not following your Path, then you are not bringing the Creative into the world. You will be uneasy and discontented, always feeling that things are not going right, and this will indeed be true. The universe will let you know in a thousand little ways that you are off track, and this will simply make you more unhappy. This in turn ripples out to others because when you are discontented, you cannot be as kind or as nurturing or as honest as you should be. You will not be able to help those who need your help, nor will you be able to receive the help you need. This causes others to pull away from their Teh. This, in turn, negatively affects society and, eventually, the world.

So, by doing something that may seem selfish to others, by following your own personal Path, True Will, or Teh, you are actually doing the work of the universe, you are setting yourself in line with the Tao, and so your contentment and your happiness will ripple out, causing harmony to grow about you. This will directly and indirectly encourage others to find their Teh as well. In short, by doing what you know deep inside you is the right thing to do and following the right way, you will benefit yourself and the people all about you as well as the universe! How do we know this is true? Think of the successful people you know in the world, the ones who are generally happy and content with the great work they do. Think about how they affect others. By observing, as Lao Tzu said, we can see that this is all true.

Why Are People Unhappy?

So why are there so many unhappy people? Why isn't everyone following their own Teh? In the *I Ching*, a number of answers are given. The first reason for error is a lack of knowledge: People simply don't know what their Teh is and our society really doesn't give people the tools to discover their unique Way.

The second reason is that while most people are born with the innate intuition, openness, and honesty they need to find their Way, their childhood upbringing, school, and other situations that impose rules and restrictions discourage and suppress the very characteristics they need in order to find happiness, to the point that when they actually do gain some freedom, they often no longer trust their instincts or the most basic and fundamental personality characteristics that make them unique. In this way they lose confidence in their Self and their own Creative spirit, and they convince themselves to continue the paths they know are making them unhappy.

The third reason is that some people choose to ignore their Teh or the Teh of others. They choose a path that involves power or influencing others to gain what they think is happiness, forcing themselves and others to do what they want them to do as opposed to what they should do. This has, to the great sorrow of most, become a standard situation in American culture. This horrifies people from many Asian cultures, where the individual's Path is considered key to the harmony of the culture as a whole. It should horrify all of us.

Every time someone is manipulated into buying something they don't need, or pushed into fighting someone they don't want to fight, or doing a job they strongly dislike, that person is being victimized and pushed farther and farther from his or her Path, or Teh. And the same goes for the person doing the pushing. He or she becomes trapped by the very power over others they covet. It becomes like a drug to them, but a drug that never really satisfies. They always need more—more money, more power, more stuff—but it will never satisfy them because they have lost the one thing that would make them happy, their Teh.

In this way, everyone is out of harmony, both the victim and the aggressor. No one wins and unhappiness spreads.

According to Taoists, this terrible situation is to blame for most of the problems in the world, and Inferior leaders (who are not following their Teh) are for the most part to blame. This is why the *Tao Teh Ching*, the most important document in Taoism, is partially written for the average person, but mostly written as a set of guidelines for political leaders. The advice is always very simple: Let people's true natures shine forth, do not meddle, do not be overly harsh or overly lenient, do not impose your will on the people, spend a lot of time listening and observing, and only act when it is necessary. And, most important, let people follow their Teh! In the *Tao Teh Ching* it is written:

> "*The more laws and restrictions there are,*
> *The poorer people become*
> *The Sharper men's weapons*
> *The more trouble in the land*
> *The more ingenious and clever men are*
> *The more strange things happen . . .*"

In other words, the farther you drift from your Center, or Self—your original openness and honesty and clarity—the more the nation drifts from the right path and so the more problems and troubles we make for ourselves. A look at today's newspapers confirms the timelessness of these observations!

This is nothing new or earthshaking. We all know this and even say things like "The tighter you hold on to something, the more you push it away" or "You can't always get what you want, but you get what you need." Yet we always feel as if the ideas of simplifying our lives, returning to our original characteristics, listening to our hearts, and finding our own Path are quaint and old-fashioned. They sound wonderful but are impractical or, at best, have to be scheduled into our busy lives, which we have been taught to divide into things we want to do and things we have to do.

Refocusing on Your Teh

Yet no matter how out of balance the world, or the country, or your city, or your job, or your family, the path of the Superior is to hold fast to the Creative, to follow the Way of your Self. This is your mission; it may seem impossible, but it is really quite simple! Of course, it's easier to do when things flow easily; the test comes when obstacles or outside forces pull and push.

Following one's Teh is a flowing experience that brings harmony and happiness, but make no mistake, it is not the easiest path or one devoid of troubles. It is work! It may be one of the most difficult things to begin, and this is often due to the resistance one faces in everyday life. But once you have found your "groove," your Way, things will ease up and you'll feel contentment, and that contentment will become the main expression of your life.

Recovering Your Way

The difficulty in finding your Way never really comes from your heart; it comes from your relationships with what is outside yourself, for once you are off your Path the way is rough and sometimes very seductive. So the real effort comes with trying to rediscover your Way and getting back on it. Remember, others have invested in your not following your true Path. Parents, children, co-workers, friends, corporations, and so on all have a stake in your following a course in life that may or may not be your Teh. These pressures are real but not nearly as powerful as you may think at first. If you truly want to get back to your Teh, you have the force of the Tao behind you. It will be hard and you must work, but it is possible to do, and once you do it, it will be such a delight that it will seem like a run downhill! Depending on how far from your Teh you have gotten, the recovering of your Way can have dramatic effects.

Families and friends also have expectations that may influence you to veer from your Teh. Your parents may push you to enter law or medicine, though that is not your path. Friends exert peer pressure, to smoke or drink, for example. These may also influence you to abandon your path. In many ways, the pressures from friends and family are harder to ignore than any other influences.

A woman I know, we'll call her V., came to me for a natal I Ching reading. Her life was a mess. Her high-tech job paid well, her boyfriend was handsome and kind, her parents were very happy with her success . . . and she was thoroughly miserable. When she realized she was making those around her miserable as well, she came for a reading to learn the root of what was wrong. V., like many, felt very guilty about her unhappiness. She had so much and everyone was telling her how fortunate she was, but she was still unhappy. How selfish! I'm sure you know people like her—you may even be one. What was her problem?

She was successful by all standards, except for the one that counted: V. was not following her Teh; she was following a path she had been made to feel was her path, yet in her heart she knew it wasn't right. Through her natal hexagram we discovered that she was an artist. She was sure this was a mistake. She protested that she had no talent and had never done art. Still, the message was clear, and it soon came out that she had always wanted to be a painter but had been discouraged long ago by people who told her it was a waste of time, that she had no talent, and that there was no money in it.

To make a long story short, she quit her job, broke up with her boyfriend, and began painting. Soon she was producing beautiful works, with little or no technical training, many based on Navaho patterns.

Within a year her life was transformed. She was fairly poor, was selling beautiful paintings, had a new boyfriend, and was happy, really happy, for the first time since she was a child.

Of course, most of us have not strayed that far from our Teh, but even being just a bit off will throw our lives and emotions out of whack and make us unhappy.

How do you get back to the right Path? As a good first step, Taoists recommend quiet meditation and breath control (calming the breath, focusing on it, and sitting quietly for periods of time) to focus on your Creative and its mouthpiece, your Self. By keeping in touch with your inner core being and reestablishing this inner link (or simply strengthening it), you will soon see where you have left your Way and where you are right-on in your life. Almost all faiths say that "The Truth is Within," and they are right.

The next step might be to consult your natal hexagram to see if you are developing your strengths and your innate talents. Simply studying the natal hexagram readings in the previous section should give you a good idea as to whether you are following your Path.

If you need more practical help in adjusting your Path, there are a number of ways for you to enter deeper into your natal hexagram and use it to help you adjust your Teh, and therefore your life.

It is important to remember that things are almost never black and white, or as radically "off" as with V. Still, readjustments, refocusing, changing some things about yourself and about your environment—all of these things will get you back into sync with your Teh and make you a more contented person.

Using Your Natal Hexagram to Rediscover Your Teh

This brings us back around to the natal hexagram and how to make it an invaluable tool in this process. The natal hexagram, being a simple yet many-leveled snapshot of the Teh you were born into, can be a sort of compass to help you follow your Way. It gives clear indications of how your Way will unfold in life, including the things you need to improve or work on in this lifetime. All this manifests as a kind of blueprint for your evolving Self and can often help point to where you need to change. Keeping all that I have said in mind, including the fact that your happiness and contentment are your responsibility and never another's, let's look at a few examples of "Teh readjusting" I have gleaned from my decades of doing natal hexagram readings.

First, let's look at someone who made the adjustment herself.

A woman I know, we will call her D., lead a fairly contented life but felt guilty because her family and friends thought she was wasting her skills and that she was shallow. It turned out that her natal hexagram was #22, Grace. If you refer back to this in the previous section, you'll see that these people are usually not seen as very deep, that they do well around the arts and around people, that they should avoid gossiping and big projects, and so on.

Well, D. had gone to college and gotten her teaching certificate as her parents had wanted her to do, but she disliked the rigors of university life and the kind of work required for teaching. She did not want to continue with this career. In fact, she borrowed money and, listening to her heart, opened up a very classy art gallery and gift shop that is even now, years later, doing very well. Her parents and others felt she was wasting her education, but she is quite happy and very good at her work. She dresses beautifully and is excellent at interacting with customers. She had some unhappiness in her life, however; she was losing friends and felt very put upon because people expected more from her. Well, it turned out she was a gossip, and, with a little introspection, she realized that she was hurting herself. I pointed out to her that gossiping or backbiting is one of the negative characteristics of this hexagram, one to avoid if you want to follow your Teh. Once she cut down on this behavior, her social life improved.

So, carefully examining your natal hexagram can give you indications as to where your Path, or Teh, lies; it will also show you your weak points and "shadow-aspects." It is these weaknesses and dark parts of your character that hold the key to how and why you fall from your Teh, for it is your character flaws which, at times enslave you to a path not your own for the benefit of another.

For example, a friend, H., has the natal hexagram #53, or Development. A quick look at this will show that his Way is to progress slowly and steadily. Because of this characteristic, he tends to be overshadowed by his faster co-workers and is sometimes seen as being a bit boring. The dark side of his character relates to an innate conservatism and the fact that he is a slow starter. He was having a hell of a time at work with pressures from others to launch new projects that he knew would fail. The nature of his job (engineering) called for precise and methodical work, at which he was excellent, but also for an openness to innovation, to which he was not entirely open.

He felt he was being vilified at work, and, after we examined his natal hexagram, we pinpointed these negative aspects as the root of his problem. He was forced to acknowledge his resistance to change and new ideas and wisely delegated the overseeing of new projects and experimental ideas to someone with a more adventurous outlook. Everything at work immediately changed for the better and he was seen as the solid bedrock worker he really was and not an impediment to innovation.

In this section I will also refer to my natal hexagram—#56, The Wanderer—in a number of places as an example of how a natal hexagram can be used to improve oneself. Since much of what I am writing about came from self-discovery, it might help to give some firsthand examples of how I've seen this Teh-adjustment process unfolding in my own life. It is one thing to simply examine your natal hexagram reading; it is quite another to analyze it and use the information in practical ways to readjust your life in a positive manner.

The most obvious shift, for me, cut right to the heart of my being and completely changed my life. I went to a university and studied history and art, getting my teaching certificate. I went on to another university to get my master's degree in ancient history and delighted in studying different cultures, yet I was not satisfied and always felt that some major part of my life was missing. When I discovered the teachings of Gurudev Dadaji and learned what my natal hexagram was, I was shocked! The path this hexagram indicated was that of a traveler, yet I had done almost no traveling in my life! Although I put it away and let it go—it seemed so wrong—I couldn't forget it completely. Years later, my then-girlfriend (now wife), who loved to travel, pushed me into a trip to Thailand, something I was sure I didn't want to do. I loved it! Not only that, but there I was in the middle of a culture I had only appreciated intellectually. A whole neglected part of myself came alive and I cursed myself for not traveling sooner!

Years later we lived in Japan for four years and spent countless days (and dollars) traveling to some dozen countries. It was through traveling and researching various traditions that I was led to write my first book, *Global Ritualism*. This led to more travel writing and a side career as a journalist and author.

Today I feel as if I have found my Teh, though I still get lost occasionally! I'm never happier than when traveling, never more alive or more in focus, except maybe when I'm doing art or writing. Later, when I reexamined my previously ignored natal hexagram, a light came on in my head—it was me! It clearly revealed my flaws and strengths, yet I had never really seen the truth of it before. This led me, after many years and much encouragement from clients, to write this book. So, if I was not following my Teh, my Will, you would not have this book before you!

I offer up these stories to show how we are all really responsible for what happens in our lives. Your life is a journey of self-discovery and your natal hexagram is like a map that indicates your unique path. You can blame others, if you wish, for your problems, but it is more often the case that you are not understanding your Self. Still, there is another point we must examine. There are times when people who are off their Teh and deeply unhappy negatively impact you. Others can pull you off your Path. Still, no matter what, any real change in your reality must start with you.

There is an old aphorism that goes: "What we do not like in others are the things we do not like about ourselves." This is very much at the root of Taoist thinking. Here is a short story to illustrate this:

Two Zen monks were wandering on a pilgrimage and they came to a river. A young, beautiful woman was stranded there because the ford across the river was too deep for her. The older monk cheerfully offered to carry her across, which he did. As the monks continued on, it was clear that the younger monk was getting angrier and angrier. He suddenly exploded at the older monk, saying, "How could you carry that woman? We monks are forbidden to touch women!" The older monk replied, "I left that woman many miles back, why are you still carrying her?"

It might be that messy people irritate you because you are messy—this is certainly the case with me! Or possibly you are angered and appalled by racism because some racism (a virtually universal flaw) lies within your heart. This is not the case completely, of course, one can be unhappy with another's behavior that is not within, but if there is a strong emotional element to your anger or disgust, chances are that the root does lie within.

This is an exceptionally hard lesson to learn, and the ancient Taoists knew that no one but your Self could really teach it to you. We rarely hear the truth of criticism from others, for it is always overlaid and colored by our own ideas and expectations. Your Ego, the biggest impediment to finding your Path, is constantly twisting and distorting information to suit its own needs and desires, which may or may not have anything to do with your Path.

This is why your natal hexagram, by nature a neutral and dispassionate look at the forces that are you, is so valuable in your quest for self-adjustment. It simply is, neither condemning nor exhorting. What you do with the information is up to you. Let me give one more example of how a friend used this information to get his life back on track. You will see how reasserting the Superior over the Inferior made all the difference in his life:

My friend B., whose natal hexagram is #4, Youthful Folly, is an impetuous, bubbling, enthusiastic, and sometimes irritating fellow. He was teaching grade school for a number of years and just loved it. His youthful and somewhat immature character fit perfectly with his job. In fact, he did it so well that he was eventually promoted to administrator, and here is where his troubles started.

He immediately clashed with all the people above him as well as the other administrative staff. He became bullheaded, wanted to change established procedures, and in general went too fast with people and projects without taking the time to really think things through or to listen to people. His brilliant ideas often died on the vine because he couldn't summon the support needed to make them happen, which only created more hostility and frustration for him and for the other administrators.

We got together at one point and really looked at his strengths and weaknesses by carefully examining his natal hexagram, which clearly pointed out that his Inferior aspects included overzealousness and impatience. This helped him to see how others were seeing him. What he then did was criticized by his family and some friends, but it was the exact right thing for him to do if he was to stay in line with his Teh: He took a voluntary demotion and went back to teaching, while keeping a few part-time administrative duties having to do with curriculum development and new projects. He earned less money, but his situation suddenly shifted from one of escalating anger and frustration to one of mending fences and working together. The person who took the job B. left was more conservative, but due to B.'s obvious innovative skills, was more open to new ideas and changes than others. In this way B. was able to work with someone whose Way included the ability to work with the more conservative elements within the system, and so many changes B. had been unable to accomplish came to pass. He was the perfect new-idea man; he was just the wrong one to carry out the new ideas.

This brings home, again, the idea that you need to think carefully about the forces of Inferior and Superior when examining your natal hexagram. As I mentioned, these are not objective ideas; in fact, Taoists believe it is impossible to have set standards for any of these things because change is the only constant. A quality, idea, person, plant, thing, and such in the right place at the right time in the right Way is a manifestation of the Superior. The same object, being, or idea in the wrong place or time or in the wrong Way manifests as the Inferior.

This is an important point and one that is key to using your natal hexagram to better understand yourself and your environment. B. had qualities that in the classroom were Superior; they were in sync with his surroundings, his students, and the school. This Superior attention to his

Teh brought him and others happiness and contentment. In a different position, however, the very same qualities suddenly manifested as the Inferior and caused all sorts of hell to break loose. Why? Because they were not in line with his Teh or with the Tao. How do we know this? As Lao Tzu said, by simply looking!

There is nothing complicated about this. B. became unhappy and everyone around him became unhappy with him! Now, his displeasing others may not have been a sure sign of the Inferior. Lawyers, for example, or political activists, tick people off all the time, yet that is what they do best and it is their Way. We need people in society to keep things changing and moving—Taoists recognize change as the only constant and stability as a temporary thing at best! But the fact that B. was miserable and felt stymied and blocked, and the fact that he wasn't accomplishing the things he wanted to, are indications that he had slipped from a Superior situation to an Inferior one and had, in the process, lost his Way, or Teh. By recognizing this and adjusting his life, he was able to regain his equipoise and contentment. How did he do this? By transforming the Inferior into the Superior through examining his Self and readjusting his Teh with Superior changes.

This is not a process that happens once a month, like a haircut, or one you can schedule in your day planner. This is a daily, hourly, minute-by-minute process that only ends with the grave. To find your Way does not guarantee that you will stay on it or that your life will be free from pain and sorrow. To live in this world is to change, grow, evolve, prosper, and eventually decay and pass away. Our Teh is our own, maybe the only thing that is really truly ours, but growth and evolving take effort and some work. Yet to follow one's Way, or Teh, is to be content and generally happy for the most part. It gives you momentum to overcome barriers and problems; it gives you self-confidence and understanding enough to weather life's sorrows. Most important, it continually renews and revives your connection with your Inner Self and furthers your manifesting The Creative in everything you do and say. In this way the Ego, while still something of a problem, becomes more of an ally and troublesome sibling than a demanding overseer or jailer.

Readjusting Your Life with Your Natal Hexagram

The process of focusing on your natal hexagram in order to get yourself back on track (back to your Teh) is referred to as "readjustment." To lead into this, I want to continue my Taoist sailing analogy (bear with me!):

Visualize your life as a sailing trip. What do you do when rough weather hits? When you get too near a reef? When the wind shifts direction? You make adjustments. You might trim the sail, come about, stow all the gear, and "batten down the hatches," or stay safely in the harbor till the rough gales sweep past. All of these things are analogies for various hexagrams in the *I Ching*. Look at hexagram titles: Retreat, Nourishing, Gathering Together, Return, Shocking, Biting Through, Youthful Folly—they (and the other fifty-seven hexagrams) could all be orders from the captain of your boat. When you seek the oracle, it tells you how the weather is and what's coming up and how to trim your boat!

Your natal hexagram is your boat. It, like all other vehicles, has natural tendencies that influence how it will sail. It may ride a bit low, have a tall mast, a small mainsail, a narrow cabin . . . you get the idea. How it handles on the water will be how it manifests the Creative in your life. Your Self is the captain and should make the decisions and the Tao is the sea—how the two interact determines the quality of the voyage. It is no wonder that some people are said to sail through life while others simply drift or are hijacked or run aground! If the Inferior are the crew of the ship, then the Superior is the captain or Self, and a correct interaction between the two creates a harmonious, ever-shifting Teh—one hell of a great sail trip!

This is a long way of saying that your journey, or Teh, requires constant watchfulness and constant adjusting. What may work for you in one situation (being tough at a meeting) will not work in another (dealing with a crying child). As Westerners we are conditioned to feel somewhat helpless when tried-and-true strategies don't work or when flexibility is called for that runs counter to rules or standards. Once you have gotten past this block, once you accept that everything is indeed relative and that you and your life can really shift direction at any time and go in a new direction, when you accept that the pivot of all of this is your Self, your unchanging/ever-changing True Will, then you are ready to make adjustments to your life using your natal hexagram.

We have discussed how you can examine your natal hexagram reading in light of specific situations and problems. This is fairly straightforward and is accomplished by rereading your natal hexagram with an honest eye. Doing this, while focusing on your current problems, will often lead to clear insights and ideas. Still, this is often not enough to really find the things you need to do or change.

Since I cannot meet and give each reader a private natal hexagram reading, I will show you how you can do this for yourself.

What follows are several methods for using your natal hexagram to help you improve your life, as many of my students have. The first, Process A, only requires a fairly short time and will yield some general ideas for readjusting your life and maybe a few specific ones. I recommend this process as a beginning step, as a way people who are basically happy with their lot in life can make things better and maybe discover a few other talents they didn't know they had. Think of this as a tune-up exercise, one that you can do at any time to get general advice about your progress in life.

The second method, Process B, is a more complex and in-depth reevaluation of your life, your Path, where you are going, who you are, and so on. It is to be done when you are feeling acutely off track or deeply unhappy, either with your life in general or with a specific Inferior situation. Think of it as an in-depth Teh-therapy session! I recommend this process for anyone who feels stuck or seriously confused about their life. This process requires more time and energy, but it will yield many more ways to adjust your life and give a number of specific pieces of advice on how to move from a place of discontent to a place of contentment.

You may conclude from Process A or Process B that your problems or unhappiness stem from other people. They may also be confused and off track; they may be cruel and aggressive, or they may just be clueless. In this case, simply working with your natal hexagram is helpful but it's not always enough. You first have to decide what you will do about the relationship—this is the most important step. After that, if you need to, you can then make a comparison of your natal hexagram with another's natal hexagram, and then take some practical steps to adjust the relationship so that it no longer hurts you. It is also possible to use this process to improve an already good relationship. You need not wait until things are bad to make them better!

These processes are basically analytical and passive in nature, exercises of exploring and understanding, though they will, hopefully, lead to positive and practical actions. If you want to explore more mystical ways of using your natal hexagram to better yourself, then check out the meditations and visualizations that follow this chapter.

Having said this, let us begin with Process A.

Process A: Self-Improvement

You'll need some paper (a journal or diary is ideal), a pencil, about half an hour of peace and quiet (good luck!), and this book.

First, turn to your natal hexagram in the earlier part of this book. Let's look at your Traits. Go down the list and copy them onto a piece of paper. Think honestly and clearly about yourself and your character as it is now. As you do, rate each of these traits in terms of how strongly they really appear in your persona and how they affect your day-to-day life. You will be rating them on how positive or negative these traits are now in your life. How you rate them completely depends on how you see them in terms of your life. This can be very relative: If you are a counselor, being aggressive may rate as a negative trait. If you are a salesman, it might be a positive. It is up to you. Rate them in this way, with plus and minus signs:

+ a positive character point (It is true)
+ + a very positive character point (It is very true and developed)
+ + + one of your best character points (It is very true and very developed)

- a negative character point (It is true, but you have worked on it)
- - a worse character point (It is really true and you are somewhat working on it)

- - - a really negative character point (It is very true and you indulge it)

If any trait does not really fit you at all, or if it does not seem to affect you one way or the other, then mark down the following:

n/a it doesn't apply to you (you cannot relate this to yourself)
/ it is true but is neither good nor bad (a neutral point)

Now, before going any further, do you think people who know you would rate these traits in the same way? Think carefully. Try to be objective. Maybe you don't think you're an aggressive person, for example, but others say you are. So, you may want to make changes in your ratings to take into account how you affect others and how they might rate your traits. Think back on what others have said to you. This does not just apply to negative traits! You may, for example, not think you are very kind, but maybe others tell you all the time how kind you are. If so, consider changing that "+" rating next to Kind to a "+ +" or even a "+ + +."

Now, look at your list.

The traits listed as "+ + +" are already well developed and don't need more attention just now.

The traits listed as "+ +" are those you are already trying to improve, and you should continue to do so. We are not so interested in these traits in this exercise.

The traits rated "+" are important. These are traits you know are positive in yourself, but you're not utilizing them! Off the top of your head, think of three ways you can boost or better utilize these positive aspects of your character in a creative manner.

The traits rated "/" and "n/a" are also important. You may think the "/" traits are neutral, but are they? Think about them carefully. How can they be emphasized or worked on so they become positive attributes?

The "n/a" traits also need to be reexamined. Ask yourself: Would others who know me really think these traits are not applicable? Have I worked them out or are they just plain incorrect? All these things are possible, but a second look may be in order.

Now to the negative traits! The "-" traits show that you recognize these as problems and have more or less worked them out for yourself, so they are not so serious.

The "- -" traits are those you are now working on. Think about how you can further mitigate them and eliminate them as blockages in your life, or focus on how to use them in a positive manner. Having a temper, for example, indicates a passion to get things right. If channeled correctly, this could become a good trait.

The "- - -" traits are clearly the ones you are having the most trouble with at this time, and so they are probably the root of your most serious concerns now. These are the things you need to work on. Off the top of your head, think of three ways you can deal with these hard traits and bend them into more positive directions, or at least mitigate them so they are not such harmful parts of your personality.

Take your notes and the suggestions you wrote concerning your "+" traits and those you wrote about your "- - -" traits and look at them. These are important. Next, reread the Life Lessons part of your natal I Ching reading. Do any of your notes or suggestions relate to any part of your life lesson? What specific suggestions would help you further your life lessons? Chances are several will leap up immediately as things to do or things to change. Put a star next to these.

Then, in a similar way, reread your Positive Tendencies from your natal hexagram reading and compare them to your "+"- rated traits notes and the suggestions they generated. Which ones connect? What positive courses of action do they suggest?

Do the same with your Negative Tendencies and the "- - -"-rated traits and compare them with the suggestions you noted down earlier. Which ones connect? What positive courses of action do they suggest?

Think of practical applications of these ideas—can you add any more general or specific suggestions on how to specifically improve yourself or how you can have a happier, more creative life based on the conclusions you have before you? Write down, on a clean sheet of paper, the most obvious general and specific suggestions you made for yourself; choose one and begin to implement it!

This is a simple process that can easily be done once or twice a year to fine-tune your Teh and push your personal evolution a bit. It is amazing how things shift as well. You may think your traits and how they rate are static, but nothing is unchangeable, and that goes for you as well. You may have serious trouble with excessive energy, for example, but as you mature and get older, you will probably learn to control and channel this energy more wisely without even realizing it. Anger may change to drive, pickiness may become thoroughness. All things change, and with a bit of monitoring and analysis you can consistently change them for the better.

I'll walk you through a Process A evaluation using my own natal I Ching hexagram: #56, The Wanderer. If you want, take a look at the reading for #56 to refresh your memory.

Here are my natal hexagram traits and how I rated them as part of myself as of January 1999. I have also noted, in parentheses, what my ratings were last year; look at how they changed!:

	1999	1998
Visitor and wanderer	+	(-)
Always moving	-	(- -)
Driven	++	(-)
Hyper	/	(- -)
Interesting	++	(+++)
Amusing	+++	(++)
Frenetic	-	(- - -)
Fascinating	++	(+)
Studies many cultures	+++	(+++)
Easily detoured	- -	(- - -)
Spontaneous	++	(+)

Looks before leaping	-	(- -)
Kind	+	(+++)
Extroverted	++	(+)
Nips things in the bud	+++	(+)
Tends to quarrel	-	(- - -)
Decisive	+	(N/A)
Deals with things fast	++	(+)
Cautious (paranoid?)	+	(- -)
Intelligent	+++	(++)
Quick-tempered	- -	(- -)
Mystic	+	(/)

Here is what I wrote down in my notebook as I was following the process:

Visitor and wanderer: Note that this changed from negative to positive! I think this is because I had moved back from living overseas, where I saw this attribute as something negative, that kept me from being part of the culture. Now I see this as an attitude that makes me more respectful of others and of customs; it also gives me constantly fresh views of what is common.

Suggestions: Find things to connect me with my culture. Treat my neighborhood like a foreign country and explore. Get involved more with my neighborhood, meet my neighbors, and so on.

Kind: Notice that I went down in my estimation of how kind I was! I'd always thought of myself as a very kind person, but after really looking at my actions and how others see them, I became convinced that I needed to be kinder, no matter how busy I was.

Suggestions: Slow down and notice others more. Say something nice to someone in my family every day. Praise people who do something nice or do a job well. Give more to charity.

Decisive: I really thought this was not part of my makeup, but then I started taking on new responsibilities at work as well as other teaching jobs and freelance writing. On looking back, I realize that I indeed have the capacity to be decisive and I'm pretty good at it, but I need to develop it more.

Suggestions: Write down work decisions I make in a clear and concise manner and check them later to see how well I did. Have S. [a co-worker] be my reality check on fast decisions. Take on responsibilities at work that necessitate fast and accurate decisions.

Cautious: I improved here by learning to trust people more and to not be so suspicious, but it's hard for me.

Suggestions: Give people the benefit of the doubt more. Trust two people at work I'm not so sure of with more duties. Avoid excess cynicism.

Mystic: I never thought this dreamy, impractical, spacing-out part of my character was useful, but I'm beginning to think it is. So it went from neutral to a small positive.

Suggestions: Try to incorporate this mysticism into my art, my poetry, and my writing more often. Discuss philosophy with my wife and friends more. Read about different mystics and magical cultures and people. Focus on my intuition more. . . .

A Final Note

Sometimes an adjustment requires a lot of work and may be somewhat intense. Other times a life-shift simply requires a small change in the way you see or do things. Never forget, the goal is to be more in harmony with your Self and your life, to be happy.

Process B: Adjustment

Process A looks at your life and your characteristics with an eye to changing yourself in general for the better, like a health checkup. Process B looks at seriously adjusting your life as a result of unhappiness or an Inferior life situation that you need to change, like a serious medical consultation or an in-depth therapy session. The best way to change unhappiness into positive feelings is to rediscover your Teh, and so reassert your True Will. This process helps you do just that. Process B is for finding out how you got off course and how you can correct it.

The fact is, only you can make changes in yourself that will help you out of a bad situation; therefore the place to begin is with your Self, your Teh, and your attachments in your life. This process really works, if you can detach from your Ego and your unhappiness and give it your full attention. Remember, according to the Taoist worldview, everything happens for a reason, and that reason usually involves a lesson of some sort. Here is a quick way to discover what your immediate lesson is and how to move beyond it. When you are ready to begin, get your notebook, a pencil, this book, and at least one quiet hour alone.

Problems Statement: Start by writing down why you are unhappy and why you feel misdirected. Use general as well as specific statements. Focus on yourself inwardly: What are you feeling? What is really going on? What are you lacking? Try to write this out. Chances are that simply doing this for a few minutes will bring you some flashes as to what the Inferior aspects are in your life at the moment and possibly some idea about their roots.

Dreams Statement: Next, without a lot of thought, without any restrictions, write some statements about what would bring you the most happiness right now. Be outrageous if you like; make it a fantasy if you want. Do not write "Well, if it were possible I'd . . ." Do not use the words "want" or "if." Really daydream before you write. What are you daydreaming about?

Positives/Negatives: Finally, get a new piece of paper and divide it into two parts. On one part, write "Positive" and list the most important things you do or encounter that currently bring you happiness. On the other part, write "Negative" and list the important things you do, feel, or have to deal with in your life that bring you suffering or unhappiness.

Simply doing this exercise often leads to some amazing Self-discoveries on where your life is going and how it is "off" from where you want it to be. Note down any flashes of inspiration, no matter how silly or random they may seem.

Analysis of Process B

Now we begin the process of adjustment. Using a new sheet of paper, note down your conclusions and plans of action.

Analysis of Problems Statement: Analysis of Problems Statement: Look at the first thing you wrote about your problems and what is making you unhappy. Compare your problems with the negative tendencies listed in your natal heagram. Ask yourself these questions and write down the answers.

- How are my negative tendencies creating my own unhappiness?
- What positive tendencies am I not utilizing in my life now that I should use to make myself happier?

You will want to break the behavior cycles. Look especially at the life lesson in your natal hexagram for clues on how to do this. Decide how you can stop making stress, problems, and unhappiness for yourself. It might be as simple as turning off the TV, getting more exercise, or being less self-critical. Or it might require a big life-change you simply don't want to face.

Analysis of Dreams Statement: Now look at your fantasy or the second thing you wrote about what you'd love to be doing now if you could. Without making any judgments, compare it to your positive tendencies listed in your natal hexagram and analyze the connections between the two by focusing on the question: What creative talents or projects am I not working on that I should? Write down your conclusions in simple statements.

Emphasize the creative! Look at the positive and practical steps you can take to be more creative. OK, maybe you'll never play flute for the Philharmonic or be a big Hollywood star, but you can take flute lessons or enroll in an acting class! Maybe simply reading more novels or cooking at home less would do it; take some creative and positive actions. Who says you can't write a novel or paint a mural?! Only you hold yourself back.

Analysis of Positives/Negatives: Look at your natal hexagram reading, at the list of traits and at the tendencies. Compare these attributes, point by point, with the positives and negatives lists. See how many, if any, of the traits and tendencies, positive and negative, can be linked with the specific things you have noted. If you can find such links, then underline all the positive and negative items that have such connections. Then note down what traits and tendencies link with each underlined item. For example, in my last Process B analysis, I have in the negative section:

"Always fighting with co-workers." So I underlined it and added links and connections from the traits and tendencies sections of my natal hexagram reading. It ended up looking like this:

"Always fighting with co-workers"

(Tends to quarrel, quick-tempered, may be argumentative, may be picky, has a big mouth)

When you have done this for all the underlined items in your list, you will have a pretty good idea of where the ongoing imbalances in your life are coming from. They are the Superior and Inferior parts of yourself in action. They are parts of yourself that you must come to terms with by either accepting them or by working on them. They are, more or less, known quantities—that is, there is nothing new here. Look at them in terms of things to improve or turn around. They also, in very personal ways, tell you the root causes of some of your problems from your point of view.

Now, in the case above, I still felt that my co-workers were at least partially to blame for these fights, but seeing how this problem linked with my own natal traits and tendencies shocked me a bit. It helped give me a handle on my own propensity to be at least partially responsible for the fighting!

This process of underlining and matching positives and negatives will be a bit painful, but it will also bring very pleasant surprises. You will see how many innately positive qualities you have, and most important, you will see what positive qualities you are not using.

Accept yourself and all your flaws, including your Inferior aspects as listed in the traits. Sometimes simply accepting that you are hyper or a bit arrogant or overly shy can remove it from the negatives list. We all hate some things about ourselves. I dislike my wavy hair and my impatience. I can work on both of these, but only once I accept them as part of me. Once you've accepted a negative trait as part of yourself, think about how you can work on making it a more harmonious part of your life. It is not so diffi-cult to take it a step farther and not only accept a trait but also work on mitigating its negative repercussions. The most hyper person can count to ten to slow himself down a bit and the shyest person can make more of an effort to be friendly. One strategy is to do projects or things that directly address those issues.

A hyper person may take yoga, a shy person might join Toastmasters. This is perfectly in keeping with Taoist thought which states that opposites should be brought together to create a harmonious union or balance. Sleepy? Drink coffee. Being a bit too arrogant? Humble yourself by doing something new and difficult.

It should be noted that positive traits can also become inferior! Too much of a good thing, Westerners call it. It is possible to be too kind to chil-dren, thus spoiling them, or too cheerful with people who are suffering, thus angering them. Keep this in mind when looking at your positive traits: Even the best quality can become Inferior or damaging in the wrong place or at the wrong time. Could this be the case with any of the positive traits on your list? Think about it, and, if so, tone down the trait you might be overdoing.

Important: Note down the positive qualities in your natal hexagram reading that are not represented on your positives list. For example, when I did this I was just getting interested in traveling and did not list it as a pos-itive in my life. After studying my natal hexagram reading, I realized that this was a big positive tendency that I simply wasn't exploring.

There will be a number of items on both the positives list and on the negatives list that you have not underlined because you could see no link with a natal hexagram trait or tendency. These are usually either neutral (one of mine was gardening) or they are positive. On the other hand, if they are negatives, they are quite important.

Some of the things you note down may not fit this assessment exactly—they may not relate directly to a listed trait or tendency. Here is how to deal with such items.

They are especially, but not exclusively, non-natal roots of your current unhappiness. In other words, they are not originating from your inner Self. Put an asterisk (*) next to these and put them out of your mind for a moment; we will return to them later.

How you proceed is up to you. You have some very specific problems now in front of you as well as reasons why they exist. No one can tell you exactly how to change your life, to readjust it in a positive manner in order to become happier, but some clear indications are now in front of you. Look at what you have written. Review all your notes and then write down some basic conclusions as well as some specific steps you can take to minimize the negatives and maximize the positives in your life. Look for things you are not doing that would bring you happiness. Decide which of the things that are problematic you can do without, avoid, or just ignore.

Final Analysis: Imposing Outer Negatives

Return to studying the negatives that have an asterisk next to them, the items that do not link with anything when compared to traits and aspects from your natal hexagram.

These are the things that are bothering you to one degree or another that are not generated from your natal hexagram. If the ones you underlined are not innate parts of your being, then they come from one of two places: (1) You are either allowing specific non-natal imbalances in your environment to influence your life (Negative Yin) or (2) You are letting other people impose their will (Negative Yang) over your Teh. While these negative influences can be considered Negative Yin or Negative Yang, they are not coming "from you" but from outside of yourself. Being aware of this often makes dealing with them easier to figure out. Here are some guidelines.

Negative Yin problems: You are allowing your environment (other people, places, events, things) to affect your Teh. An example of this might be commuting in heavy traffic. On bad-traffic days I can arrive at work irritable, unhappy, and angry. Why? Because I allowed my environment to pull me off my Teh. I've allowed my Ego to take over from my Self and dictate how I should feel and react. Then I intellectualize it by saying that I'm dumb for allowing it to bother me! So I feel even worse! What an Inferior situation I have created for myself.

The problem here is the Ego and how it tends to personalize our environment. No one was out to get me on the freeway, but that is how I reacted. In the case of Negative Yin problems or hassles, the first step is always to step back, to remove yourself mentally or physically from the situation or environment until the Self, your higher being, can reassert control over the Inferior aspects of your situation—in my case, anger and impatience with slow traffic. One can then avoid the situation or find a way to focus on your Self and rise above the button pushing. For example, I simply started taking the bus to work a few times a week, and, when I do commute in terrible traffic, I blast loud rock music and get out my aggression that way! Note that the negative situation may call forth negative aspects from your natal hexagram, but the situation does not originate with your negative aspects.

Negative Yang problems: These are those stresses, problems, and hassles that are caused by others actively attempting to impose their will on you. These are often the most difficult problems to deal with. In the next section, we will be discussing how to use natal hexagrams to get along better with difficult people in your life, but now, let us just look at a worse-case scenario where another person is inflicting problems on you.

The first step, as with Negative Yin problems, is to step back and disengage. Take a look at your traits; how is this person using your traits to get at you? If, for example, you are very kind, are they using this to make you work overtime? If you are very neat, are they intentionally letting you do all the housework because they know it's a pet peeve? Step back and look at how you are unconsciously helping them make you unhappy! In most cases, it really does take two to tango, and you're likely allowing that person to make you unhappy for one reason or another. The real problem, then, is the feeling of helplessness, the feeling that you are powerless to do something about it.

You will never make someone do or stop doing something, but you can do three things to immediately stop them from warping your Teh and interfering with your True Will:

1. Stop doing! The *Tao Teh Ching* says that we should cultivate the art of "Doing without Doing." This sounds silly but reveals a profound truth: Sometimes simply ceasing an action causes great change. By refusing to argue with someone, the argument generally stops. By refusing to clean up after someone, the mess they are making readily becomes clear to all and the situation reaches a point where some change is inevitable. Refusing to offer kindness to those who take advantage of it will send them off to find another person to take advantage of. Simply being silent can often communicate more than a thousand words, and often when you stop complaining about something, the problem moves away because you have moved on. This is called "detaching."

2. Remove yourself! Avoid the perpetrator. Do something else. The victimizer is getting something out of causing you problems or controlling your behavior. The most obvious answer to the problem of being stuck in a job that is simply wrong for you is to change jobs or to at least take a vacation. We often end up doing things that deeply bother us, that are not part of our Teh, because we are tricked into thinking that we "must" do them. In fact, Taoist philosophy constantly shows that we limit ourselves, that in fact the Tao is all things, and so, when we are flowing with it, all things are possible.

    Everything in the universe will tell you when you shouldn't be somewhere and shouldn't be the victim of someone. Listen! Follow your heart. Avoiding is not running away. It might be as simple as not talking with an unpleasant person more than is necessary or moving your desk or transferring to a different department. One can mentally as well as physically avoid a person. Within a more complex relationship, such as a sibling relationship or marriage, avoiding has much more serious ramifications, ranging from giving one another more "space" to divorce. The only constant is holding fast to the Self, focusing on the Creative, and following your Way. No one ever said it would always be easy.

3. Adjust the relationship between you and the problem person. This can take two different forms, depending on how close you are to the offending party. The two options are: Change the Relationship, and Begin Getting Along.

Change the Relationship: This is a difficult thing to do, it requires a lot of effort, and you should really contemplate it before embarking on this particular Path. The Tao tells us that all things happen for a reason and when they are supposed to happen. Even errors and clinging to the Inferior are part of the Tao. It is a way of learning and we are here in this life to learn and to get better at navigating our Teh in order to evolve as well as to become positive growth-oriented helpers of others who are seeking to do the same.

As usual, the attitude we strive for is clearly seen in Nature. The bee is fed by flowers and in turn helps them pollinate. We are all part of a grand, ever-flowing design of give and take. Energy that does not flow becomes stagnant. It is often best to take things as they come, remember the impermanence of things, and do your best to improve yourself while keeping to your Teh.

Yet there are times when we are destined to be with certain people and we know that our Teh is connected with that person. Yet maybe things have gone awry, off track, become somehow dysfunctional in this relationship. It might be a relationship with a parent, a co-worker, a boss, a good friend, a mate, or a mentor. If this is the case, and it is your Will to work out the problems between you and not just call it quits, then do so.

Begin Getting Along: Smoothing over problems and working things out is called, in the *I Ching*, "Getting Along." This basically means to take the irritating or overbearing nature of a less intense relationship and to somewhat transform it into a more bearable situation. It means taking a terrible or unworkable relationship with someone who is victimizing you in some way and adjusting it to create a situation where there is a middle ground and the situation becomes acceptable. In short, it is the difference between being able to work with someone while still following your Teh and not being able to work with someone without being pulled from your Teh. This requires less effort than a real change in relationship in that you simply want to keep your Will intact while still getting along. It does not ask the other person to really change, only to stop actively damaging you. You don't have to like each other! Though easier, it is still somewhat tricky and requires some effort on your part.

Process B: Example

What follows are highlights from the notebook of a student who did the Process B exercise. They are included here as a practical example to show how the whole process comes together. This excerpt includes some of her notes and analysis at the end. We will call this person G. All the words, except where noted, are hers.

Problems Statement: I feel completely worthless in my hospital job. Many co-workers are rude to me and it is boring. My boyfriend is not willing to commit to me emotionally even though we love each other. I want to help people, but I do not feel I'm helping people now. I'm overweight and do not like my appearance. I feel stuck and unsociable. I'm sad too much.

Dreams Statement: I want to be a famous doctor like on *ER*. I want to save hundreds of people's lives. I want to be thin and glamorous like Ginger Rogers in a musical and have tons of people admire me!

Positives/Negatives:
Positives

Growing flowers
Long walks at the beach
Helping others
Healing people

Loving my cats

Talking on the phone

Romantic dancing

Reading romance novels

Watching romantic movies

Meeting kind people

Eating fresh vegetables

Cooking

Negatives

Hate doing desk work

Hate arguing with my mean boss

Having work dumped on me by lazy co-workers

No patience with regulations red tape

Being made fun of

Overeating

Drinking too much sometimes

Waiting in traffic

Having silly arguments

Falling for lies and gags

Gossiping

Being depressed about my boyfriend not committing

Sometimes not caring about others

Notes

Flashes: A lot of my problems are connected with my job! I need a new one. Also, I think that I should be dealing directly with people more, not doing so much paperwork. I need to be a bit more assertive as well, I guess. I think I eat too much because I feel powerless and I want to nurture people, but I can't, so I nourish myself too much.

Analysis of Problems Statement:

- How are my negative tendencies creating my own unhappiness?
  I really shouldn't be working where I am. It makes me negative toward

myself and others. I think I'm too maternal; I want to tell people what to do and they don't like it. Maybe I complain too much. Maybe I need to keep my mouth shut more, I think it annoys my co-workers.

- What positive tendencies am I not utilizing in my life now that I should use to make myself happier?

I'm usually so positive and I'm pretty nice. I really love taking care of pets and baby-sitting the neighbors kids. I think I'm really a healing person. I think I really want to mother people or have my own kids soon. I can be a good teacher, I think I can be good at being a boss (initiating beginnings) instead of just taking orders. My life lessons tell me that I should mind my business more and get more organized. This is so true! My current job requires too much talking and busy work, I really am no good at these things.

Analysis of Dreams Statement:

I really want to heal and help people, I am an open-hearted, loving, nourishing, and giving healer, like my natal hexagram says. I need to get a job that uses these skills—I'm sure many negative things would stop if I did. Am interested in alternative healing, maybe I can get a job in that field. I think I'd feel better about myself, not binge eat so much and feel like going out more. I've always wanted to learn ballroom dancing, I can do that!

Analysis of Positives and Negatives:

[Note: All of the attributes in parentheses are from G's natal hexagram, #27, Providing Nourishment.]

Positives

Growing flowers (Open-hearted, Loving, Maternal)

Helping others (Nourishing, Healer, Provider)

Healing people (Nourishing, Healer, Provider)

Loving my cats (Open-hearted, Loving, Maternal)

Talking on the phone (Wonderful friend, Fun, Caring)

Romantic dancing (Sociable, Loving, Unsophisticated)

Reading romance novels (Sociable, Loving, Unsophisticated)

Watching romantic movies (Sociable, Loving, Unsophisticated)

Meeting kind people (Altruistic, Loving, Sociable)

Eating fresh vegetables (Nourishing, Healer, Provider)

Cooking (Nourishing, Provider, Loving, Open-hearted, Good friend)

Negatives

Hate doing desk work (Excessive perfectionist, Disorganized, Forgetful)

Hate arguing with my mean boss (Meddlesome, Big-Mouth, Haughty, Condescending)

* Having work dumped on me by lazy co-workers

No patience with regulations red tape (Meddlesome, Taking good to extremes, Too idealistic, Haughty, Disorganized)

* Being made fun of

Overeating (Don't cope with real world, Take things to extremes)

Drinking too much sometimes (Don't cope with real world, Take things to extremes)

* Waiting in traffic

Having silly arguments (Condescending, Big-mouth, Simplistic, Meddlesome)

Falling for lies and gags (Gullible, Simplistic, Disorganized)

Gossiping (Big-mouth, Meddlesome, Simplistic, Condescending, Paternal)

* Being depressed about my boyfriend not committing

Sometimes not caring about others (Haughty, Condescending, Detached)

Notes

Well, I sure need to keep my mouth shut more, both with chatting and with eating! I'm just so frustrated at not being able to say positive, kind things to people more often. I can see that my lack of sophistication gets me in trouble, especially when I try to be uppity or condescending! I can also see some cool stuff about myself now. I really am pretty friendly and fun, kind as well. I shouldn't worry so much about trying to be hip or witty and just be myself. I like simple stuff, so what?! I don't have to be so thin or aristocratic, I'm really not those things. I need to find ways to help others more. Maybe volunteering. But I have to get a job where I can be more emotionally giving and less intellectual, that just isn't me! I have to accept that I'm naturally disorganized and not get so hung up on it, too. I need to go out more, get my girlfriends and go to some hot romantic movies, and grab my boyfriend and go dancing!

Final Analysis: Imposing Outer Negatives

[These items were given an asterisk on G.'s list—that is, she did not link these items to her natal hexagram.]

1. Having work dumped on me by lazy co-workers
2. Being made fun of
3. Waiting in traffic
4. Being depressed about my boyfriend not committing

Notes

I think that all of these do not come from me. I think 3 and maybe 2 are negative Yin, I think that they are produced by a bad environment. Traffic I can't do anything about, but maybe I can take a bus to work or (new idea!!!) listen to romance novels on tape or something! Being made fun of, I think, is mostly because of my really lousy working environment. Maybe it is a reaction to my gossiping too much. It doesn't seem to be really people attempting to attack or dominate me, just petty meanness.

1 and 4, however, are definitely negative Yang. Co-workers do take advantage of me and I do let them. I think I'll just stop letting them dump on me, it isn't so hard, really, to say no! Hopefully I'll move from this crappy job and then it won't be a problem anymore.

My boyfriend is another matter. We love each other, but I really feel he is using me in some ways. I think I need to look at his natal hexagram and work stuff out with him or we won't stay together."

This ends the exploration of Process B and the Self-focused natal hexagram exercises. You have now been given several specific ways to proceed with removing yourself from an Inferior, unhappy situation. You may also have come to the conclusion that your problems are also being caused by another person, someone who may be imposing upon you, someone you cannot simply walk away from or ignore. G.'s boyfriend is a good example.

To review, you should first go through the things about your problem that are rooted in your natal aspects and come to some practical course of action to address what you have discovered. G. went on to find a new job in alternative health working with patients, and she is much happier. Next, look at the asterisk-marked aspects that are not natal aspects and decide where they originate and how you can remove or avoid them in your life since they are making you unhappy. If you keep coming back to the fact that another person is the root of your unhappiness, then you must decide. Will you avoid this person? Leave this person? Or do you need to do something to change the relationship between you and this person? The action you take is up to you. If you want to take real practical steps to improve your relationship with another person, the next section will help you.

Using Natal Hexagrams to Improve Relationships

Why do we care about other people? Because we are attached to what they feel, say, and do. This might be the result of an emotional bond (friendship, love, dislike, hate) or it may be because they are in a position to influence us (boss, co-worker, teacher, mentor, parent). In any event, before you go any further with seeing how you can create more harmony between you and another (which might mean getting them off your back!), let's examine the Taoist view toward all interpersonal relationships.

> "Peace is easily maintained
> Trouble is easily overcome before it starts
> The brittle is easily shattered
> The small is easily scattered
> Deal with it before it happens
> Set things in order before there is confusion"
> —Tao Teh Ching

Self-Check: Nipping Things in the Bud

It is far easier to stop problems before they happen, both in your own life and between you and another person. The first step in clearing up and improving relationships is to examine how you influence such relationships. With a dispassionate eye, look at your behaviors and your natal I Ching traits with a view towards nipping interpersonal problems in the bud. All of us are more powerful than we give ourselves credit for and can use our power to heal or help all our relationships. All that is needed is a bit of awareness and a desire to be positive. Let me give you examples from my own natal hexagram. I will list the traits assigned to my natal hexagram (#56) and show how I have managed to end problems with others before they start by focusing on how these traits affect my relationships.

MY TRAITS (AND MY COMMENTS)

Visitor and wanderer:

Because I usually (unconsciously) see myself and my relationships as transitory (even though they're not!), I can sometimes irritate others—like my wife—by inadvertently using words that communicate this. Others sometimes feel that I am not committed to a project or job because of this attitude, even though I am. By realizing that this is how I come off, I can put people at ease about these things up-front and therefore it does not have to become an issue.

Always moving, Driven, Hyper, Frenetic:

My restlessness drives some people crazy, especially if their natal hexagrams indicate that they are calmer or more sedentary people. I have learned to tone it down and to adapt a calmer and steadier demeanor around others. Well, I try, anyway! I also realize that as I get more excited or frenetic in conversations or discussions, more sensitive people will begin to get defensive and irritated. I have learned to catch myself and lower my general energy level when interacting with others.

Interesting, Amusing, Fascinating, Studying many cultures, Extroverted, Intelligent:

I know that I am somewhat witty (and can write books!) and that I have traveled a lot and done a lot of things. I love entertaining and conversing, but I must also be very careful not to become an egocentric windbag or be seen as pedantic! I realize that some people will always see me as full of myself, though I view it as simply being playful, but by carefully watching others' reactions (and by learning to shut up and listen more!), I can focus on being interesting and not overbearing.

Easily detoured, Spontaneous, Looks before leaping:

I know I'm horribly forgetful, easily distracted, and tend to do things on a whim. I have learned to live by my datebook, have paste-up notes all over my desk, force myself to spend set amounts of time on projects, and to limit distractions. I'm also learning to get advice from my wife and friends before launching into a new project or work—this has saved me more than once from leaping to disaster!

Kind, Mystic, Open-minded:

I try to emphasize these qualities, but not to the point of being taken advantage of (which happens) or being naive. I also need to keep my feet on the ground and focus on the practical in life. I have a tendency to get too theoretical or spiritual in conversations, something I always monitor, especially if it's inappropriate (like at work!).

Nips things in the bud, Decisive, Deals with things fast:

These are great qualities, unless they lead me to make snap judgments about people or things and I happen to be wrong. I've learned to get a second opinion about almost every quick decision or sudden situation I am faced with. Simply counting to ten can often help. I try never to second-guess myself because these are essentially positive qualities that are very useful in general, though I often do need to explain why I made a decision so quickly to people who need to mull things over or who are, by their natal hexagram, less decisive.

Tends to quarrel, Quick-tempered:

These are overtly negative traits, but I have learned to use these tendencies in positive ways. For example, I recently represented my co-workers in a meeting with the company president. I did not lose my temper, but I did argue passionately, clearly, and concisely (using my more positive traits) for some changes we needed. I find that I am rarely harassed on the street. Though I spent a lot of time in New York, I was never mugged because, I think, I projected these traits as a kind of "don't mess with me" psychic armor!

On the negative side, my sometimes volcanic nature has led me to adopt some anger management strategies and simply learn to control my temper.

Cautious (paranoid?):

I do not feel that I am paranoid, but now I am aware that others may perceive me as such. By being aware of this trait, I have pushed myself to be a bit more trusting and to give people the benefit of the doubt in general.

By simply being conscious of my traits and how they might cause problems with people I interact with, I have improved my relationships in practical ways, and so can you. You can avoid many, if not most, of the interpersonal problems that can crop up without even looking at someone's natal hexagram. Using your traits in this way, to increase harmony and eliminate problems before they even begin, is a practice Taoists call "restraint." All things—traits, attitudes, emotions—in moderation! There is a time and place for everything, even losing your temper. You moderate your traits and interpersonal skills by focusing on your past experiences combined with what the inner voice of your Self tells you is True. This is called Virtue by the Taoists.

> "In caring for others and serving heaven
> There is nothing like using restraint.
> Restraint begins with giving up one's own ideas.
> This depends on Virtue gathered in the past."
> —Tao Teh Ching, vs. 59

I can go farther with the "nipping it in the bud" methodology I have outlined here by examining the other parts of my natal hexagram reading, and you can do this for yourself as well. The Life Lessons give very clear directions on improving relations with people and help us approach situations, people, and relationships in such a way that problems can disappear before they even begin.

Dealing with People Who Bring "Inferior" Elements Into Our Lives

The *I Ching* tells us that by being more sensitive, by taking responsibility for resolving disputes, and by being nicer and a bit humbler, we can generally make all relationships easier. This is, of course, much easier when working with people you feel close to. Improving loving relationships is one of our main duties as human beings; we all really know this is true. Removing or transforming Inferior elements in all relationships is the way to do this. Yet we are sometimes confronted with Inferior people, people who enter our lives and bring with them Inferior elements, attitudes, or feelings. Keep in mind that "inferior" as we have seen is a relative label and that no person is completely "inferior." They may seek to push you from your Teh; they may try to impose their Way on you. They may simply drain you of the Creative energy or push your Negative Trait buttons! In any event, the Taoist attitude is that one should never shirk a confrontation if such is called for, but as in Tai Chi, an art that reflects the Tao, what you do with the negative energy directed toward you is the key to overcoming or avoiding it. This is determined by what you do with your own energies.

So, when I am first confronted with a personality clash, an obstinate or hostile co-worker or relative, or any other problem involving others, I specifically look at what I am bringing to the relationship that might be causing or worsening the situation, and then change my approach. The other person will always, either consciously or (more likely) unconsciously, notice the effort I am making to balance the forces between us and he or she will often, without realizing it, begin to moderate themselves as well.

So, examine your natal hexagram with this in mind. I suggest that you write down your nip-it-in-the-bud strategies, much as I did above. Keep these notes and refer to them when interpersonal problems crop up.

In this last section we explored how to do this. Following is another, more active way to use your personal power to improve a relationship. It has nothing to do with natal hexagrams, but it is an exercise that has proven so effective that I feel it should be included here.

Mirroring

Next time you have an argument with someone, in the middle of the fight, suddenly lower your tone of voice. Surprisingly, the other person will almost always follow suit and lower his or her voice as well. This illustrates the idea of mirroring—that is, causing change in others by changing ourselves. It is a powerful and effective interpersonal tool that can be found in Tai Chi as well as some popular psychological practices.

It is rare when we can influence others directly to spur them to manifest more positive qualities—no one can make other people Superior if they insist on sticking with Inferior behavior or attitudes. That has to do with them fitting together the pieces of their Self by themselves. We must each find our own personal Way of harmony. Though you cannot make others be nicer to you or more pliant or even happier, you can use your personal power (Chi) to help them to improve themselves, if they are sincere and willing to do so. The best way to do this, the Taoists declare, is to become a mirror of the Tao for them.

This means that your being and behavior, in specific and in general, should let them see the positive and negative qualities they are projecting and of which they might not be aware! It is within your ability to show them these things. You can do this by the Creative expression of your own Self as you unfold this growth in your life. It is the best thing you can do. When done correctly, it will make them aware, without their even realizing it, of their Inferior habits and qualities and so point the way for them to change. Whether they act on this information or not is up to them.

It has already been explained how you can use your natal hexagram to find and work out problems for yourself. It is not the Taoist way to depend on what others do or say for you to find harmony or your Teh. Always remember, others cannot make you angry, unhappy, tense, or sad; you make yourself experience those feelings by your reaction to what others do or say. The choice of how you react to people is definitely yours to make.

For example, if you encounter bigots who make disparaging remarks, the most natural reaction is to get angry. Are they making you angry with their negative Yang aggression? No, you are making yourself angry. They are Inferior in that their baser thoughts are ruling their Self; they are not balanced but hateful. You could choose to feel pity instead, or boredom, or ignore the insult completely and feel nothing. To be free enough from social and parental conditioning is to see that your choices are the first steps in influencing others. If you cannot control your own reactions to what others throw at you, then you cannot be removed enough from the situation to effectively mirror to them what they are doing and so cause some change.

One effective way to mirror problem people is either to be completely silent and let the words return to those who uttered them, or to simply repeat what they said back to them with no added feeling or words. Let them hear, with no emotive input from you, exactly what they said. Their ego might simply rage on, but their Self, their inner Spirit, will hear how Inferior they sound, and you will feel the negative energy return back to them.

Let me give a more complete and concrete example. When children repeatedly steal cookies from a cookie jar, they may be doing so for a number of reasons. Possibly they want attention, they may be hungry, they may crave the sugar, they may be testing Mom, they may simply be bored or, it is possible that their big sister might even be putting them up to it! The most common reaction for parents is to get angry and yell, thus stopping them. But have the children really learned much? Will the behavior stop? Behaviorists say no, they will simply act out in another manner or be sneakier in stealing the cookies. So what should Mom do in this case? There are always three options.

First, she could simply give the kids the cookies and request that they ask next time. Second, she could punish the behavior. Third, she could discover the root of the negative behavior and deal with that—in other words, discover if they're hungry, bored, needy, being manipulated, and so on.

Any of these are acceptable responses, depending on the situation. Remember, all is relative. One situation is never like another! There are no set rules. Yet how one reacts, according to Taoist thinking, is far more important than what one says.

In each of these cases, the children's actions should be mirrored. Many people, especially children, act unconsciously and become defensive when confronted because they really don't know why they did something or said something. To yell "Why did you steal a cookie?" will either get you that predictable defensive reaction (Yang: "I wanted it!") or cause a retreat (Yin: "I don't know . . .?"). By being a mirror, one gets around both of these responses. In this case, the mom should simply state, in neutral tones, what is happening. For example, "You took cookies." This leaves room for kids to make a natural response, and remember, the goal of all this is to return to our Superior qualities of being natural, open, kind, and so on. Where the interaction goes from here depends on many things; if the neutral tone and detached attitude is clung to by the mom, it will usually work itself out in a natural and nonconfrontational manner.

This same strategy works with lovers, bosses, co-workers, parents, and so on. It is a very simple trick but it has great depth. It also helps to mirror the stance of people, their body language, and facial expression, but not their vocal tone, especially if it is negative. At the same time, visualize yourself as a mirror; everything they see is them, you are safe and protected behind the mirror. It is remarkable how effective this can be.

Dealing with Problem People Using Their Natal Hexagrams

OK, you've tried working with your traits, you've tried being as Superior and harmonious as you can possibly be in your interactions. Even mirroring is of limited use because you interact with the problem person all the time and the two of you are just like oil and water. Yet some sort of relationship has to be worked out that does not pull you from your Way or put you in jail for homicide, justifiable or not. Now it is time to seriously look at the other person's natal hexagram.

Think of the people who are imposing on your life. Think of exactly how they are driving you crazy or torturing you. You must try to rise above their negative Yin or Yang and carry on with the business of your Teh, but if this proves impossible, or if they are very near and dear to you, you have to decide how you wish to change the relationship. It is time to pull out the big guns of their natal hexagram!

The Blending Way

The best approach to take when using two natal hexagrams to better a relationship between the two people is called the Blending Way. It is really the most Taoist approach in that it aims to create more harmony than already exists. It is not a me-versus-them approach at all. Think of yourself and the problem person. Try to objectively view the two of you as a meeting of complex forces. The optimum path here is finding ways in which tension can turn to harmony. This is not as difficult as it seems, and often great tension can transform into great friendship. Many hexagrams show this clearly (look, for example, at Critical Mass). You know from experience that antagonism and powerful dislike can change to love and vice versa.

But heed this warning: If you attach too much to the other's growth or evolution, you will pull yourself out of whack and end up becoming an Inferior person. To reiterate, you cannot change another. You cannot find another's Path for him or her. You cannot grant harmony to another. Each must find his or her Way. But you can create more harmony between you and another.

Not Just for Problems!

"... having and not having arise together
difficult and easy complement each other ..."
—Tao Teh Ching

Even the most loving friends, relatives, or mates have points of stress and periods of disharmony in their relationships. If you have never thought "I'm going to kill him (or her)!" at some point in your life about a loved one, then you are not human. No relationship is perfect, and since the only constant is change, then we (and our relationships) are always changing and rearranging ourselves. This is good, this is life, this is the flow of the Tao. That which does not accept change is doomed to pass away, including relationships. In this light, the process of creating more harmony between yourself and another person should not simply be seen in the light of working things out with someone who is being difficult or overbearing. The time to solve problems is at the beginning of troubles, not when they become critical.

It is important to keep in mind that all relationships can be improved, no matter how good they are. Real communication only occurs between equals, and this equality is determined by the depth and completeness of the understanding between two people. As we form and work out relationships between people, it is always like a square peg in a round hole in some ways; there will always be places where you and the other person completely agree and understand each other and places where you don't. There will always be things about the other person that really bug you and vice versa.

Why Look Up Another's Natal Hexagram?

Points of ease and points of contention between any two people can clearly be seen when comparing natal hexagrams. This may be for the purpose of making a good relationship better, for overcoming a hard or difficult relationship, as we previously mentioned, or it can be used to find out how to make a new just-beginning (or yet-to-begin) relationship flow smoothly and be positive on all levels.

If you know that a new co-worker is entering your office or that your friend is marrying someone you don't know, or that you have a new stepbrother, you should try to look at their natal hexagram. By studying their natal hexagram and comparing it with yours, you will be forearmed and aware in your dealings with them and so will be able to stop any personality clashes between the two of you before they begin. This is, of course, the best possible way to solve relationship problems in advance! So, as we now explore the process of critically comparing two natal hexagrams with the intention of improving relationships, keep in mind that there are three possible reasons for doing so: First, to make an already good relationship better on all levels. Second, to save, mend, or at least neutralize a difficult or even terrible relationship with someone you need to deal with.

And third, to form a positive and equitable relationship with someone important who is entering your life in a position where getting along with him or her is paramount.

OK, are you ready? Breathe deeply, focus on the relationship you wish to improve, then get out your pad and pencil. Here we go!

Comparing Natal Hexagrams to Improve Relationships

First, find some quiet time and a quiet place to work this out. Have at least three sheets of paper to write on. One should be marked "Notes," another should be marked "Work Space," and the third should be divided into two parts and should be marked "Comparison."

The Notes sheet is for you to note down ideas, strategies, ways of making the relationship better, things to keep in mind, conclusions, and so on.

The Work Space sheet is your scribble page, for doing the math necessary to get the Natal Hexagram, for plotting out good and bad points, and for doodling.

The Comparison sheet is for listing the results of comparing your natal hexagram with the other person's.

Never fear, an example of this whole process will be given at the end of this explanation. Now we begin.

Part 1

Using the formula in this book, figure out the other person's natal hexagram, then find it in the appropriate section. Next, reread your natal hexagram. This will give you a fair idea of where you are starting in regards to the relationship between the two of you. It gives a good overview, and some ideas or strategies might suggest themselves right away. Meditate for a moment on both of you, each a composite bundle of thoughts, feelings, traits, and tendencies. Study both natal hexagram readings. What are the obviously positive points between you? What aspects are clearly conflicting? You will get some insights and ideas about your relationship right away. Write them down on your Notes page. Use your intuition and listen to your inner voice; sometimes first impressions are the most important and truthful. Note: Often the hardest or most difficult aspects between two people are reflected in negative traits or tendencies that they share in their natal hexagrams.

Part 2

The next step is to look at both readings and see if either of your natal hexagrams are noted in the compatibility section. If not, then there is more freedom in changing the relationship. If you are on either the compatible or incompatible list of the other person, it simply makes things a bit easier or a bit more difficult, depending on the situation.

- If you are on each other's compatible list, it will be quite easy to set things right and improve the relationship. Just a shift in attitude or a little extra effort will quickly work wonders.
- If you are on each other's incompatible list, then things will be harder to fix, but then again, it helps explain why you are having problems with your relationship to begin with! The focus, again, will be on the trigram you have in common; this is helpful in that it clearly shows where and why you both clash. You see in each other things you do not care for about yourself or things that you have already worked on that the other person hasn't.

For example, the top trigram of my natal hexagram is LI, Fire. I tend to be incompatible with those who have a top trigram of LI because both are in the Heaven (Yang) position (top) and both are very fiery and aggressive. It is like adding gasoline to a fire! I may see that other person as arrogant, overbearing, loud, and temperamental—all qualities that sometimes apply to me. Now, I have really worked on my temper and rarely show it, but encountering this other person's temper will irritate me to no end, either because that person has not mastered it as well as I have or because like calls to like and that person's temper will evoke my own as well!

There is, however, good news here. This Fire/Fire clash can be shifted easily, especially if we are both angry at the same thing or feel passionate about the same subject. So, in a way, this incompatibility can work to your advantage in "flipping" the relationship from poor to good. You just have to find common points of interest and get your energies moving in the same direction instead of against each other. In this situation, a person you can't stand can end up becoming a very close friend.

If you are on each other's incompatible list, put down on the Notes page exactly what trigram you share and whether it is in the top or bottom position, this will be important.

If you are not on each other's compatible or incompatible lists, then neither of you has a predisposition toward the other; you start off more or less neutral, though, as we will see, certain trigrams work together better than others. There is no predisposition toward strong feelings one way or the other and so you will be working on mostly improving general feelings or attitudes, but then again, this may be exactly what is needed and what you are after. If your relationship is basically good, then minor changes are all you want anyway, and if it is a really bad relationship, then you only want to change things enough so you get along and can stand each other, right?

Part 3

Draw your natal hexagram on the top left side of the Comparison page and the other person's natal hexagram on the top right side of the same page. Draw them fairly large and clearly so you can see the trigrams. Now begins the process of comparing the trigrams.

Look at the trigram list and look up your trigrams and the other person's trigrams, then write what they are next to at the top and bottom of each natal hexagram. Look at which trigrams are in the same position.

Trigrams are the key elements to each hexagram. The upper trigram reveals the basic nature of a person's Conscious Mind; the lower trigram reveals the basic nature of a person's Unconscious Mind. How two trigrams interact, as you discovered in the first part of this book, determines the unique character of the Self in any natal hexagram reading. When comparing two natal hexagrams, we must also look at how the two people interact and, importantly, how the elements of their character interact. We all interact with others on two levels, the conscious level and the unconscious level. You may like some people (a conscious reaction) and get along with them, but always feel uneasy or distrustful of them for no apparent reason (an unconscious reaction). This is an example of compatible upper trigrams and incompatible lower trigrams.

These, of course, are very general comparisons, points, and suggestions, but they may be enough for you to better a relationship without going any farther in this process. Remember to always compare across— your upper trigram with the other person's upper trigram, your lower trigram with the other person's lower trigram.

What follows are some general points of contention or hard aspects that may cause personality problems between any two trigrams. If the two trigrams being compared are in the upper, or Heaven/Yang, position, then these problems will be outwardly evident. If the trigrams in question are in the lower position, then the problems will be of an unconscious nature and much harder to overtly pin down or see. In this case, simply being aware that you or the other person are being subconsciously influenced negatively by this clash can help you deal with problems that come up.

Points of contention will be listed by trigram. These will give some clear root causes of possible problems with the person with whom you are comparing natal hexagrams. Simply identifying the root causes will help clear the way for making things better. After this list, a specific example of how to translate this information into practical solutions will be given as a model.

Root Causes of Contention Between Compared Natal Trigrams

K'UN/Earth with . . .

* K'UN/Earth: Passive aggressiveness, Smothering, Reacting without thinking, Not being straightforward, Simplifying complex things, Being too physical, Money issues

CHEN/Thunder: Feeling slighted or ignored, Different modes of communicating, Conservative vs. radical, Passive vs. active, Calm vs. agitated

TUI/Lake: Having too much fun, Indulging, Impracticality, Clash of moods, Laziness

CH'IEN/Heaven: Pecking order, Emotional balance, Direction, Seriousness, Respect

SUN/Wind: Depth, Pace, What is true/not true, Long-range plans, Conversational style

K'EN/Mountain: Lethargy, Non/miscommunication, Differences in values, Strange energy, Spirituality

LI/Fire: Styles of conveying information, Dependency, Commitment, Creativity, Aesthetics

K'AN/Rain: Focusing on the negative, Worrying, Neediness, Secrets, Selfishness

CHEN/Thunder with ...

*CHEN/Thunder: Duties and responsibilities, Power, Movement and planning, Intellectual aggressiveness, Listening

TUI/Lake: Intense feelings, Opening up too fast too much, Hurt feelings, Inappropriateness, Differences in speed

CH'IEN/Heaven: Visions and goals, Status, Aggression, Organization, Creative style/presentation

SUN/Wind: Methods of work, Morality, Humor, Letting things go, Affecting others

K'EN/ Mountain: Patience, Being obstinate, Communicating clearly, Way of thinking, Nontangibles

LI/Fire: Getting sidetracked, Too much talking, Lecturing, Telling vs. showing, Disrespect

K'AN/Rain: Foolish actions, Prioritizing, Distrust, Uneasiness, Transference

K'UN/Earth: Pecking order, Emotional balance, Direction, Seriousness, Respect

TUI/Lake with ...

*TUI/Lake: Lack of motivation, Obsequiousness, Eroticism, Overdoing things, Excessive hedonism

CH'IEN/Heaven: Lack of focus, Effectiveness, Leisure time, Emotive style of communication, Manners

SUN/Wind: Sincerity, Quantity of conversation vs. quality, Complaining, Interpersonal borders, Stamina

K'EN/Mountain: Inaction, Differences in humor, Nonverbal communication, Responsibility for others, Atmosphere

LI/Fire: Desires, Language, Decisiveness, Clear communication, Enjoyment

K'AN/Rain: Inappropriateness, Emotional muddiness, Insecurity, Cynicism, Intuition

K'UN/Earth: Having too much fun, Indulging , Impracticality, Clash of moods, Laziness

CHEN/Thunder: Intense feelings, Opening up too fast too much, Hurt feelings, Inappropriateness, Differences in speed

CH'IEN/Heaven with . . .

*CH'IEN/Heaven: Power politics, Seriousness, Flexibility, Excessive strength, Lack of emotion

SUN/Wind: Rebelliousness, Styles of action, Immediacy vs. long term, Drive (too little/too much), Timing

K'EN/Mountain: Apparent effort, Passivity vs. aggressiveness, Caution, Goals, Delegating responsibilities

LI/Fire: Misplaced energy, Intellectual arguments, Learning methods, Artistry, Content vs. form

K'AN/Rain: Pessimism vs. optimism, What is/is not realistic, Risks, Concerns, Judgments

K'UN/Earth: Pecking order, Emotional balance, Direction, Seriousness, Respect

CHEN/Thunder: Visions and goals, Status, Aggression, Organization, Creative style/presentation

TUI/Lake: Lack of focus, Effectiveness, Leisure time, Emotive style of communication, Manners

SUN/Wind with...

***SUN/Wind:** Simplification of ideas and emotions, Flightiness, Arrogance, Quarreling, Pinning down issues/ideas

K'EN/Mountain: Permanence vs. being transitory, Structure/form, Pace and criteria of work, Truth, Relevance

LI/Fire: Inspiration, Focused communication, Exchanges, Perceptions, Sharp vs. soft wit

K'AN/Rain: What is real, Rating problems, Process of making decisions, Detachment/attachment, Motivations

K'UN/ Earth: Depth, Pace, What is true/not true, Long-range plans, Conversational style

CHEN/Thunder: Methods of work, Morality, Humor, Letting things go, Affecting others

TUI/Lake: Sincerity, Quantity of conversation vs. quality, Complaining, Interpersonal borders, Stamina

CH'IEN/Heaven: Rebelliousness, Styles of action, Immediacy vs. long term, Drive (too little/too much), Timing

K'EN/Mountain with. . .

*K'EN/Mountain: Immobility, Excessive stubbornness, Refusing to listen/see/hear, Extreme passivity, Perverse attitude, Extreme spirituality, Disapproval

LI/Fire: Energy levels, Speed of processing information, Dependency, Personal styles, Value of discussion

K'AN/Rain: Depression, Inaction, Focusing on inconsequentials, Lack of communication, Ignoring each other

K'UN/ Earth: Lethargy, Non/miscommunication, Differences in values, Strange energy, Spirituality

CHEN/Thunder: Patience, Being obstinate, Communicating clearly, Way of thinking, Nontangibles

TUI/Lake: Inaction, Differences in humor, Nonverbal communication, Responsibility for others, Atmosphere

CH'IEN/Heaven: Apparent effort, Passivity vs. aggressiveness, Caution, Goals, Delegating responsibilities

SUN/Wind: Permanence vs. being transitory, Structure/form, Pace and criteria of work, Truth, Relevance
LI/Fire with . . .

*LI/Fire: Egocentrism, Finishing projects, Long-term planning, Intelligence vs. wisdom, Neediness, Tempestuousness, Volatility

K'AN/Rain: Very different viewpoints, Dismissiveness, Lack of consideration, Narrowness of focus and understanding, Making ideas clearly understood

K'UN/Earth: Styles of conveying information, Dependency, Commitment, Creativity, Aesthetics

CHEN/Thunder: Getting sidetracked, Too much talking, Lecturing, Telling vs. showing, Disrespect

TUI/Lake: Desires, Language, Decisiveness, Clear communication, Enjoyment

CH'IEN/Heaven: Misplaced energy, Intellectual arguments, Learning methods, Artistry, Content vs. form

SUN/Wind: Inspiration, Focused communication, Exchanges, Perceptions, Sharp vs. soft wit

K'EN/ Mountain: Energy levels, Speed of processing information, Dependency, Personal styles, Value of discussion

K'AN/Rain with . . .

*K'AN/Rain: Destructiveness, Dishonesty, Distrust, Fear, Problem solving, Interpreting meaning, Gut reactions

K'UN/Earth: Focusing on the negative, Worrying, Neediness, Secrets, Selfishness

CHEN/Thunder: Foolish actions, Prioritizing, Distrust, Uneasiness, Transference

TUI/Lake: Inappropriateness, Emotional muddiness, Insecurity, Cynicism, Intuition

CH'IEN/Heaven: Pessimism vs. optimism, What is/is not realistic, Risks, Concerns, Judgments

SUN/Wind: What is real, Rating problems, Process of making decisions, Detachment/attachment, Motivations

K'EN/Mountain: Depression, Inaction, Focusing on inconsequentials, Lack of communication, Ignoring each other

LI/Fire: Very different viewpoints, Dismissiveness, Lack of consideration, Narrowness of focus and understanding, Making ideas clearly understood

Example: Comparing Trigrams of Natal Hexagrams

Here I will compare my natal hexagram (#56, The Wanderer: LI/Fire over K'EN/Mountain) with that of my "difficult friend," whom I will refer to as T. His natal hexagram is #36, Darkening of the Light: K'UN/Earth over LI/Fire. Using the trigram points of contention given above, I will show point by point what the trigrams revealed the problems between us were and how I used this information to improve our rocky friendship. T. and I have known each other since we were kids and are like brothers, but our relationship, though close, is not an easy one. Here are our two hexagrams:

HEXAGRAM 56   HEXAGRAM 36

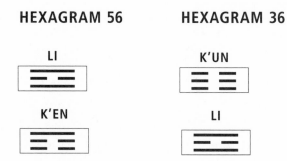

LI

K'UN

K'EN

LI

Here is an analysis of the top trigrams, the "conscious" roots of the problems between us. It is broken down by the points of contention:

LI

K'UN

LI/Fire

K'UN/Earth

Styles of conveying information: I am very energetic and positive; he is morose and pessimistic. I communicate with humor and fairly directly, always asking questions. T. is often silent and stewing. He only communicates problems after they have been eating at him for a while, often by exploding. I finally was able to discuss with him how his outbursts made me not want to be around him or discuss things with him. He felt I was shallow and chatted too much, not giving thought to what I was saying. We realized how different our communication styles were. Now I pointedly ask him yes-or-no questions about his thoughts and feelings, something he is comfortable with, not general "How do you feel?" questions. He is trying to communicate problems and frustrations outwardly more often, not holding them in so long.

Dependency: I wasn't aware that this was a problem between us, but when I brought it up, T. had a lot to say. It turned out that he felt I constantly relied on him for a number of things. Being introverted, he simply didn't mention this irritation, but it continually bothered him. We worked it out that he would ask me to contribute more when he felt I should and I in turn would not get defensive. This removed a huge stress from our relationship that I didn't even realize was there.

Commitment: Here the problem was less one of actual inner commitment to our friendship than outer communication of such. Whenever we had a quarrel, he would say "Go to hell" and other dismissive, get-lost-type statements. Yet if I actually did take off, he'd call me later all upset because I had taken him at his word and left! I couldn't understand, until I looked at this, that what he said and what he really meant were not the same things. I asked him to express his anger and need for some sort of affirmation of our friendship in different ways, and, after a time, he did.

Creativity: I like lots of input and conversation as I sketch out ideas for drawings or writings I'm doing. My art comes spontaneously to me and I assumed all people were creative in this way. T. is very different; it takes him days and days to write and rewrite a simple poem or do a simple drawing. Creativity is a difficult and painful process for him, something I just didn't think about when he blew up at me about art or writing. Later, after analyzing this, I realized that I'd been constantly rubbing his nose in this difficulty he has with my style of creativity and so I toned it down a bit and gave him more time and more room in which to be creative.

Aesthetics: In general, T. and I have completely different tastes, even down to the women we married, how we dress, where we live, and so on. Yet we have learned to be a bit more open to each other's tastes, though not a whole lot! The trick was finding a few things—like Picasso, jazz, and pottery—that we could agree on. Keeping aesthetic discussions to what we both like has eliminated many arguments, but not all of them!

Here is an analysis of the bottom trigrams that represent the "unconscious," or hidden, roots of the problems between us and the points of contention that go with them:

K'EN

K'EN/Mountain

LI

LI/Fire

Energy levels: It is very interesting that even though I was diagnosed as hyperactive as a child (LI/Fire!), I prefer my surroundings calm and subdued. T. is the opposite. He is volcanic. On the surface he is very calm and quiet, but he is often exploding inside. His hidden fiery nature often made me uncomfortable; he always seemed edgy and ready to blow up even though outwardly he was usually calm. Looking at this, I realized that I simply needed to accept that these feelings were unconsciously sparked by his inner character and that this is simply how he is.

Speed of processing information—personal styles: On a deep level, T.'s mind and my mind work very differently. I like to study something carefully, let it seep into my mind, and then intellectually reorganize ideas. T., on the other hand, lets visions and feelings erupt from his unconscious mind in a very unorganized manner. Logical arguments rarely work with him and we got increasingly frustrated by each thinking that the other person did not understand basic things about reality! The key here was finding common ground between my intellectual, organized musings and his almost visionary outbursts and setting a few ground rules for our discussions. This made us more comfortable with each other's modes of processing data.

Value of discussion: I love to chat, and furthermore, it is how I work out deep issues for myself. It is also how I come to know someone on a deeper level—through intellectual bantering and the exchange of information. Because I am so orally centered, it is of great subliminal import for me to get a handle on someone through discussions. So, on an unconscious level, I need this to feel comfortable with someone; it is how I size them up. T., on the other hand, thinks such chitchat is a waste of time. Even his letters are usually only a paragraph long. He believes in stating the key points of what he has to say and that's it. Conversational style, manners, and the nonverbal components of discussion mean nothing to him. This causes us great unease with each other: He thinks I talk too much; I never feel I know what he's about. This is a hard one; we have simply talked about this issue and he's agreed that when I really need comments from him, he'll give them, and I in turn will not keep expecting him to talk more than he is comfortable.

There are no easy answers in this kind of process of working things out. In some cases it was one-sided; he didn't see a point of contention at all and so I simply adapted to it. We did agree on many of these things and are both doing our best to work them out. We have greatly improved our friendship. We still have a difficult time of it and there are some points of contention I have accepted will just not satisfy either of us, but, in the long run, this trigram analysis has helped quite a bit. Many things that cause bad feeling between two people are simply miscommunications or misperceptions. You can see this in the analysis above. Often just becoming aware of a problem or issue is the biggest step to solving it, especially if both parties are willing to make the effort.

Part 4

When you wish to understand and improve a relationship between two people, one other thing needs to be checked out. This concerns who is more Yin and who is more Yang in the relationship. Keep in mind that a person being more Yin or Yang does not translate into them being good or bad! Though Yin is often described as passive, a Yin person in a relationship can do more harm than a typically Yang, or active, person. Both Yin and Yang can be very negative and very harmful. Just think of someone telling a serious lie or forgetting to take an important message! These are aspects of negative Yin and can be just as bad as any typically negative Yang behavior, like yelling or critiquing someone.

The technique for getting this information is very simple, just look at the Yin and Yang lines in each hexagram you are comparing. The person with the most solid or Yang lines is more Yang in the relationship; the one with the most broken or Yin lines is more Yin.

If one person in a relationship is more Yin, look for them to be more passive aggressive in the relationship, less truthful about their feelings, more inclined not to do things that are important, or to ignore, intentionally forget, or even edit things said and done. Sneakiness, stewing, being cold, and ignoring are negative Yin attributes. If you are the Yin person in the relationship in question, examine how honest and up-front you are in dealing with the relationship. Are you being negative Yin? Get clear on what you are doing to add to the problem, even if it is not easy to pin down. It may simply be that you are being misread and misunderstood; the other person might think you're not honest or have a bad attitude when that is not the case at all. In this situation, being more open and forward and simply getting reality checks from the other person on what they think or feel about you is helpful.

If one has more Yang than Yin lines, they are more likely the overt cause of relationship problems, though that might not be the real truth. It is always easier to blame the Yang person in a problem relationship because they are more obvious in their thinking and actions. They are more likely to show their feelings, openly criticize, and be aggressive or overbearing. If you are that person, right away try to tone down your feelings before approaching a problem. Listen more and get the other person to talk about problems first. This is, in any event, a helpful strategy when resolving conflicts, but it often falls to the Yang person in the relationship to begin the fixing process and the Yin person will often follow the lead and be supportive and nurturing. Remember, Yin and Yang here have nothing to do with gender! Also, remember that every relationship, like everything else in this world, shifts from Yin to Yang and back again. A Yang person can be very Yin at times, and vice versa. Yet when we are looking at root causes of relationship problems, we must look at the natal hexagrams; these give us basic Teh, or Way of Being, patterns for people. By going to the roots of people's natal hexagrams, you can almost always get to the root problems of their relationships.

Example

In my case, again returning to my problem friend T., we can clearly see that I have one less Yin line than he does (I have three broken lines, he has four). This indicates, more often than not, that I am the more Yang component of our troubled relationship, even though he is bigger, stronger, and more intense than I am! Yet his aggressiveness is volcanic (for more information, review the reading for his natal hexagram, #36) and his power is often internalized, thus causing outbursts. What irritates him about me is that I am always talking, emoting, discussing, pushing to go somewhere, see something, hurry up, and so on. His pace is slower, he likes quiet, he prefers to ruminate about things and be the strong, silent type. Because of this, when looking at how to save our faltering friendship, I realized that I would have to take the lead, and I did. This triggered some defensiveness, a lot of evasion, and some ignoring, but finally quite a bit of revealing of thoughts and feelings that I had no idea he harbored!

Part 5

Final Evaluation

All these processes may seem like an overly complex way to simply improve a relationship, but as I mentioned earlier, you need to decide beforehand if actually analyzing and fixing such a relationship in this way is worth the trouble. You can often simply get along better by just looking at your own natal hexagram and operating from that situation, as discussed in an earlier section. Just doing Part 1 and Part 4, and possibly Part 2, will give you more than enough relationship information advice to work things out with another person on a superficial level, like with a co-worker you are not very close to or with a boss you don't care so much about. Part 3 is really a more involved and complex way to compare and improve a more serious relationship. It requires a bit of mental commitment, time, and thought, some things you may or may not want to invest in the relationship at all! Yet it is a fascinating process and I recommend that everyone try it at least once. When doing this analysis, you will really begin to grasp the power of the natal I Ching hexagrams and the depth of knowledge they can impart to you.

Remember the old adage, "Knowledge is power."

Taoist Meditations and Visualization Exercises

This section is provided for those people who want to go one step farther in using the powers of the trigrams and the hexagrams to better their
lives. If you are satisfied with simply learning about yourself, your friends,
or your family, then the first part of this book will satisfy you. If, on the
other hand, you wish to actively change yourself through hexagram and trigram meditations, visualizations, and other exercises, then read this section.

Just as it is not necessary for you to be a Hindu to benefit from Yoga,
it is not necessary for you to be a Taoist to gain great insight and practical
benefits from these exercises. You are your own best counselor, therapist, or
healer. Self-knowledge is the most important knowledge. In the following
pages you will find a number of practical, active, fun, and maybe even life-
changing exercises that use Taoist principles and the natal hexagram system
to help you substantially improve your own life. Think of these exercises as
ways to take back personal power that has always been yours and use it to
become a happier, healthier, more balanced person.

The section is divided into two parts. The first is strictly concerned
with exercises and visualizations that use your natal trigrams and your
natal hexagram to help you grow and evolve. The second part contains
some general Taoist meditations that have proven very helpful for my students over the years. I hope both parts are interesting and helpful.

Feel free to pick and choose which meditations you want to try, though
it is recommended from experience that you do the natal trigram exercises
before attempting the natal hexagram exercises. This is simply because the
trigram exercises prepare your mind for the hexagram exercises. All of
these exercises have been done in numerous classes with great success; may
they help you as you grow and evolve in joy.

Natal Trigram and Hexagram Meditations

Natal Trigram Meditations

The purpose of this exercise is simply to use the trigrams in your natal
hexagram as psychological triggers to better understand and analyze your-

self. A surprising amount of self-knowledge can come from this easy exercise, and though we may not always like some things about ourselves, by facing the more difficult aspects of our personalities we can change them for the better.

The goal here is really twofold: to imprint your natal trigrams into your unconscious mind, and to further understand yourself on a deeper level. It is recommended that these be done to completion before other meditations or visualizations in this chapter are attempted. The reason for this is simple and is similar to installing software into your computer, though in this case the software is your natal trigrams and the computer is your mind. Once they have been successfully "installed," you can quickly call up your natal hexagram for more complex meditations and visualizations.

But first things first!

Preparing the Natal Trigrams

You will need, for many of the following exercises, a few simple things:

- A package of plain white index cards
- A wide-tip water-based black marker
- Incense, candles, or whatever else you'd like to add atmosphere
- A notebook or pad on which to write your notes
- A quiet time and place to do your meditations

On two of the blank white index cards, using a wide-tip black Magic Marker, draw the two trigrams of your natal hexagram. Look up the trigrams (page 15). On the back of each card, note down what each trigram represents. For example, if your hexagram is # 56, The Wanderer, like mine is, then you would have two cards like so:

Card 1:

(front:)

(On the back:)
LI: Fire - (Top Trigram)

Card 2:

(front:)

(On the back:)
K'EN: Mountain - (Bottom Trigram)

Sitting 1: Imprinting the Natal Trigrams

In this exercise you will concentrate on really understanding the trigrams of your natal hexagram on a deep level. Thus you will be making connections to the Yang and Yin aspects of yourself. By imprinting the trigrams and memorizing them and exploring the feelings and images they call up, you are paving the way for further, more serious meditations. This exercise is designed to unlock the powers of the natal trigrams within you.

Sit quietly in a room with low background lighting and simply stare at the first trigram as long as you can. Close your eyes every so often to see the afterimage of the trigram. Keep doing this until the afterimage is very clear to you when your eyes are closed and you can hold the image steady in your mind. This may take some practice and a bit of time. If it isn't working or you're not relaxed, try again another time.

When you are clearly able to hold the trigram in your mind's eye, totally relax all your muscles, breathe deeply, and feel the power of the trigram fill your consciousness.

Now comes the important part: Let your mind run free while holding the image of the trigram steady. This takes a little practice. It is a lot like daydreaming. Think about what this trigram represents. My top trigram, LI (Fire), conjured up images of flames and glowing embers, rushing people and bright sunrises. After thinking about what your upper trigram means, let images spontaneously arise; make a mental note of them but do not try to change or manipulate them. You are training your mind to understand and relate to this trigram. When images stop coming or when you start having trouble holding the trigram image in your mind, it means that the process is coming to a close. This can happen at any time and it signifies that you are all done with the sitting.

When you finish any of the meditations in this book, it is important to reabsorb the Chi, or energy, that you have put out. In a practical sense, you need to return to an alert and conscious state. This can be done with a simple exercise called the Returning Chi: Put your index finger to your lips, inhale deeply, and see the focus of your meditation (in this case, the trigram) being absorbed into your heart, into a point of light. Exhale and open your eyes.

After every meditation, it is important for you to write down for future reference the images that came to you during the meditation. The various images you get during meditation are like dreams; they have meaning on a deep level. When you do this, do not try to analyze the images, just note them down and let them go.

When this last visualization has been done to your satisfaction, do the same exercise with your lower natal trigram after you have taken some time to study what it represents. This trigram represents your Inner Character.

Repeat the process as noted in Sitting 1, meditating on your lower trigram, relax, breathe deeply, and let your mind go as before. This lower natal trigram will teach you about your inner, or subconscious, mind and the way it works; it is the manifestation of yourself as Yin. In my case, my lower trigram is K'EN, or the mountain. When I first sat and worked with my lower trigram I got some fun images, including: a table, Mount Baker, a house, a Yogi meditating, a big rock, a dark forest, and a pyramid.

Of course, close with the Returning Chi exercise. You have now imprinted both of your natal trigrams into your deep mind and you are ready to really unlock the hidden powers of your natal trigrams and your natal hexagram.

Sitting 2: Empowering the Natal Trigrams

When you are ready to really empower yourself using your natal trigrams, get into a meditative, relaxed situation as before and again take out your natal trigram cards. Meditate on your upper trigram again. Close your eyes and bring forth the mental image of that trigram. Now, also bring forth all the images, feelings, thoughts, and emotions you have come to associate with that trigram, including many of the thoughts and images you received through that trigram in Sitting 1. Now comes the tricky part: You must hold the image of the trigram in your mind while visualizing yourself and how you live, work, play, love, fight, and so on. See all your outward words and actions in terms of this trigram, then ask yourself:

- What are the positive qualities of this trigram in my outer life?
- What are the negative qualities of this trigram in my inner life?

You will receive all sorts of interesting thoughts, ideas, and insights about yourself as images and feelings swirl about the image of the trigram held in your mind's eye. Do not attach to any one image or insight, just focus on yourself and how you live and act. Just let the images come.

When the exercise naturally seems to end, again do the Returning Chi exercise and write down what you discovered about yourself through your upper natal trigram!

In my case, focusing on my upper natal trigram, LI, I came up with the following images of things I do, say, and feel:

Laughing, thinking quickly, talking too fast, having lots of ideas, being creative, getting angry quickly, yelling too much, being cheerful a lot, being very friendly and outgoing, being critical, being sharp-tongued, being impatient, encouraging others, figuring things out quickly, being a hard worker for short bursts of time, being jittery, being high energy, always rushing around, trying to do too much, feeling high and low very quickly, being easily offended and hurt, smiling a lot, being assertive, being aggressive . . .

As you do this exercise, it is important that you not attach emotionally to any of the images or thoughts that come or in any way try to deal with them. The whole idea is to push the ego aside and, using the trigrams, get an insightful, objective look at how you live and work and function in the world. Remember, according to Taoism nothing is good or bad in and of itself. Getting angry at someone who deserves it is acceptable; feeling depressed when you are hurt is also acceptable. Nothing in and of itself is negative unless it blocks your flowing, your growth, your evolution.

After you have finished meditating on your upper natal trigram, focus again on your lower natal trigram and do the same meditation.

When I sat and worked with my lower trigram, K'EN, in this way, the images I saw concerning myself and my life were:

Being solidly built, having a stocky body, eating too much, being stubborn, being surly, being passive aggressive, being loyal, being strong, working hard, sitting around too much, being hedonistic, brooding, suppressing fears, being a bit of a bully, ignoring advice, being very supportive, being generous, being conscientious, ignoring problems . . .

Of course I ended with the Returning Chi exercise and I noted down these images.

Analyzing the Trigram Meditations

Sitting 1 and Sitting 2 should be very natural meditations and not at all forced or pushed. You should be very passive, just receiving images and information and not attaching any kind of emotion to them. This may take some practice and some time. A few memories or images may emerge that are painful and hard to deal with. You can end a sitting at any time with no harm to yourself; just do the finger-to-lips reabsorbing at the end to earth yourself. The key to making this work is to keep most of your attention and focus on the image of the trigram in your mind as the other thoughts and images come and go. If your mind begins to wander away from the trigram, stop the sitting.

If you find issues coming up about yourself that you don't want to deal with at the moment, then just stop and do the meditation another time. Because this process bypasses the ego by focusing on a simple primal form as a trigger (a trigram), a surprising amount of repressed information may emerge. Though initially painful in some cases, knowledge of the self is the key to all growth and evolution. To finally see some patterns in our behaviors or attitudes that may be holding us back from our full potential means that we can then move on to correct imbalances or at least be more appropriate in our functioning. Since the only negative in the Taoist path is that which restricts or goes against the Tao, the process here is not the very Western attack/eliminate process at all—it is acceptance and understanding and, where necessary, rebalancing. Still, before adjusting can come, Self-discovery must be completed.

The first step, in Sitting 1, is to deeply understand the two trigrams that make up your natal hexagram and what they mean in general and to you and your unique unconscious mind. You are introducing these trigrams to your deep mind in order to assure success with future meditations.

The more personal meditations (Sitting 2) are more important. They give you clear information into how you Are your natal trigrams. What does this mean? It means that you are a special and unique blend of forces, and now, through meditation, you can really see how those forces flow through you to create the patterns and experiences in your life. What good is this? Well, you will gain three practical benefits from these meditations.

First, you will immediately gain perspective on who you are and what you do. By using the trigrams as foci, you remove your ego from the meditation, thereby allowing yourself to clearly see your thoughts and deeds.

During this meditation, you will often start a bit and silently say, "Do I really do that? Do I really come off that way? Do I say those kinds of things?" You will be able to see yourself as others do. Second, you will gain insights and flashes concerning your character and your life that may seem to come from out of the blue. Because you are opening yourself up and asking your deep mind for wisdom, you will surely receive it. The trigrams form bridges into the deep mind; you will be amazed at what comes strolling across them!

Lastly, you will gain some very clear images and ideas on how to better your life immediately. Once you are aware of a behavior or an attitude, you can most easily change it, especially if you can link it with a trigram. For example, when I begin to lose my temper, I always say to myself, "Don't be so LI! Cool that fire!" and it works! It gives me an easy handle on aspects of my own personality.

Now that you have completed the process of deeply understanding your natal trigrams, pat yourself on the back and think about the notes you have written. You can always do these exercises again—in fact, I recommend it. There is always more to learn!

Balancing the Natal Trigrams

Now that you have a deep understanding of the two trigrams or powers that make up your Natal Hexagram, you can gain further understanding of your Will and facilitate the balancing of Heaven and Earth within yourself and your life.

The ancient Taoist sages talked a lot about Heaven and Earth and balancing the two. In fact, sometimes they saw the universe as one big hexagram; the top two lines were Heaven, the bottom two lines were Earth, and the middle two lines were Humanity. We have already seen that Heaven is a code for Yang and what it means and that Earth is a code for Yin and what it means as well. If we are each a unique blending of Yin and Yang (Heaven and Earth), then it follows that keeping our lives on track—that is, following our Path—is a matter of harmonizing those two forces in our selves and in our lives.

We know that the upper trigram is the Heaven place and the lower trigram is the Earth place, and your natal hexagram reading in the first part of this book clearly tells you how these two interact. It is also true that as you move through your life, your Natal Hexagram is altering and changing. Your job, of course, is to improve yourself and your life by uncovering your true nature while working on the negative aspects and utilizing the positive aspects of your natal hexagram. The key here is to maintain Harmony between the different parts of your being as represented by Yin and Yang.

This exercise will help you perform a reality check on the relationship between your conscious mind (Heaven, top position) and your Unconscious mind (Earth, bottom position). A balanced and harmonious relationship between these two is vital to your functioning. If you ignore your unconscious, your hidden roots and dreams and urges, you will inevitably begin to sabotage yourself and do things unconsciously that impede your conscious "outer" life. On the other hand, if you ignore your conscious mind and focus too much on your fantasies, dreams, desires, and "inner world," then you will waste your time and all sorts of problems will occur in the "real" world due to your lack of attention to the practical day-to-day necessities of life.

This simple meditation will tell you whether you are placing more stress on your outer (Yang/conscious) world or on your inner (Yin/unconscious) mind. You will need a white card or piece of paper with your natal hexagram drawn on it with the same wide-tip marker you used before!

Relax. Do deep breathing for a minute or so. Slow your mind and center yourself. Stare at your natal hexagram until you can close your eyes and hold it in your mind's eye. This may take a little time. It is a bit harder to do than visualizing a trigram, but if you have mastered visualizing your trigrams, then the process will be much easier.

When you can hold the image of your natal hexagram clearly in your mind, you are ready. Now, look carefully at the image of it in your mind. Either the top or bottom trigram will most likely be clearer, brighter, easier to visualize or possibly even larger.

Remember which trigram is "stronger" than the other, and open your eyes.

If it is the upper trigram, it means you are focusing too much on the conscious or outer world and neglecting the inner/unconscious world. If it is the lower trigram that is clearer, brighter, or stronger in appearance, then the opposite is true.

Here are some ways to help balance these two parts of your being. Periodically checking yourself by visualizing your natal hexagram will show you how you are progressing. The goal, of course, is to have the entire visualized hexagram all the same in intensity, size, focus, and so on when you meditate on it. If this is the case, then you are successfully balancing Heaven and Earth in your being, well done!

If you have overbalanced Heaven/Yang/conscious (upper trigram):

- Pay attention to your dreams and write them down.
- Schedule more quiet, relaxing daydreaming time into your life.
- Do more right-brain things—dabbling in art, listening to music, playing silly games.
- Take a break or a vacation and focus on sensations and feelings.
- Plan time for more passive entertainment, like watching videos or movies.
- Let more people do things for you, pull back a bit from so much socializing.
- Meditate, do Yoga, and so on.
- Return to nature and simply experience it.

If you have overbalanced Earth/Yin/unconscious (lower trigram):

- Pay attention to your daily schedule more, get a day planner, organize your life better.
- Do fewer things that others want or tell you to do and do more things you want to do.

- Write down several things you always talk about or fantasize about and plan a day and time to Do them! Do one at a time.
- Look about your home or workplace and schedule times to get projects done that you have neglected.
- Socialize more with people, read more about the world (nonfiction), and spend more time doing "active" things. Turn off your TV!
- Return to nature with the object of learning something concrete: identifying birds, learning about trees, or whatever interests you.

Unlocking Your Complete Natal Hexagram

Just as the trigram meditations are sort of warm-up exercises (though vital ones!), a way of training your conscious and subconscious to accept and use the trigram images to communicate to you, the following natal hexagram meditations represent the payoff! Here the goal is intense, concrete self-discovery through meditation (call it therapy if you like), and this can readily be accomplished by doing some simple meditations while focusing on your natal hexagram.

Though this may seem a bit complex at first, never fear, it's really simple. These "sittings," as I call them, have worked well for hundreds of people and you can do them all by yourself. The results range from simple Self-understanding and important insights to spiritual breakthroughs. Though confronting some of the unpleasant parts of yourself may not be much fun, the process is gentle and you can usually overcome or improve your negative character aspects once you confront them with just a little effort.

The process is simple. You will first "imprint" your natal hexagram into your deep mind, just as you did with the trigrams. You have already begun this process if you have done the previous exercises. The pattern is basically the same as with Sitting 1 and Sitting 2 in the natal trigram meditations section. After visualizing your natal hexagram, you will open your mind to imprinting images and attributes related to that hexagram. Next, you will open your mind to viewing yourself and how you interact in your life with others through the lens of your natal hexagram.

These visualization exercises will give you important insights into key attitudes and behaviors that are both positive and negative. The images and feelings will be more specific to you and your life than those evoked by the trigram meditations. They will bring together many of the feelings, thoughts, images, and insights you gained from your natal trigram meditations into a more centered and cohesive whole.

By comparing your natal hexagram reading in the first part of this book with the meditation-induced insights and images you gain from these meditations, you will see how much you have evolved in your life and what specific behaviors and attitudes you need to work on to become a better person!

This sounds like a tall order, but you will be surprised how easy it all is and what a powerful, interesting person you really are. You have the power to use your natal hexagram as a jumping-off place to improve your life in any way you choose.

Imputting the Natal Hexagram

As in the previous exercise, carefully draw the full natal hexagram on a blank index card and study it. Make sure you go back and study your natal hexagram reading as well before beginning this exercise.

As mentioned, my natal hexagram is # 56, The Wanderer, so I drew this card:

Sitting 1B:

Focus on the hexagram with a relaxed, open mind and unwavering gaze for as long as possible. When you close your eyes, the afterimage should be clear. Keep opening and closing your eyes until the afterimage is solid and you can keep it steady in your mind's eye. This will be harder to do than with the trigrams because it is six lines instead of three, but with a little practice and patience you will soon have it down pat.

As in the first trigram sittings, close your eyes, focus on the image of your natal trigram, and let it trigger images naturally. Let them flow out of, around, and over the hexagram image in your mind and do not seek to control or manipulate this flow of images.

End your meditation, when you wish, with the Returning Chi exercise.

Here are some of the images that came to me:

Windswept ruins, a mountain hiking trail I know well, a lantern hanging on a tree, stars, a lone tree on a hill, a leaf in a stream, an old man walking over a mountain, a candle on a cake, a tightrope walker, the Fool card of the Tarot, my passport, a boat going down a river in Thailand, a prayer flag flying from a peak, a hotel all closed up, a baby all alone in the woods . . .

When you are done with the sitting, put your finger to your lips, inhale, and see the hexagram being absorbed into your heart and into a point of light. Again, do not analyze these images, just note them down in your diary right after the sitting.

Later, before doing a second sitting, go back in this book and find your natal hexagram reading and study the attributes carefully at least once, if not a few times. You will most likely get some interesting insights regarding the images you received and some of your traits. Free associate. The most unlikely images will trigger various emotions and ideas. For example, to me, the light in the tree symbolized not giving up, continuing my studies. The closed hotel reminded me of some emotional issues I was suppressing and it spurred me to deal with them. These sorts of images and the connections they make are often very personal but should always be noted down.

Sitting 2B

When you are ready, sit comfortably and begin the sitting as before. Focus on the natal hexagram and burn it into your mind until it is clearly there when you close your eyes. Empty your mind of all thoughts and focus on the hexagram, then call forth your Self, the center of your very being, and feel your whole body, mind, and spirit enter the hexagram. The idea is to picture yourself as an observer and the hexagram as a sort of lens through which you are observing yourself. View your daily behaviors as you go through life, all focused through your hexagram. Then, open yourself to inner thoughts, images, feelings, insights, and revelations. It may take a couple of tries to get this, but it works. Many different people have had great success with this exercise, so don't despair if it takes a bit of effort.

You want to be focusing on the hexagram as you call up your True Will, your Path, your Self. Keep yourself open and relaxed, focus all your conscious mind on your natal hexagram and on visualizing yourself. In this way you will simply receive what the hexagram is saying about "you" and your specific traits. Don't struggle with anything that flows forth. Any distractions or weird interruptions in your visualizing should be ignored; that is just your ego, an unwelcome distraction. Try to be the Taoist impartial observer, watching yourself and your life from a distance. As usual, reabsorb your hexagram using the finger-to-lips practice after you are done.

As the images of Self flow, take a dispassionate note of them as they go by.

End the sitting with the Returning Chi exercise and note down your results.

Here are some of the images I received from meditating on my natal hexagram:

I'm daydreaming about traveling, feeling restricted in relationships, being picky at work, laughing a lot with friends and family, traveling in Japan and China, making maps, being foolish about rules, impatiently demanding things, offending someone without noticing, helping a friend through a rough time, being very faithful to my wife, playing too much, tickling my son, forgetting appointments, snapping at a student, losing work due to bragging, meditating on a hill, daydreaming . . .

It is important that you now review your natal hexagram reading given earlier in this book. Compare the images you saw with those traits noted in your natal hexagram reading. You want to think about and then note down the following:

- Positive traits manifesting in your life
- Negative traits manifesting in your life
- Positive traits not manifesting in your life
- Negative traits not manifesting in your life

Let me show you how this broke down concerning my natal hexagram and how this helped me. Sitting 3 and Sitting 4, done with my natal hexagram, The Wanderer, yielded a lot of images and some very clear realizations. This was especially true when I compared my sitting notes with my natal hexagram reading. Here are some of the insights I received the last time I did this:

Positive Traits Manifesting: I am often: expressing my love of traveling, being friendly and funny, working hard to help others, working on expressing my spirituality, being a good mate and father, and being playful.

Negative Traits Manifesting: I still have problems that I need to work on concerning: losing my temper, keeping my feelings suppressed, being too rowdy, offending people, being too picky, being absentminded, and being too proud.

Positive Traits Not Manifesting (I found these by comparing my notes with the traits in the reading for my natal hexagram, #56.): I need to cultivate: being more decisive, being more diligent at my job, really traveling instead of talking about it, being kinder to everyone, and nipping more problems in the bud.

Negative Traits Not Manifesting (I found these by comparing my notes with the traits in the reading for my natal hexagram, #56.): I'm not: as hyper as I was, as quick-tempered, as foolish, or as self-centered. (All things I have worked on, good for me!)

So, this gives me a clear and fairly easy-to-grasp idea of how I am now as opposed to the characteristics and traits I manifested at birth as symbolized in my natal hexagram. This gives me clear goals to work for in self-improvement. Call these "self-therapy" sessions or Taoist meditations; for all intents and purposes, they are the same. By learning to use your natal hexagram to tune in on your psyche and your unconscious, you will forever be able to get a remarkably clear reality check on who you are, how you are evolving, and what you can do to continue growing.

There is no limit to the number of times you can do these exercises. In fact, after doing them once or twice, you can simply "check in" with your natal hexagram when riding a bus or having a cup of coffee to see what issues need work. You will also be creating a stronger bond with your inner Self, and this will lead to spiritual discoveries and insights.

The following are a few other simple Taoist rituals that may help you in your life. They are included here so that you may use some simple Taoist techniques, modernized just a bit, to reduce stress, center yourself, protect yourself from whatever forces are imposing on you, and generally lead a happier, more prosperous life as you focus on your real work: evolving mentally, physically, and spiritually.

Natal Hexagram Self-Knowledge Meditations

The universe is the Tao and it manifests as Yin and Yang. In our lives these two essences can exist as our outer or conscious mind and our inner or unconscious mind. Your natal hexagram, because it partakes of both worlds, can be a unique tool for gaining wisdom from the universe through both your Yang/consciousness and Yin/unconsciousness. Following are ways to ask and receive clear answers and wisdom from the worlds of Yang and Yin using the power of your natal hexagram.

Your natal hexagram, in these meditations, represents the point where you and the universe connect. It symbolizes the key to helping you develop your Self, or Center, and therefore helping you to follow your Teh, or Path, in a harmonious manner.

Sometimes you may feel stuck, blocked, or frustrated with things in your life. This may call for a quick and honest understanding of the root of the problems as they exist in the primal Tao, or universe. The root of any problem will lie in one of two places: the conscious mind (Yang), or the subconscious mind (Yin). These two exercises are designed to spur clear and decisive psychic understanding in order to help you grow and overcome problems. They are also lots of fun to do, even if everything is going fine in your life! Try them and see.

These two exercises, while seemingly simplistic, often trigger deep insights and strong emotional releases. They are designed to help you get on with the process of following your true path and being a harmonious and happy person as you channel the Creative in your life.

Yang Self-Knowledge Meditation

You will need a mirror at eye level, at least one square foot in size, but a larger mirror will certainly do. You will need to place a chair or comfortable cushion before this mirror so that you are staring into it. It should reflect only your face and nothing distracting in the background. You will also need a wide-tip dry erasable black marker.

Draw your natal hexagram on the mirror; make sure the whole thing is about eight inches by eight inches or so. When you are done, you should be looking at your face with your natal hexagram in the center of it.

Before we begin, a word about mirrors. Mirrors have been sacred Taoist amulets from the dawn of prehistory; in fact, small polished metal mirrors were sacred in many different ancient cultures, from Egypt to Mesoamerica, and such a magical culture as that of Tibet still utilize small mirror-charms to remove evil. In Japan, the round mirror is the symbol of the sacred Sun Goddess, the most powerful Being in Shinto mythology, and the light a sacred mirror sheds is said to banish all evil. In African-based religions and their offshoots, such as Voodoo, the mirror is said to be a gateway to other worlds, especially to the world of the ancestor spirits and the Loa, or gods. Because in Taoism the mirror is often a symbol of the Tao (in that it reflects all things while being itself nothing), it is an appropriate tool for meditation and spiritual self-discovery. Here is how it works:

Get comfortable sitting in front of the mirror. Make sure you will be alone with no distractions for as long as you want to pursue this exercise— at least half an hour is suggested, though an hour is better. You will be surprised how quickly time can pass during this practice. The room should be dimly lit; a candle or two is perfect.

When you are ready to begin, close your eyes and imagine a ring of light about you. Mentally cast away and banish all cares, worries, problems, and so on. Breathe deeply, calmly, and with measured breaths. Silently repeat a phrase about wanting to know yourself through your natal hexagram, in my case I often mentally say, over and over: "I seek to know Self."

You can also ask about a specific problem or issue concerning yourself. For example, one I recently used was: "How can I eliminate my writer's block?"

For each of us the sentence will be different. It is up to you and will focus your mind and Self on the issue at hand.

Do this for a short time until you are really calm and centered and quiet, then let all fade away and be quiet outwardly and inwardly. Close your eyes. Breathe deeply and relax. Visualize your natal hexagram, then, when it is clear in your mind, open your eyes and focus on the drawn hexagram on the mirror before you.

Do not strain! Relax completely. Let the image of the mirror hexagram go in and out of focus, it doesn't matter. Just keep your gaze on the mirror. After a time, your vision will blur and strange things will appear in the mirror. Don't let anything startle you, they are merely daydreams and imagery from your own mind. Let the experience flow naturally, don't hold on to anything. Keep silently repeating the phrase you have chosen.

When you have gotten your answer, or feel that the experience is over or that you've had enough (or your legs begin to fall asleep!), close your eyes. You will see a strong glowing afterimage of your natal hexagram. Inhale deeply and calmly three times; as you do so, see the image of the hexagram get pulled into your body and sit glowing in your heart until it fades away.

Again, imagine a ring of light about you, dispelling all fear and problems and negativity. Then arise and find a notebook or some paper and write down what you saw, felt, and experienced!

This is a powerful exercise that almost always gives clear answers to questions or insights into problems or projects. If you do it a number of times, you will find that it gets easier and easier to connect with your Self and to get information about yourself and your life. I find that I am even able to ask simple questions through my natal hexagram and I get answers in the mirror in the forms of flashes of intuition and images.

Here is a short synopsis from some notes on one session a friend (we'll call her S.) did using this exercise. Her question was "Why am I feeling blue?" Her natal hexagram is #14, Possession in Great Measure. Here are the images she got:

A dragon, fire and ice, a fir tree, a musical note [heard], rope, a black horse, ashtray, a cat litter box [!] . . .

After reviewing her natal hexagram reading, she noted down a few conclusions about what her Self was telling her:

Dragon—The creative power, to be more creative (one of her traits) and find more ways to do art, which she loves but hasn't been inspired to do lately.

Fire and ice— She is swinging to emotional extremes too much, she realized that she needs to moderate herself more.

Tree— A symbol of spirituality for her, of sitting, meditating. One of her life lessons is to focus more on the spiritual. She is planning to take a yoga class.

Musical note— Could be that music is something that will benefit her more or she may need to find more harmony in her life.

Black horse— This represents freedom for her, the urge to travel, and also simply her love of horseback riding, which she had to give up for the winter but which she misses and will return to.

Ashtray— She feels "burned out," like she is doing too much. She needs to cut back on her duties and to organize her time better.

Cat box— She never feels her house is clean enough and it would help her to clean out more things from her life and dump all the old ... stuff! ...

Of course, all of these symbols have special meaning only to S., but after a little thought and after referring back to her natal hexagram reading, it became clear to her that several of these images were telling her how to get back on track in her life. Many were simply telling her things she knew already deep down. This is the point of the exercise.

Yin Self-Knowledge Exercise

This exercise has to do with taking your natal hexagram right into your unconscious mind and seeing what your unconscious mind has to say about how you are doing in your life and how you can improve things. This exercise seems quite easy, but as with all things concerning dreams and remembering them, it may take a few tries. The reward will be worth it, though, I guarantee it.

Dreams are one of the greatest and most neglected tools for self-discovery and self-improvement we have. Whether you believe as Freud did— that our unconscious minds are just giant depositories of our repressed desires, frustrations, and fantasies—or if you are more of a Jungian—and believe that the unconscious holds the keys of mythology, visions, and personal evolution—dreams are still an important tool for personal growth. By planting certain symbols or ideas into the unconscious, we can cause it to talk back and give us a dreamtime take on any number of things. In this case we are focusing on the natal hexagram and asking the Dreamtime for specific images and advice on fulfilling our Teh, or Will. Often it will come up with things that our conscious mind has forgotten or suppressed as well as positive courses of action. As with the previous exercise, you can also focus on a specific problem or question if you want an answer to a current conundrum or problem.

To do this exercise, all you need is the ability to remember your natal hexagram (write it on a card if you need to practice) and a bed! Here is how it works:

Make sure that you are tired and will fall asleep easily. Don't have any coffee, tea, sugar, or alcohol before going to bed. Lie on your back, get comfortable, and begin to breathe deeply. Relax your whole body. As you become sleepy and comfortable, imagine a ring of light about you. Mentally cast away and banish all cares, worries, problems, and so on. Breathe deeply, calmly, and with measured breaths. Silently repeat a phrase you have selected, as in the previous exercise. In my case, I might silently say: "I seek to know Self." You can also choose another sentence or question, as in the first exercise. My friend F. used the phrase: "Where should I live after college?" He then dreamed of the desert. He now lives in Arizona!

As you silently repeat the phrase you have chosen, snuggle in your bed, close your eyes, and imagine a door in your mind's eye. Make the door any shape, color, or style you wish. When you can clearly see the door and hold it in your mind, visualize your natal hexagram on the door in bold black lines. Hold that image until it is extremely clear and solid and until you are just about to fall asleep . . . then open the door, enter and fall asleep! It may take a little practice to get the timing down.

When you wake up the next day, before you do anything else (important!), write down your dreams. Compare the images and actions in your dreams with your natal hexagram reading and with what is happening in your life. You'll find some amazing information in your dreams. If you had no dreams, or you can't remember any, try it again. It seems to work with just about everyone, but not always the first time. Perseverance pays off.

I recently did this exercise and I will quote from my diary what I experienced:

Very sleepy so went to bed about midnight. I lay on my back and visualized a door. I could see it clearly, it was big and white with almost Greek-looking columns on the sides. It had four panels and looked a lot like the door of the old house I lived in when I was a kid. It was harder to visualize my natal hexagram (#56) on the door, but when I imagined it as painted on in matte black paint, I could suddenly hold it clearly. As I started to fade, I opened the door and I fell asleep.

Dreams: First, I was in a cabin in the mountains with a lot of people I don't know, but it was some foreign country and I was doing my best to learn their weird language. Suddenly I was in a vast valley, still in the mountains, very alpine area, cold, cloudy, and far in the distance was Mt. Everest! I was in Nepal! An older man with a beard came out of the lonesome cabin and told me he was living there for years studying the mountain and photographing it . . . then I woke up.

Most of my interpretations of this dream are personal. I really want to visit Nepal, for example, but a few points became clearer after I referred back to my natal hexagram reading, something I suggest you do. My hexagram is Fire over Mountain and my dream of the brightly sunlit Mt. Everest is a clear symbol of that. I also interpreted the dream to mean that I must learn to listen to people more and learn to "speak their language"— that is, to speak to people the way they want me to, not the way I want to. I think the old man represented my Self, or he was a symbol of a higher part of myself. He was telling me to "study the mountain"— that is, to focus more on the calm, meditative, staid, stable side of my persona and emphasize stability more in my life. Very good advice for a new homeowner!

This will, I hope, give you some indication of what this exercise can do for you. The communications you get from your unconscious mind will, no doubt, be very personal, often symbolic, and possibly hard to decipher at first, but if you keep studying your natal hexagram (and your Self!), things will almost always become clearer. Pleasant dreams!

Natal I Ching Affirmations

Before going any further with the mystical (or psychological) subject of meditations and visualization exercises, we should discuss the easiest and maybe most effective way to use the information in your natal hexagram reading to better your life: affirmations.

Affirmations, as they are commonly understood, are simply not used in the most effective manner by most people. By definition, an affirmation is a phrase or sentence that directly sums up what a person wants to change for the better in his or her life. This phrase or sentence is put on a piece of paper, stuck to the bathroom mirror, attached to the refrigerator, carried in the wallet, taped to the dashboard, or whatever. The idea is that constantly seeing this affirmation and, more importantly, constantly repeating it will prime the person on both a conscious and unconscious level to make the targeted change in his or her life. If repeated enough times, it will actually modify behavior and attitude.

Some generic examples I've seen are: "I will accept my life and all it holds," "I am getting better and better every day," "I feel love and give love and accept love."

Such general affirmations are all well and good and can't do any harm—unless they cause the person to become depressed because they are not feeling enough love—but they are not specific enough.

The problem with most affirmations is not the theory, which is basically sound, but that most of them are too generic. Briefly, the reason affirmations can work is that our brains are somewhat programmable. If we repeat something enough times, it will sink into the unconscious mind and cause changes to occur. This is why repetitive advertising is so effective.

True belief, that which is both conscious and unconscious, is immensely powerful. It can heal people or make them ill, attract others or repel them. This is why parents must be careful what they repeat to their children. A child who is constantly told he or she is smart will likely grow up with good grades and great self-confidence, no matter what his or her IQ might be. Of course, the opposite is also true.

Most affirmations are not repeated/read enough and they are too general. The first shortcoming can easily be solved by more focus. When you have settled on an affirmation, expect to spend a month to a year on it, not just a day or two. Focus clearly on what you want to change and do so by repeating the phrase several times a day. How many times is enough? As many times as possible. If you can connect something you do daily, like meals or brushing your teeth or checking your e-mail, with a schedule for "programming" affirmations, you are more likely to do them consistently and therefore get results. Consistency and repetition are the keys.

Now, most people want to change too much too fast; they want to be thinner, smarter, richer, and nicer all at once! Real change, that which lasts, occurs slowly and in a focused arena of life. Also, it is impossible to make someone who is genetically short or big-boned any different. This goes for personality types as well. A person who is overly energetic can become calmer and a person with little motivation can acquire more drive and ambition, but a leopard cannot change his spots. In short, think clearly about who you are and what you want to change: Is it realistic? If not, then you are "going against the Tao" and more or less doomed to failure. Everyone can change, but the first step to changing yourself is to know who you really are and what you are all about. It is easy to get lost here, because what our parents or society thinks we should be (and programs us to believe!) is not necessarily who we really are nor where our Path must take us.

So, the first thing to do is to review your natal hexagram reading, then, after accepting the positive and negative about yourself, look at what can be improved. A likely place to start is the life lessons. Here you are clearly given the things you need to work on in your life. From these you can create powerful and tailor-made affirmations for yourself. For example, if you look at the life lessons for my natal hexagram, #56, you will see why I crafted the following affirmations for myself:

I shall be more sensitive to the needs of others
I shall be more appropriate in my dealings with others
I shall resolve all disputes in a calm manner
I shall be humbler when dealing with others

When I'm going to work with these affirmations, I pick and focus on only one of them at a time. For example, I am currently working on a variation of the first affirmation, being more sensitive to the needs of others. I started about three months ago and I will continue for at least three more months. I repeat it quietly when I'm commuting in the morning (a stressful time) and also when I drive home at night. Others have noted a positive change in this part of my personality. The affirmation I am using is:

"I will be kinder to others."

Look at your natal hexagram's life lessons. You will find that you are able to write several affirmations that fit you and the things you need to work on. Choose one and begin! Other affirmations can be created from the traits list or even from the negative tendencies list in your natal hexagram reading, but I recommend that you begin with the life lessons section since these comments go to the heart of the work you need to do in this life. The fact that it comes from your personal natal hexagram shows that what you are choosing to work on is what you need to be working on anyway; it is part of your Path, or Way, and so is in line with your True Will. In this way you know that you are flowing with the Tao, and it is said that he who moves with the Tao has the universe behind him!

General Taoist Meditations

There were three basic goals in traditional Taoist spiritual practice: The first was to protect the individual or family or clan from negative forces or misfortune. The second was to understand and know the Tao and to accept one's place in society and the world by finding and following one's Path. This, it is said, leads to a good life. The third aim was to further evolve the Self and the spirit so as to eventually transform oneself into an immortal (i.e., a balanced, long-lived, powerful, and happy being) by becoming one with the Tao.

Whether you look upon these as spiritual or material goals is almost beside the point when we think in practical terms. You can see Taoist practices as helping you come to terms with your conscious and unconscious mind, your inner Self (spirit), your Shadow (darkside), and your ego: In short, all the aspects of your psyche.

The same goals that motivated ancient Taoists reflect the goals most of us have today, but we usually word them differently. We want to be protected from bad luck and misfortune, we want to know our place in the world (and make it a nice prosperous place!), and we want to become better, healthier, happier people. Think of these as modern takes on ancient wisdom or simply see them as two ways of seeing the same goals. The fact is, using some Taoist visualization techniques will positively change you and your view of the world around you.

If you wish to try some of these exercises, keep an open mind and remember what the *I Ching* always tells us: "Perseverance furthers." Anything done well and with the strength of Will shall succeed. Even if you don't become immortal, it could very well improve your life in practical ways. (If you do become an immortal, please let me know!)

Now let us examine several Taoist exercises and how they can be adapted and used with great effectiveness by people today. The earliest geometric forms used for Taoist meditations in China were the Square, representing: Yin—Earth, and the Circle, representing: Yang—Heaven. When the two are combined, as they are in may forms of Chinese art and even in Chinese coins, it denotes the balance and power created between Yin and Yang as one becomes the other becomes the other and on and on. The famous Temple of Heaven in Beijing rises gloriously above the valley atop two huge, marble levels: The first is a square; this rises up and gives way to a level that is round and another that is square. This culminates in the Temple, which is itself round and contains a square altar. It was here that the emperor communed with the powers of Heaven and Earth combined, for the good of his nation.

Taoists thought of the mundane world and the life they built in this material reality as a "square," often represented by the four directions or by a square seat or throne. The square in this system is the primal form of solidity and of form (Earth).

Taoists thought of this solidity, the physical mundane world they lived in, as residing in the center of the ever-expanding sphere of the cosmos, the ever-manifesting magical circle of abstract thought and spirit (Heaven).

As they merged their physical, material world with the ever-infinite spiritual universe, they integrated the square and circle, the cube and sphere. By doing this they become the Yin/Yang or Tai Chi.

To accomplish this, ancient Taoists concentrated on stilling their minds, using controlled breathing to cycle the energy through their bodies, and thus they would become so centered that they could touch the universal mystery by becoming the circle and square (Yin and Yang) combined. It is also interesting to note that ancient Western alchemists and philosophers referred to the perfect Soul as "the circle squared."

So, what does the Taoist sage or alchemist residing upon his sacred mountain have to do with us and our busy modern lives? Just this, the simple techniques and visualizations the Taoist sages used for understanding, identifying with, and finally manipulating these forces of nature can be used by you, here and now, to better your life.

Centering of Self as Heaven/Earth

One of the most pervasive causes of anxiety and unhappiness in our hectic, modern society is the feeling of being disconnected or rootless. Some people refer to this as feeling lost, unfocused, not being "together," or not being "centered." In our fast-paced, somewhat fragmented world, this is a common malaise, one that affects all of us at one time or another. Stress, excessive demands from work or family, lack of a grounded home-life, or emotional turmoil are common causes of this "out of it" feeling. Many people misdiagnose this as mild depression (not to be confused with clinical depression, a serious medical diagnosis). Others fear they are becoming overly alienated or neurotic.

From a Taoist viewpoint, a person who feels this way is simply removed from his or her Center or has lost his or her balance within the flow of the Tao that is the unfolding, flowing world around us. The cause could be any of a thousand things, but often it is simply attaching to one external thing or another, thus losing the Self amid the chaotic environment around us that pushes and pulls.

A very simple cure for this condition is to meditate and rediscover your true Center. You cannot seek balance and harmony outside yourself. The more unbalanced you become by reaching out of yourself for a calm center, the more your outer world will become unbalanced. Why? Because your inner world is a reflection of your outer world and vice versa. So, from both a psychological and a spiritual point of view, by pulling back to your Center, the beginning place of your true Self, you will recover your balance and your sense of perspective. You will become more rooted in the world and in your life. It really works.

Here is a very simple exercise for accomplishing this. It is also a good exercise to do before any other spiritual practice, including the other exercises in this book.

The Centering Meditation

You will need at least fifteen minutes of uninterrupted quiet in a softly lit room or, better yet, outside in a park or in the woods. The exercise is in two parts; experiment.

Sit quietly and comfortably.

Breathe in and out, calmly and deliberately.

Slow your breathing and deepen it, take full breaths that fill your lungs, and when you exhale, exhale all the air in your lungs.

Relax your body with every breath.

When you are ready, visualize light above you and shadow below you.

Above you is Heaven, below you is Earth.

Still your mind.

Now, breathe in slowly, and as you do so, pull into your body energy, light, and glowing power from above you, from Heaven.

See it fill your heart and from there fill your whole body.

Now exhale slowly.

As you do so, feel the energy flow through you, down through your body, into the Earth.

At the end of your exhalation feel the power of the Earth under you, supporting and nourishing you. Feel your roots deep in the Earth.

Now, reverse the polarity.

Inhale slowly and carefully.

See the strength, security, stillness and calm of the Earth rise up and fill your heart and then fill your body.

Exhale slowly, see the Yin/Earth energy pour up into Heaven, dispersing amid the light.

Do this cycle three times.

(Inhale Heaven, hold at heart/body, exhale to Earth.

Inhale Earth, hold at heart/body, exhale to Heaven.)

Then, still your mind and your breathing.

See the power of Heaven entering you from above.

See the power of Earth entering you from below.

See them meet in your heart.

Inhale deeply. See the two forces as Yin/Yang, forming the Tai Chi in your heart.

You are relaxed and are now reconnected with the Tao as it flows from Heaven to Earth and back again. Let it flow through you.

After this, become as still as you can. Close your eyes if they are not closed already.

Visualize a large solid cube under you. It is a throne or seat of sorts and it is very dark. Feel how solid it is, feel its density and depth. It is the densest, heaviest stone in the world, and you are solidly anchored to it. It fills you with a sense of stillness, security, solidity. This square is the soul of matter; hard, solid, strong, immobile form. It earths you. As you breathe deeply, all your stresses and worries flow into the cube. It absorbs them without a problem. All negative feelings, ideas, thoughts, and experiences flow down into the cube; it is the power of Earth and it will take all you don't need and "earth" it.

You are now the center of all matter and solidity.

Then, solidly centered on the square, imagine the world about you, the whole world, as a vast cosmic sphere that goes on forever and ever all about you, reaching out to the ends of the universe. It encompasses all the things in your life, in reality, in the cosmos, and it is constantly shifting, flowing, moving, and fluctuating as things are born, die, move about, and so on. Everything in this infinite sphere is energy, changing, transforming, reproducing, withdrawing—all energy in a multitude of forms. Feel how all these forces of energy make up your day, call for your attention, pull you this way and that, call to you, attract you, repulse you, and so on. But, here you are firmly seated on this square of pure Matter, and all is still. You can see the energy forms of the world and the universe move about you, but you are not affected by them.

You are the center of all energies and change.

Now, visualize the sphere slowly contracting, as the square expands. You do not move, you are a still center of light. Breathe deeply.

Now you become the square, and as it slowly merges with the sphere, you become the sphere, the chaotic all-embracing flow of energy patterns, as well.

Yet you are neither the square nor the sphere; you are the union of the two. You are Matter and Energy, yet both of these only exist where you are, and where you are is the center.

There is only energy and matter and neither can be destroyed; one merely changes from one to the other. At your mental command, the sphere becomes the cube and the cube becomes the sphere. As the center you balance the two. Breathe deeply and see both forms merge within you to form a shining point of light, your Self. It glows in your heart. Hold to this, nothing else.

Place both hands over your heart. You are one with your Self.

That's it. Yet once you have done this simple visualization exercise, you will be reinforcing your inner understanding of the flow of the Tao. Yin and Yang (Matter and Energy) can only manifest through you. Most of us realize that the universe is not a vague impersonal force, but we stop short of realizing that the world is not real unless it manifests through us.

This is not New Age thinking; it is solidly based in Taoist philosophy as well as quantum physics: The observer always affects what he is observing. Perceptions are everything and reality is what we perceive. If you feel centered and operate from a place where you are the center point, where matter shifts to energy and back again, then you will be very comfortable and will feel much more connected and right with your life and how it unfolds. In short, this exercise is to basically rediscover the fact that you are the center of your own life, that you have been "giving your power away" to the "10,000 things" that are simply ephemeral changing manifestations of the Tao. You are not your job or your family or your hobbies or your desires— you are a timeless, changeless center of the world, you are the Tao.

It is important that you grasp this if you wish to go further with the exercises we are exploring here. This is not intellectual philosophy, but a state of consciousness that transcends intellect. And it is not an attitude that pulls you from the world to be a saint or guru! In fact, Taoism has always stressed the practical and the mundane. We need not "find" anything; we simply need to remember our primal beginnings, to see the world again as a wondrous place like every child does. A child naturally balances the Yin and Yang; he or she instinctively knows that the world is a magical place of flowing matter and energy that can be influenced by your mind. It is when we learn that things are solid and inflexible and that life is full of responsibilities and desires and problems that we lose our center.

Yet all is not lost; your Center and the innocence it preserves is right there where it's always been. You have but to peel away the onion layers of the artificial world and all the mental constructs that you are taught are real and there you are, in the Center of your life again.

Pa Kua Meditation

The following exercises use the trigrams to improve the psychological and/or spiritual forces within you and within your life. Because the scope of this book is limited, we will simply explore the basics of using Pa Kua visualizations in two ways: first, for protection from misfortune, negative energies, and negative people; second, to attract positive energies, prosperity, and wealth.

I am quite sure that as you explore the Pa Kua, a number of other meditational uses will occur to you; go for it! It is my hope that a future volume
may contain additional Pa Kua explanations and exercises, but for now, let
us concentrate on two simple objectives of Pa Kua visualizations: protection and prosperity.

So, what is the Pa Kua? It is a circular arrangement of all eight trigrams
and it is considered the most powerful magical Taoist charm:

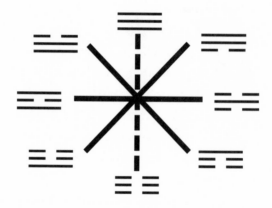

Taoists often simply make a Pa Kua charm by drawing or carving it, or
by painting it on wood, metal, or stone and then hanging it over the door
or window. Often the Yin/Yang symbol is seen in the center or there might
be a small circular mirror. These symbolize the Tao and the primal source
of all things. These Pa Kua charms can be found in any Chinatown and they
are very useful for meditation or to simply put up over your door to keep
nasty salesmen away! The Pa Kua in the following exercises, however, will
be created in your mind! Here's how.

The first thing you must do before you can begin the Pa Kua meditations is memorize the eight trigrams. This can be done very quickly with a
minimum of effort.

Take eight index cards and draw the eight trigrams on them. Refer back to the trigram list in the first part of this book (page10). On the back of each card, in pencil so it doesn't bleed through, mark what each trigram represents from the trigram list. For example, on the back of the card that has this trigram:

CH'IEN

You will write something like:

CH'IEN/ Heaven

Creative, strong, firm, light, ruler, cold,
serious, organizing, powerful, intensely focused,
centered, aggressive, assertive

When you have all eight cards done and in front of you, study them by simply focusing on each trigram and then turning the card over and focusing on what it represents. In a very short amount of time you will have them more or less memorized. When you can look at any card and remember the name of the trigram and what it generally represents, then you will have finished programming your conscious and subconscious with these symbols. Of course, you already know two of them well, the two that make up your natal hexagram!

Be aware that your ego might kick up a bit of fuss; no one likes to be superseded or put upon, and your ego is no different! Ignore all distractions until you have all eight trigrams down pat; then you will be ready to do all sorts of amazing things with these simple yet potent symbols.

It is said that the Pa Kua easily protects one from bad luck, psychic attacks, and evil spirits (even if they take the form of neighbors or co-workers!).

Aside from being a charm, the Pa Kua was aligned with all the directions like so:

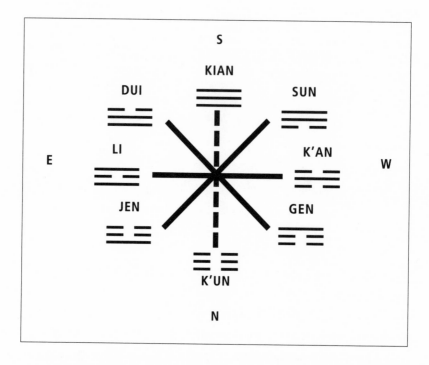

For you scholars out there, this is called the Primal Arrangement and was created during the earlier phase of the formation of the I Ching during the Chou dynasty.

The Pa Kua is always potent as a mental and/or spiritual protection for banishing negative people, energies, or situations when visualized as a protective circle. This is called Pa Kua Projection and this is how it is done:

Sit comfortably facing east, and then, clockwise, place the trigram cards about you in the Primal Arrangement as noted above. As you place each card, close your eyes and visualize that trigram floating in space in that direction; CHEN to the north, SUN to the northeast, K'AN to the east, and so on.

You may need a little practice to clearly visualize everything, and it is OK to refresh your memory by opening your eyes and checking the card in front of you once in a while. Go slow at first: Look at the card, shut your eyes, "place" it to the right direction, open your eyes, check, close them again, and so on. When you can hold the trigram in your mind in the proper direction, put the card down in that direction and move on to the next one.

Eventually you will be sitting happily with all eight Trigrams glowing about you in your mind's eye. This is far easier than it sounds because the trigrams are such simple images, but it will take a bit of practice.

When you have the Pa Kua floating about you, breathe deeply a number of times and visualize the Yin/Yang (Tai Chi) as glowing in your heart. Now you are the Pa Kua, the center of the universe.

The benefits of this visualization are threefold. First, it will banish or eliminate any negative energy, stress, bad feelings, and such from your body and mind.

Second, it will help you balance all the subconscious elements of your personality as symbolized by the trigrams. By getting all the trigrams to appear, the forces within you on which you are focusing too much or not focusing enough will simply balance out. This is why it is important to focus on each trigram individually, one at a time and with equal intensity.

You will find that certain trigrams are stronger than others and are much easier to call up in your mind while others are harder to hold. The "easy" trigrams are stronger parts of your psyche at the moment, the hard-to-hold trigrams are weaker forces in your psyche at this time. These can point to imbalances that need correcting.

The third thing becoming the Pa Kua does is it protects you from the harmful energies, actions, and emotions of negative or unhappy people, places, or things. This is what we have been aiming for, and once you've gone through the trouble of getting the Pa Kua visualization down, you are done with the hard part. Activating it for protection is easy!

Pa Kua Protection Visualization

When you find yourself in a difficult situation, under assault from your environment or another person or simply in any state of mental, physical, or emotional distress, do this:

Close your eyes for a moment and conjure up all the trigrams around you, each in its proper direction. Do this with eight deep breaths, one trigram appearing with each exhalation, glowing at the right direction and fiercely protecting you. Finally, visualize the Tai Chi (Yin/Yang) glowing in your heart. Feel the glowing power of the Tai Chi pushing all negativity and pain out of your circle and see and feel the trigrams forming an impenetrable wall about you through which nothing negative can pass. Relax. You are safe.

When you feel that it has done its job and you are home or in another safe place, close your eyes and take eight more deep breaths. Visualize each trigram returning to the Tai Chi in your heart with each inhalation. When done, see the Yin/Yang (Tai Chi) become a point of light and disappear within your heart. You should feel really good after this.

Attracting Prosperity with the Pa Kua

Projecting the Pa Kua can also be used to attract the positive as well as repel the negative. This is how it works:

Close your eyes for a moment and conjure up all the trigrams around you, each in its proper direction. Do this with eight deep breaths, one trigram appearing with each exhalation, glowing at the right direction and emitting attractive golden light. When they are all placed, see each trigram as a magnet. Inhale three times as deeply as you can. With every inhalation, see the golden light pour from the surrounding universe through the eight trigrams and flow into your heart. Silently ask for whatever it is you want. Do this each time. Finally, visualize the Tai Chi (Yin/Yang) glowing in your heart with a gold light. Feel the glowing power of the Tai Chi attracting all that is positive and especially what it is you desire most.

When you are done, close your eyes and take eight more deep breaths. Visualize each trigram returning to the Tai Chi in your heart with each inhalation. The idea is to "absorb" this energy into your physical body, just like a cup of water dissipates throughout your system when sipped. When done, see the Yin/Yang (Tai Chi) become a point of light and disappear within your heart. You should feel really good after this.

This is an excellent exercise for attracting business opportunities or to do before addressing a group of people. Good luck!

On this positive and happy note, we must depart. So ends the section on meditations and visualization exercises. There are, of course, hundreds of other exercises and meditations I could expound upon, but these are enough to begin with. May you have success and happiness in all that you do and may you ever flow with the Tao in harmony and peace!